HUMAN PERCEPTION AND DIGITAL INFORMATION TECHNOLOGIES

Animation, the Body, and Affect

Edited by
Tomoko Tamari

BRISTOL
UNIVERSITY
PRESS

First published in Great Britain in 2024 by

Bristol University Press
University of Bristol
1–9 Old Park Hill
Bristol
BS2 8BB
UK
t: +44 (0)117 374 6645
e: bup-info@bristol.ac.uk

Details of international sales and distribution partners are available at bristoluniversitypress.co.uk

British Library Cataloguing in Publication Data
A catalogue record for this book is available from the British Library

ISBN 978-1-5292-2618-8 hardcover
ISBN 978-1-5292-2619-5 ePub
ISBN 978-1-5292-2620-1 ePdf

Cover design: Blu Inc
Front cover image: Anatolyi Deryenko - Alamy
Bristol University Press uses environmentally responsible print partners.
Printed and bound in Great Britain by CPI Group (UK) Ltd, Croydon, CR0 4YY

FSC
www.fsc.org
MIX
Paper | Supporting
responsible forestry
FSC® C013604

Dedicated to my mother, Yōko Tamari, and the memory of my father, Keisaburō Tamari

Contents

List of figures   vii
List of web links   viii
Notes on contributors   ix
Acknowledgements   xiii

Introduction: Human Perception and Digital Information Technologies   1
Tomoko Tamari

PART I   Animation and Consciousness
1   Pastures New: Atmospheres, Mud, and Moods   29
           Esther Leslie
2   The Neurodynamics of Technically Mediated Motion: 42
           Perceptual vs. Conceptual Animation in Artworks of
           Nam June Paik and Bill Viola
           N. Katherine Hayles
3   Moving Images and Human Perception: Affect in Hand-   62
           Drawn Animation and Computer-Generated Imagery
           Tomoko Tamari
4   New Punctums, Proto-Perceptions, and Animated   86
           Entanglements
           Tony D. Sampson

PART II   Affective Experience and Expression
5   On Pixar's Marvellous Astonishment: When Synthetic   111
           Bodies Meet Photorealistic Worlds
           Eric S. Jenkins
6   Player and Avatar in Motion: Affective Encounters   131
           Daniela Bruns

PART III Data Visualization: Space and Time

7 Animation, Data, and the Plasticity of the Real: From 153
   the Military Survey of Scotland to Synthetic Training
   Environments
   Pasi Väliaho

8 Chronoclasm: Real-Time Data Animation 171
   Sean Cubitt

PART IV Image Formation and Embodiment

9 Deepfake Face-Swap Animations and Affect 195
   Mette-Marie Zacher Sørensen

10 Deepfake Reality, Societies for Technical Feeling, 213
   and the Phenomenotechnics of Animation
   Mark B.N. Hansen

Index 239

List of figures

4.1	*Barthes's Punctum* by Mikey B. Georgeson	87
4.2	*Thrum II* by William Bishop-Stephens	101
4.3	*Thrum III* by William Bishop-Stephens	105
4.4	Detail of *Thrum III* by William Bishop-Stephens	106
7.1	US Army's 'mixed reality' environment	155
7.2	Paul Sandby, *Plan of the Castle of Dunbarton*, c.1747	158
7.3	Illustration from Roger de Piles, *Cours de peinture par principes* (1708)	162
7.4	Constantijn Huygens, Jr., *View of the Ijssel*, 1672	164
9.1	Andreas Schmelas and Stefan Stubbe, *Artificial Smile* (2010)	197
9.2	Daito Manabe, *Face Visualizer*, performance, 2008	199

List of web links

Chapter 2

Image of Nam June Paik's *TV Buddha*
https://explore.namjunepaik.sg/artwork-archival-highlights/tv-buddha/

Chapter 5

Impact images: When photorealistic worlds collide with synthetic characters
https://theimpactimage.blogspot.com/

Notes on contributors

Daniela Bruns is an independent scholar and worked as a University Assistant at the Department of Media and Communications at the Alpen-Adria-University Klagenfurt (AAU) in Austria. She holds a diploma in media theory and cultural studies and a bachelor degree in economics from the University of Klagenfurt. She was the organizer of the annual Game Pics Event at the AAU, which was an art project that experimented with reflections on in-game imagery, and consultant for video game ratings for the Federal Chancellery of the Republic of Austria. Her main research interests include cultural studies, popular culture, serious gaming, and video games between escapism and activism.

Sean Cubitt is Professor of Screen Studies at the University of Melbourne. His publications include *The Cinema Effect* (MIT Press, 2004); *EcoMedia* (Rodopi, 2005); *The Practice of Light* (MIT Press, 2014); *Finite Media: Environmental Implications of Digital Technologies* (Duke University Press, 2017); and *Anecdotal Evidence: Ecocritique from Hollywood to the Mass Image* (Oxford University Press, 2020). He is a co-editor of *The Ecocinema Reader: Theory and Practice* (Routledge/American Film Institute, 2012) and of *Ecomedia: Key Issues* (Earthscan/Routledge, 2015), and is series editor for Leonardo Books at MIT Press. His research focuses on the history and philosophy of media, political aesthetics, media art history, ecocriticism, and practices of truth.

Mark B.N. Hansen is the James B. Duke Professor in the Program in Literature and in the Department of Art, Art History and Visual Studies at Duke University, as well as co-founder of Duke's Program in Computational Media Arts and Cultures, and co-founder/director of the s-1: Speculative Sensation Lab. In work that ranges across a host of disciplines and areas, Hansen mines philosophical resources in order to explore the technological exteriorization of the human and the technical distribution of sensibility currently underway in our world today. Hansen is the author of *Bodies in Code* (Routledge, 2012); *New Philosophy for New Media* (MIT Press, 2004); *Embodying Technesis: Technology Beyond Writing* (University of Michigan

Press, 2000); and most recently *Feed-Forward: On the Future of Twenty-First-Century Media* (University of Chicago Press, 2015). In dialogue with French philosopher Gilbert Simondon, Hansen's current research theorizes information as a process of individuation across biotic–abiotic divides and at multiple scales.

N. Katherine Hayles is the Distinguished Research Professor at the University of California, Los Angeles, and the James B. Duke Professor Emerita from Duke University. Her research focuses on the relations of literature, science and technology in the 20th and 21st centuries. Her twelve print books include *Postprint: Books and Becoming Computational* (Columbia University Press, 2021); *Unthought: The Power of the Cognitive Nonconscious* (University of Chicago Press, 2017); and *How We Think: Digital Media and Contemporary Technogenesis* (University of Chicago Press, 2015); in addition to over 100 peer-reviewed articles. Her books have won several prizes, including The Rene Wellek Award for the Best Book in Literary Theory for *How We Became Posthuman: Virtual Bodies in Literature, Cybernetics and Informatics*, and the Suzanne Langer Award for *Writing Machines*. A member of the American Academy of Arts and Sciences, she has been recognized by many fellowships and awards, including two NEH Fellowships, a Guggenheim, a Rockefeller Residential Fellowship at Bellagio, and two University of California Presidential Research Fellowships. She is currently at work on *Cognizing Others: Human Futures with Our Nonhuman Symbionts*.

Eric S. Jenkins is Associate Professor of Communication at the University of Cincinnati. His research focuses on the relationship of affect, media, and consumer capitalism. His first book, *Special Affects: Cinema, Animation, and the Translation of Consumer Culture* (Edinburgh University Press, 2014), illustrates how early cinema and animation capitalized on the special affects of these media to create new modes of consumerism. His forthcoming book, *Surfing the Anthropocene: On the Big Tensions of Virtual Life*, diagrams how digital media repeatedly expose users to issues with a global and epochal scale but do so in a rapid, skimming manner signalled by the term *surfing*. The book contends that the tension between the speed and the scale of digital media shapes online experience today, especially in relation to the political activities of citizens, such as following the news and deliberating on social media. This tension accounts for the common expressions of anxiety, angst and disgust that digital and social media frequently generate.

Esther Leslie is Professor of Political Aesthetics at Birkbeck, University of London. Her books include various studies and translations of Walter Benjamin, as well as *Hollywood Flatlands: Animation, Critical Theory and the*

Avant Garde (Verso, 2002); *Synthetic Worlds: Nature, Art and the Chemical Industry* (Reaktion, 2005); *Derelicts: Thought Worms from the Wreckage* (Unkant, 2014); *Liquid Crystals: The Science and Art of a Fluid Form* (Reaktion, 2016); and *Deeper in the Pyramid* (with Melanie Jackson: Banner Repeater, 2018).

Tony D. Sampson is a critical theorist with an interest in the philosophies of media technology. His publications include *The Spam Book* (Hampton Press, 2009); *Virality* (University of Minnesota Press, 2012); *The Assemblage Brain* (University of Minnesota Press, 2017); *Affect and Social Media* (Rowman and Littlefield, 2018); and *A Sleepwalker's Guide to Social Media* (Polity, 2020). Tony is the host and organizer of the Affect and Social Media international conferences in east London and a co-founder of the public engagement initiative the Cultural Engine Research Group. He works as a reader in digital communication at the University of Essex.

Mette-Marie Zacher Sørensen is Assistant Professor in the Department of Aesthetics and Culture at Aarhus University. Since 2014 she has been working on the project 'Technologies of the Face in Contemporary Art', funded by the Danish Council for Independent Research. She has arranged two international seminars gathering scholars and artists within the field of new media art: 'Shy Faces – Digital Subjects and Acts of Disappearing', and 'Facial Machines and Obfuscation in an Age of Biometrics and Neural Networks'. She has published the articles 'Quantified Faces: On Surveillance Technologies, Identification and Statistics in Three Contemporary Art Projects', in *Digital Culture and Society* 2(2) (2016); and, with Thomas Bjørnsten, 'Uncertainties of Facial Emotion Recognition Technologies and the Automation of Emotional Labour', in *Digital Creativity* 28(4) (2017), and in *The Uncertain Image* (edited by Ekman, Agostinho, Thylstrup, and Veel, Routledge, 2019).

Tomoko Tamari is Senior Lecturer in the Institute of Creative and Cultural Entrepreneurship, Goldsmiths, University of London. She is managing editor of *Body & Society* (Sage). Her long-standing research interests focus on consumer culture in Japan and Japanese new women, which will be discussed in her forthcoming book *Women and Consumer Culture: The Department Store, Modernity and Everyday Life in Early Twentieth Century Japan* (Routledge). She has published 'Body Image and Prosthetic Aesthetics' in *Body & Society* 23(2); 'Artificial Intelligence and the Materiality of the Body' in *Divinatio* 51; 'Human Perception and the Animated World' in the *Glossary of Animation Today* of the research group of Animate Assembly. She is currently working in the following areas: body image and technology; artificial intelligence and creativity; digital archives and memory; and human perception and the moving image. She is the organizer of the online seminar 'AI and

Society Series' (https://www.tomokotamari.com/ai-and-society-series) at Goldsmiths, University of London.

Pasi Väliaho is Professor in History of Art and Visual Studies at the University of Oslo, Norway. He is the author of three books which map the contribution of screen media to histories of knowledge and capitalism from the early modern period until today: *Mapping the Moving Image: Gesture, Thought and Cinema circa 1900* (Amsterdam University Press, 2010); *Biopolitical Screens: Image, Power, and the Neoliberal Brain* (MIT Press, 2014); and *Projecting Spirits: Speculation, Providence, and Early Modern Optical Media* (Stanford University Press, 2022).

Acknowledgements

My interest in moving image and human perception started back with my first conference paper, 'Moving Image and Affect in Digital and Analog(ue) Animation' at the 'Affective Fabrics of Digital Cultures: Feelings, Technologies, Politics' International Conference, held at the University of Manchester in 2010. Since then, I have been fortunate to have had several opportunities to present papers on relevant topics, and I have benefited from useful feedback from many of my colleagues and mentors. Especially I would like to thank Mike Featherstone for his inspirational conversation and helpful suggestions. I faced many difficulties and unforeseen problems in the process of publication, but Ryan Bishop, David Beer, Matthew Fuller and N. Katherine Hayles kindly gave me practical guidance and suggestions which were incredibly helpful. I must say that I very much appreciate all the contributors to the book, who have been patiently working with me for years. At Bristol University Press, editor Paul Stevens' suggestions gave me confidence, and in the production process, Freya Trand, Sarah Green, and Georgina Bolwell have been very supportive, and especially the help of my *Body & Society* colleague, Fern Bryant, has been irreplaceable. Finally, I'd like to acknowledge that the book could not have appeared without my partner Mike's deep understanding and his sacrifices in our everyday life.

Introduction: Human Perception and Digital Information Technologies

Tomoko Tamari

'The body is our general medium for having a world.'
Maurice Merleau-Ponty (2002/1945:169)

The main theme of Maurice Merleau-Ponty's philosophy is 'the world of perception'. He was interested in the world that appears to us via our bodily senses. The body is continuously communicating with the changing environment to shape our sense of the world. Yet the changing environment today is characterized by the digitalization of everyday life. In seeking to respond to this contemporary situation, this book seeks to better understand the ways that digital information technologies form and influence human perception and experience.

Contemporary computational media increasingly govern our experience through their capacity for externalizing our knowledge and memories, mining data from our behaviour to influence our decision-making, and also by creating emotionally rewarding sensory pleasure (Stiegler, 2015). The digital networks continue to expand their capacities, becoming faster, more efficient and more accurate. At the same time, their devices offer affective encounters. This is a particularly pressing issue that confronts us, given our growing dependence on computational platforms and software, which have become essential to contemporary everyday life and are now almost impossible to eliminate. In this light, it can be argued that the computational media *embedded* environment is becoming inseparable from *embodied* human experience.

The emergence of ChatGPT is clearly reinforcing this situation. As many have already discussed, ChatGPT can influence the human capacity for decision-making and knowledge formation. This new digital environment means that human perception is becoming a product of human–machine

1

symbiosis in a new type of media ecology (a key issue addressed in Esther Leslie's piece, Chapter 1).

The expanding digital media environment has generated a large amount of research and scholarship within various fields that relate to digital information technologies, such as digital media, digital computation, digital archives, digital geographies (Ash et al, 2016), digital art, digital health, digital theatre and museums, big data, and data visualization.

For some, this suggests the possibility of a new ontology and epistemology for the social sciences and humanities that has led to the emergence of the digital humanities. The term digital humanities has been used since the early 2000s without, as yet, an established consensus about its definition among scholars. The term is, however, often used in various disciplines, such as sociology, media, art, philosophy, geography, and literature to incorporate digital information technologies into the research terrain.

One of the growing areas in digital humanities is new media studies, which has been developed by theorists, critics, and artists who 'focused on media and networks from a poststructuralist or cultural-critical perspective' (Liu, 2012:9). This collection also shares this focus on various digital media and their influence on society, but it engages more specifically with the interrelation between digital media technologies and human perception through three key components: animation, the body, and affect.

Animation, the body, and affect

Advanced digital computerization has not only redefined static photographic images but also cinematic and animation moving images, especially since screens are now essential everyday devices (computer displays, mobile phones, digital billboards, and so on) influencing not only ways of living but also ways of thinking and sensing the world. Thus, animation can no longer be simply defined as moving images based on the artificial arrangement of photography or a recording of real-time movement.

Animation in this collection, therefore, encapsulates not only modalities and 'techniques' of moving images in both 'frame-by-frame' analogue images and digital 'information'-based images, but is also treated as a concept that can elucidate the formation process of human perception. Animation is an illusory movement that can evoke paradoxical traits such as intangibility and palpability, immateriality and materiality, and actuality and virtuality. We sense animation as an actuality in the mind but see it as an illusion on the screen. The emotional, sensory, and psychological experiences point to the importance of affective perception.[1]

As mentioned at the beginning, according to Merleau-Ponty our affective perception is produced through our bodies. This is why this book seeks to discuss the body in relation to affect, which could enable

2

us to better understand the relation of human perception and animation. Although a comprehensive overview of the various orientations of affect is provided by Gregg and Seigworth, they argue that there is no final notion of affect theories, and it is always in 'the not yet of never-quite-knowing' (Gregg and Seigworth, 2010:9). This is because affect can be an ever-processual entity induced by complex communication between the body and the ever-changing environment. It is, therefore, not easy, and even perhaps inappropriate, to produce a general definition of affect. In this book, then, the discussion of affect focuses specifically on psycho-physical sensations and the array of mental processes that occur in dynamic interaction between human perception and moving images in both analogue and digital formats.

Today, human perception in the brain can be 'seen' through advanced medical technologies. More precisely, some argue that it could be possible to examine the impact of moving images through observing complex neurophysiological mechanisms in biological cognition processes. Advanced medical technologies, such as MRI, which makes it possible to see micro detailed brain activities, can provide confirmation of some of the scientific theories of the brain.[2]

In fact, brain imaging studies show that the right frontal insula and anterior cingulate in the brain produce for human emotion (Blakeslee and Blakeslee, 2007:190), and therefore some scientists consider that 'affect' can be explained through neural processes and mechanisms. This can be understood as neuroreductionism, which has been contested by some other neurocognitive theories of emotion (Pitts-Taylor, 2016:4). These theories are based on the idea that 'the body (not just a brain) is mediator and repository of memory and emotional valence' (Pitts-Taylor, 2016:4).

The centrality of the body is also emphasized by computer scientists and biorobotics scholars who are investigating artificial intelligence and comparing it with human intelligence. Pfeifer and Bongard argue that the body is embodied intelligence. Unlike an algorithmic-based cognitivistic view of intelligence, their 'embodied approach' envisions 'the intelligent artifact as more than just a computer program: it has a body, and it behaves and performs tasks in the real world' (Pfeifer and Bongard, 2006:18).

Moreover, theories of affect also use cognitive and neuroscientific accounts of presubjective (nonconscious) and emotional experience. They emphasize the significance of the body (gut feeling, for example), which plays a key role as an interface between cognition and environment.

Further understanding of the role of the body has also developed in theories that discuss the biological body as being always both materially and socially cultured (biocultural), and argue that bodies are not just responsive to their environment but have their own agency which is 'the quality of the forms of responsive self-transformation' (Frost, cited in Tamari, 2021:89). This research sees the body as a biological and social entity and can help to avoid biological determinism.

All these theories and debates imply that it is not so simple to grasp human perception by envisaging it as part of the bodily 'organic' mechanism, since it is a rather complex bio-social constitution. We can see a human as entailing an embodied being-in-the world and as an organism which has the capacity to live with their own agency, projecting their own subjectivity onto the environment. This is what Jakob von Uexküll called '*Umwelt*'.

Hence, the aim of the book is to avoid overemphasizing or underestimating both neuroreductionism and biological determinism to better understand affective and embodied experiences in ever-changing environments; that is, in the era of the digital information society. Dichotomizing the two approaches or favouring scientific and technological accounts over cultural accounts, or social constructionism over biological accounts, does not capture the plasticity, multiplicity, complexity, density, and specificity of human perception. In effect, these two approaches, which used to be contested, now need to be considered as inevitably involving each other.

The collection therefore draws on the broader scope of pieces written by scholars who have not only been working in the fields of digital media but also on affect and body studies and trying to make a bridge between them. The authors were invited to contribute to the book based on their academic expertise and their individual interests and thematic fields. Their individual approaches not only address the dominant and mainstream topics on digital media, but they also offer attempts to refine and apply new categories of animation to digital media theories and affective experiences. Hence, although all the pieces discuss the wider implications of contemporary computational media, they consistently focus on animation (moving images) as the key concept, and the body as the related field to analyse the role of affect in human perception.

Overview of the book

The book consists of four parts: animation and consciousness; affective experience and expression; data visualization: space and time; and image formation and embodiment. The collection addresses a wide array of theories and orientations that bring together media theory, philosophy, science and technology, visual culture, computation and algorithms, big data, psychology, neuroscience, and the body.

Part I: Animation and consciousness

The first part provides the theoretical foundation for the book by considering the critical implications of computerization. The concept of animation in this part treats not only 2D screen animation, but also other moving image modalities and their relation to the dynamics of (non)consciousness. In addition, this part considers 'animation' in terms of the complex relationship between nature, the humanities and technologies.

The collection begins with Esther Leslie's provocative investigation of the negative implications of bio-techno integration into human life and the natural environment.

In her chapter, 'Pastures New: Atmospheres, Mud, and Moods', she considers the intelligence of the liquid crystal to argue that screen-devices deliver endless types of animations in physiology. The body today is digitized and quantified, and is only accessed through machines (liquid crystal devices). If the body is data, life can be controlled. Computational biology (bioinformatics) has been applied to bio-experimentation for dairy cows. Cows are monitored, physically and mentally controlled, and genetically modified for profit. For Leslie, this could be a lesson for our future in advanced digital information society. She considers digital technologies work to deceive the senses, produce affect, and construct imagery. Hence, digital technologies generate various social phenomena, what she calls 'animation'. Furthermore, she introduces the idea of 'radical atoms', atoms which are re-engineered through the idea of the liquid crystal. Whereas physical objects are fixed and solid, 'liquid crystals' are transformable. This proposal 'extends the flatness of pixel painting … into the dimensionality of pixel sculpture'. It remains at the dream level, but Leslie indicates that if 'computers can control the existence of matter', then images of the world could be remade by computers. Leslie grapples with the central theme of the book: the changing relationship between advanced digital technology and human life.

In contrast to Leslie's exploration of the atomic level of computational body coding, Hayles, Tamari, and Sampson focus more on the cognitive processes of human perception.

In 'The Neurodynamics of Technically Mediated Motion: Perceptual vs. Conceptual Animation in Artworks of Nam June Paik and Bill Viola', N. Katherine Hayles emphasizes that knowing the recursive dynamics between nonconscious and conscious cognition is important for understanding 'the neurological basis for animation's motion effects'. In the brain's recursive architecture, she explains that 'information is processed first by nonconscious cognition', which 'discern[s] patterns in information too dense and noisy for consciousness to process as anything other than chaos'. She defines 'perceptual animation' as 'traditional animation achieving motion through the perceptual processing of nonconscious cognition'.

In contrast to this, in discussing Nam June Paik's artworks, she identifies one of his works, *TV Buddha*, as 'conceptual animation'. *TV Buddha* not only illustrates the cognitive recursive cycle of meditation/reflection, but also shows how neuronal processes create 'the impression of motion' at 'the high level of the massive recursivity of meta-consciousness.' Furthermore, in discussing Bill Viola's high-speed video art, Hayles indicates that the viewers experience feelings 'many hundreds of milliseconds later than the corresponding bodily emotions'. In this process (slowed down in speed to view), stillness and motion can be seen as a continuum, and feelings could be linked directly through 'nonconscious affect'. Hayles expands the concept of animation and brings together neurodynamic and neuroscience approaches to open up new ways of understanding the moving image of human perception.

Focusing on Japanese animation cinema that has been widely acclaimed as an art form, in 'Moving Images and Human Perception: Affect in Hand-Drawn Animation and Computer-Generated Imagery', Tomoko Tamari discusses human perception of animation by scrutinizing 'the affective effect' in the dynamic relations between moving images and human conscious–nonconscious cognition. The chapter explores the differences between digital aesthetics created by computer animation and analogue aesthetics in hand-drawn animation. While computer-generated imagery (CGI) refers to the process that involves mathematical calculations within computers to create verisimilar naturalistic images, the traditional hand-drawn animation method involves symbolic expressive forms created by the animator's spatiotemporal sensitivities. Drawing on Hayles's discussion of the 'cognitive nonconscious', Simondon's notion of 'technical mentality', and biosemiotics, the paper argues that there might be an inevitable incompatibility in the image-formation process between human perception and algorithm-based CGI. To explore this assumption, the paper focuses on the questions of 'selectivity' and 'abstraction' in both the neuronal and the technical, and emphasizes the significance of 'noise' (incompleteness and ambiguity) and 'time' (speed, duration, and delay) for human perception by exploring the nature of cognitive systems. The chapter further considers the expansion of digital computer technology and its integration within human life by analysing the 'recursive dynamism' of human perception and CGI. Tamari argues that embodied digital experiences could recursively become part of our environment and influence conscious–nonconscious cognition: in effect, they could become a significant part of the constitution of human perception in our digital computational society.

In contrast to Tamari's phenomenological approach towards human perception, Tony D. Sampson develops a nonphenomenological approach in 'New Punctums, Proto-Perceptions and Animated Entanglements' to conceptualize affective experiences of animation. Sampson introduces Jenkins' claim (2013) about 'another punctum' and explains that Jenkins conceives the importance of the presubjective experiences of animation through affect theory. Developing Jenkins' idea of a new punctum, Sampson argues that 'an analytical transition from the problematics of phenomenological thinking to an affective mode of movement event' is needed for capturing human perception of virtual images. Critiquing the brain's synaptic plasticity model of proto-perception and neurocinematic experiments, Sampson argues that the crudity of the cognitive effect model cannot be simply detected, this is what Franco Varela called 'structurally coupled systems' in the relationship between moving images and perception.

Furthermore, by considering how we can understand the experience of 'real' movement or that of illusory moving images, Sampson points out the limitation of phenomenological approaches and draws on Whitehead's nonphenomenology. For Whitehead, human experience is entangled with brains, minds, bodies, and images in the duration of events. The illusory moving image is 'declared in the percipient encounter with events'. Hence, the percipient experience of movement is 'a felt experience of the intensity of the event'. In conclusion, Sampson extends Jenkins' 'another punctum', which is developed by the concept of affect, by adding the concept of the event, and shows that the new punctum reveals nonphenomenological experience of material entanglement with moving images.

Part II: Affective experience and expression

In this part, Eric S. Jenkins and Daniela Bruns explore specific fields of contemporary computer graphic moving images on different platforms (digital animation and computer games respectively) in order to analyse affective effects in terms of the relationships between technology, the body, and environments. Both chapters discuss how carefully programmed digital images create affective virtuality, which influences the spectator's sense of actuality.

In 'On Pixar's Marvellous Astonishment: When Synthetic Bodies Meet Photorealistic Worlds', Eric S. Jenkins examines Pixar's cinematic techniques and 'special affects' (Jenkins, 2014): what he calls 'the marvellous astonishment'. He points out that digital images often look too pristine and soulless, and particularly that 'artificial human representation feels uncanny'. To avoid these possibly negative affectivities, Pixar developed 'marvellous astonishment': a combination of astonishment (the realistic lifelikeness of backgrounds) and marvel (the wonder of perceiving motion through an artificial form). Hence, Pixar deliberately creates 'a tension between the photo-realism of things and the unreality of the lives they are seen to lead' (Schaffer, 2004:83). At this point, Pixar creates the digital world in which '[t]he characters are synthetic but tactile, the world photorealistic but magical'. Jenkins also argues that Pixar's *Incredibles 2* suggests that individuals must be flexible and adaptable to survive in neoliberalism, just like the characters. Hence, Pixar's *Incredibles 2*, with its 'marvellous astonishment', is an 'expression' of the event that is the ideological message of consumer capitalism and neoliberal society, since 'affect shapes ideology' and not the other way round. He also shows Pixar's success is making things look realistic without reproducing reality but by producing a new digital actuality.

Following on from Jenkins' 'special affect' of CGI animation, Bruns focuses on video games in terms of the complex interactivities between the avatar (machine) and the player (human) in algorithmic programmes. In 'Player and Avatar in Motion: Affective Encounters', Daniela Bruns discusses the complex relationship between avatar and player in video games through the perspective of affective encounters between humans and machines. Drawing on Seth Gidding's remarks on the cybernetic circuits of video games in which he conceives 'the process of starting to play a video game as plugging oneself into a cybernetic circuit, where computer as well as human components are working together to create the gaming experience', she examines the executing bodies of player and avatar, demonstrates the meanings of avatars in different game environments, and explores the player's bodily sensitivity to machine activities. Bruns argues that the agency in gameplay oscillates between the dominant player's acts (such as stopping the machine's processing by pressing the pause button) and independent machinic acts (when the gaming process is taken over by the programme). She discusses intercorporeality and trans-subjectivity in terms of the relationship between avatar, player, and video game by showing the various qualities of human–machine interaction, embodiment, and affective encounters in gaming.

Part III: Data visualization: space and time

Animation can also be found in data processing. From the viewpoint of data visualization of moving images in various terrains from digital charts to financial media, Väliaho and Cubitt explore the differences between computational mediated data analysis and human perception. In both chapters, time and space are the key concepts in terms of analysing how the representation of time can be visualized in special domains by applying the techniques of animation. In this process, affective animation as visual data could also help the construction of narratives.

In 'Animation, Data, and the Plasticity of the Real: From the Military Survey of Scotland to Synthetic Training Environments', Pasi Väliaho extends the concept of animation as visualizing data in order to understand its association with topographic mapping practices. He argues that 'automatization and abstraction of perceptual synthesis and pattern recognition' of topography creates military computer simulations at the expense of the human affective element. Väliaho further explains 'tracing shadow' and 'animation' are essential not only to Sandby's chart and camera obscura projections, but also 'a clay likeness', which was produced by tracing the shadow of loved one's figure on the wall and casting it in clay. Whereas both Sandby's conceptual geometrical charts and the semi-machine projection of the camera obscura can animate 'the real' as an objective (subjectless) and actionable database, the loved one's surrogate clay double is animated by depth memory and affection. Here, imagination leads to animation. In these contexts, he argues the concept of animation should be understood as a tool for actionable world formation, and also provides an enactive attunement between the observer and their environment. In this chapter, Väliaho shows how actuality can be influenced by subjective experience with imagination, the key elements for constructing the sense of the real and the simulation of the world.

Also addressing the theme of data visualization, Sean Cubitt's 'Chronoclasm: Real-Time Data Animation' argues that exploring techniques of animation can be the privileged starting point for the analysing of chronoclasm as crises and as the changing notion and practice of time under capital. In data visualization, generative adversarial network (GAN) animation mimics imagination, not reality. GAN animation provides futurity, which is 'hovering between the "may happen" of the imagination and the "will happen" of planning, an incorporate administration and imagination'. Such subjunctive accounts of the future lead to the question of where and when the present and truth(s) exist in GAN animation. Cubitt claims that the truth practice of the 21st century is data, and truth as data aggregation is always in unstable movement, therefore techniques of animation can be useful to access this mode of truth. Such future-oriented simulation, which entails the so-called 'colonization of the future', can be also found in the debt crisis. This is a symptom of chronoclasm, which are 'crises of time that occur when practices and concepts of time come into contradiction' in various forms of animation (for example, real-time data visualization). Cubitt uses the concept of chronoclasm to explore the gap between computer-determined time and human perceptible time (and reality/truth). He shows an analytical close link between human affective responses and computer-rendered future-oriented simulations.

Part IV: Image formation and embodiment

The capacity of supercomputers to provide high-speed and huge-scale data processing makes possible not only real-time data visualization, but also the extremely sophisticated simulation of a sense of 'reality'. Given this situation, Hansen and Sørensen explore how operational technologies of human–machine coupling can create new dimensions of embodiment and affective experiences. Focusing on one of today's controversial media environments – deepfakes – the two chapters in this part theorize the negative consequences in terms of affectivity, temporality, and algorithmic reasoning.

In 'Deepfake Face-Swap Animations and Affect', drawing on Spinoza's notion of 'affectio', Deleuze and Guattari's 'faciality', Stiegler's 'tertiary memory' and Hansen's notion of 'temporality', Mette-Marie Zacher Sørensen analyses the affective effects of face-swapped deepfake moving images. She focuses particularly on two different forms of its application: 'the public speech' and 'the porn scene'. She uses 'Who are you?' (identity axis) and 'How are you/What are you doing?' (expression axis) to analyse the affective encounter of the deepfakes, and explains that 'one of the crucial aspects of deepfakes is that they separate the two axes in a more extreme manner'. Yet this condition can be reversed in terms of embodiment in affective encounters of face-swapping, particularly in pornographic scenes. It exists in artificial time, but it is experienced as 'a mode of living presence'. Hence, 'the temporal character of the deepfake face-swapped in a pornographic scene makes the difference between fake or real less relevant'. She argues that 'in the deepfake face-swapped public speech, it is possible to deny the content due to its semantic character by saying, "I never said that"', but in a pornographic scene, it is impossible to deny the event which 'happened' ('She did this'). Hence, 'identity axis' and 'expression axis' become inseparable. She shows that two axes are 'technically' separated and reconstituted, but they are closely linked in response to embodied affective encounters.

The construction processes of the deepfake and fake news largely rely on the development of algorithms. In 'Deepfake Reality, Societies for Technical Feeling, and the Phenomenotechnics of Animation', Mark B.N. Hansen focuses on the deepfake image as a good example for exploring the 'phenomenotechnics of embodiment' in fake news. Borrowing two key concepts from Whitehead, 'proposition' (lures for feeling) and 'causal efficacy' (the source of sense/perception from which it abstracts), he explores the way in which the technical operations of algorithms do not engage human contribution (bodily feeling, for instance) in larger human–technical societies. Taking cinematic animation as a 'blueprint' of algorithmic operation, Hansen explains that algorithms can only operate by reducing a multiplicity to a simple repertoire of potentialities. Algorithmic operationality 'rigidly determines the bounds of what has value', therefore 'it effectively depotentializes the very potentiality that informs its operation', which leads to 'algorithmic collapse'. Hence, it reduces the causal efficacy. Like cinematic animation's operationality, the deepfake as algorithmic subsumption of animation is '*at one and the same time* the apotheosis of the process of generativity *and* the epitome of "algorithmic collapse"'. This is the technical process of fake news, which overwrites the complex situations transformed into misrepresentation with 'solipsistic histories of feeling' and 'hijack[s] the affective, bodily experience of the causal efficacy of the world'. The deepfake is a product of the combination of superficial content and time-critical reception channels on the internet. Such a 'perfect simulacrum' is an image not received by being embodied perception but rather being *felt/sensed* by 'presentational immediacy'. To respond to such toxic consequences of fake news, Hansen emphasizes the significance of 'humanness', which implies the human capacity to grasp the partiality of abstractions and to sense the vague totality.

Contextual theoretical excursion: the body, affect, and perception

The brain and cognitive science

The issue of human–machine relationships has been a major theme for a number of philosophers (Heidegger, Whitehead, Simondon) in the previous century. What could be a new trend in 21st-century humanities is that the impact of life science, especially the development of brain and cognitive neuroscience, has established a new approach to challenge the '[C]artesian division between mind and body or the psychoanalytical conscious/unconscious duality' (Sampson, 2020:1). Victoria Pitts-Taylor succinctly explains the impact of brain science on both science and humanities, arguing that '[T]he brain is conceived as the biological ground for the self and social life, as constituting the mind and underpinning intersubjectivity' (Pitts-Taylor, 2016:1). This amounts to a new idea about the way in which the brain is both biologically and socially constructed, developed, and transformed by communicating with its environment. The so-called brain plasticity referred to by Catherine Malabou introduces the scientific concept of 'plasticity' into debates in the fields of philosophy, sociology, and cultural studies (see Angerer, 2015:124). The idea of brain plasticity provides a bridge between mind and body, since mind can be seen not just as an immaterial source of emotions and affects, but also understood as a neurophysiological entity. Hence, '[T]he mind is now widely defined as equivalent to, or as emerging from, the brain' (Pitts-Taylor, 2016:3).

For instance, there is a good deal of emerging research which explores human cognitive functions, such as self–other cognition, estimation of others' intentions along with emotions, and altruism, by using robots equipped with neural network models.[3] This suggests that today neuroscience combines the study of the organic brain along with cognitive science methods.[4] Given that concepts such as perception, attention, intention and memory have been accorded more attention and debated in cognitive science, consciousness has therefore become a key concept to explore these mechanisms. As Dehaene (2014) remarks, consciousness has been ill-defined and described in terms of information processing and its molecular and neuronal network effectuation, suggesting that the problem of consciousness has become a major issue in neuroscience research.[5] Hence, it can be said that consciousness should take the central role in perception, because it helps us make sense of our experience and creates a coherent view of the world.

It isn't, however, the whole of cognition, since 'cognition is a much broader capacity that extends far beyond consciousness into other neurological brain processes; it is also pervasive in other life forms and complex technical systems' (Hayles, 2017:9). Hayles's extended cognitive neuroscience theory has helped to ground debates on cognitive processes by focusing on the relation of life forms and computational media as well as human–machine interfaces. This also can relate to the brain's plasticity, which is the ability to transform by adaptive bodily affordances in ever-changing natural and social environments.

Affect, body, and consciousness

This focus on the interaction and communication between the body and the environment resonates with one of the core features of affect. Gregg and Seigworth remark that affect can be understood as a gradient of bodily capacity which reflects a myriad of encounters with various rhythms, modalities, sensations and sensibilities (see Gregg and Seigworth, 2010:2). What is important here is that they argue that affect can be understand as a 'bodily capacity'.

Sigmund Freud further considers affect in relation to (un)consciousness. He believes affect creates immediate contiguity and adjustment of thought and '[these processes are] close enough that sensate tendrils constantly extend between unconscious affect and conscious thought' (Gregg and Seigworth, 2010:2). Here, we can see 'affect and cognition are never fully separable' (Gregg and Seigworth, 2010:2–3). All the processes occur in the body: 'bodies are bodies with brains: neurobiological bodies', according to Pitts-Taylor (2016:1).[6]

Movement and perception

Consequently, it can be argued that 'the body is the site where inner sensations and external images meet', as Bergson claims (Angerer, 2015:52).[7] In his book *Matter and Memory* (1908/1991), Bergson conceives the body as 'a centre of action' (Bergson, 1908/1991:20). He explains how external images influence the image that he calls his 'body' and how his body influences external images. He continues:

> In fact, I note that the size, shape, even the color, of external objects is modified as my body approaches or recedes from them; that the strength of an order, the intensity of sound, increases or diminishes with distance; finally, that this very distance represents, above all, the

measure in which surrounding bodies are insured, in some way, against the immediate action of my body. (Bergson, 1908/1991:20)

Here he emphasizes movement, for the distance between external images and the body changes our perception.[8] Perception is never static and fixed, since our body as a living organism is in continuous interaction with the ever-changing environment. Hence, it can be said that our perception in the living body is in constant animation.

The question here, then, is how can we as the 'living' body apprehend our spatial perception?[9] To further this inquiry, I would like to address the relationship between the living body and the ocular process. There is a biological mechanism of human retinal perception which lies in the oculomotor system. When we see an object, it is hugely significant to 'maintain a steady gaze'. Suzan R. Barry explains that while we tend to believe that we sense the world first and then react, this is not true, since 'we cannot perceive the world in any detail without moving at the same time. [...] Perception and movement are intimately linked in a continuous two-way conversation' (Barry, 2009:70). Hence, to see an object clearly, as Barry argues, we need to develop a stable gaze in motion.

Expanding the definition of animation

This suggests that we live in an animated world. We are surrounded by countless moving images. Animation is conceptually important here. This is because animation can be seen as not only moving images but also a dynamic sensorial occurrence which can help us better understand the complex relationship between human perception and environment.

Definitions of animation vary a great deal. Animation can refer to a broad range of modalities: new types of aesthetics and various creative practices which usually engage with visual culture and technologies. Before the digital shift, it generally referred to the moving image created by frame-by-frame production, a human-made illusionary movement, rather than computationally recorded or reproduced real-time movement. Yet such a simple definition does not capture the image-making process today, given that animation production processes have been developed via increasingly 'sophisticated' technical interfaces. As a result of the intervention of digital information technology, the distinction between animation and live action becomes blurred in terms of visual aesthetics.

Clark succinctly explains today's traits of animation when he writes:

In digital media, the progression of the image is not limited to the run/stop algorithm of the film projector but can now engage in the complex if/then logic of the computer code. With this code the physics of movement can be written and distributed separately from the image itself. The code can generate the image and the image can generate the code. Just as live-action film can now be seen as a subset of animation, so too can animation be seen now as one particular simple example of image/code hybrid. (Clark, 2005:143–4)

Hence, the concept of animation should not be limited to cinematic illusory moving images but also encompass moving images created by 'image/code hybrids' in digital forms. These kinds of digital forms are now ubiquitous on screens. As screen culture penetrates into everyday life, we continuously see various types of image/code hybrid animation on screens.

In this context, we need to examine how and why 'animation will increasingly influence our understanding of how we see and experience the world visually' (Buchan, 2013:1). This book therefore attempts to widen the focus beyond animation studies to take in visual culture, digital media theory and body studies.

Animation and cinematic realism

The rapid development of computer graphics technologies since the 1980s has brought about new types of visuality, such as virtual reality, that focus on realism. The issue of realism in animation (moving images), however, existed long before the various optical devices appeared. Here, 'realism' is the concept which refers to 'the reconstruction of a perfect illusion of the outside world' (Bazin, 1967:235). This can be seen as the construction process of representing reality, an attempt at the complete visualization of reality.

This attempt inevitably accompanies the idea of cinematic realism. The meaning of 'cinematic' here is not restricted to Hollywood movies, Disney animation (see Eric S. Jenkins, Chapter 5) or computer games (see Daniela Bruns, Chapter 6), but also applies to the wider category of computer animation, such as visualizing live data technologies in stock market information, planet trajectory in the cosmos, cartography (see Pasi Väliaho, Chapter 7, and Sean Cubitt, Chapter 8) and deepfakes (see Mette-Marie Zacher Sørensen, Chapter 9, and Mark B.D. Hansen, Chapter 10). Cinematic realism can thus be observed in a variety of digital platforms and screens.

With rapidly developing production methods along with advanced computational media, cinematic realism is becoming a debatable issue that not only reflects practices of digital technologies, but also impacts on the conceptualization of reality. It is generally considered that the 'reality' of cinematic moving images is a human and/or machine-made illusion. Bazin's realism is not a natural phenomenon. In other words, such cinematic illusion can be seen as the virtual, since illusion is a deceptive or false actuality and reconstruction of the simulation of reality. If it can be safely said that the virtual is the simulation of reality through reconstruction or transformation into different modalities, we can understand that the topics of this book, such as cinema, animation, live data-visualization, cartography, art and deepfakes, can be understood as various modalities dealing with the virtual.

Actuality and affective reality

Deleuze discusses philosophical accounts of 'the actual and the virtual' in terms of the relationship between objects and images. He writes, '[P]urely actual objects do not exist. Every actual surrounds itself with a cloud of virtual images' (Deleuze and Parnet, 1983:148). This suggests that the actual can only exist with collective virtual images. In other words, 'The actual and the virtual co-exist, and enter into a tight circuit which we are continually retracing from one to the other' (Deleuze and Parnet, 1983:150). If we follow Deleuze's assumption that we live in a world of virtual images, it is clear that his concern is to unfold the process through which we perceive 'reality'.

Reality we can perceive is not *the* reality, but it can be regarded as embodying multiple realities as suggested by Alfred Schutz. He borrows William James's account of 'multiple sub-universes', which explains that reality can be considered as pluralistic. Schutz focuses on the paramount world of everyday life and argues that there are various worlds such as dreams, phantasms, science, art, religion and politics. Schutz and James developed the idea of sub-universes (James) and finite provinces of meaning (Schutz) that only appear while consciousness attends to it (Geniusas, 2020:3). If we live in multiple realities, we can add another world, which is the world of digital virtual images (for example, the metaverse), another reality of the virtual.

But then how should we perceive such virtual realities? To open up this question, we also need to consider the different properties between actuality and reality and how actuality contributes to create human perception of the reality of the virtual.

Before we discuss the relationship between actuality and reality, it could be useful to introduce the Japanese psychiatrist and philosopher Bin Kimura, who developed the phenomenology of psychopathology and published *Zur Phänomenologie der Depersonalisation* in 1963. Depersonalization is characterized as a detachment from one's own personal self, lacking bodily sensations, emotions and feelings, and disorder of the sense of space and time experience. Those subjects who are suffering from depersonalization usually do not have physical disabilities (loss of hearing or sight, for example), but have a diminished sense of 'reality'. This suggests that normal bodily functionalities alone cannot establish our sense of being in the world and sense of reality.

Kimura uses two concepts to explain these psychopathological conditions: *mono* and *koto*. *Mono* can be described as things which have distance from us (things that appear). The distance means not just physical distance (between a cup and me), but also distance in consciousness (for example, time itself is *not* a thing/*mono*, but when we 'think about' time, time is recognized through distance in consciousness, and it turns into a thing/*mono*). Put differently, we need some distance, both physically and mentally, to 'see' (and comprehend) things around us. *Mono* can be therefore described as 'things to be seen' that are 'objects' and 'objectified' things. An object always stands outside the self. Hence, Kimura writes, '*[M]ono* (things) are all objective entities, and objective entities are all *mono* (things)' (Kimura, 1982:6).

Koto, on the other hand, can be characterized as a subjective entity which does not appear as an objective one. Such a state of being in existence is, therefore, unstable and unclear for us. A pen as an object/thing has a size and colour. A pen, therefore, is *mono*, while 'a pen on the desk' is a situation or condition (in context) which evokes subjective image, sensation, and interpretation. Then the pen becomes a subjective object. We can therefore see the pen as *koto*: a way of 'appearing' that is different from that of *mono*.

Furthermore, no matter how we perceive *mono*, *mono*'s existentiality remains. The pen's being in the world remains, whereas *koto* only appears via someone's subjective experience and image. It can be said that *mono* is an objective being, whereas *koto* is a subjective being. Yet *koto* cannot be separated from *mono*, since *koto* derives from our subjective experience with *mono*. Kimura therefore conceives that *koto* emerges between subjective state and objective state (Kimura, 1982:10). Interestingly, this can resonate with Bergson's explanation of the concept: an image's existence that lies between a representation (subjective) and a thing (objective).

We usually try to make sense of our experience in everyday life through applying both *koto* and *mono* processes. All things around us appear in front of us as both objective and subjective beings. Hence, we can perceive things as not only simple objects, but also lively, sensory and affective objects. People who have depersonalization syndrome, however, often have a problem with *koto*. They can 'see' an object (or a thing) but cannot 'sense' the affectivity of an object. In this light, Kimura considers that *mono* can be viewed as 'reality' and *koto* can be seen as 'actuality'.[10] For him, reality is a 'given reality' which we do not have the agentive capacity to generate or transform, whereas actuality is an '(affective) reality' which is evoked by subjective action and experience (Kimura, 1994:29). This indicates that those who have depersonalization can be alienated from their 'actuality' in the world in which they live. They have lost affectivity in a given reality. This suggests that we cannot make sense of being alive in a given reality without the sense of actuality.

Affect and phenomenology

Actuality can therefore be understood as affectivity evoked by subjective consciousness. This is what Husserl's phenomenology emphasizes as its significance, which was explicated as (subjective) 'life of consciousness' (*Bewusstseinsleben*, Hua XIV 46, cited in Moran, 2013:37). Husserl's approach was based on the criticism of scientific rationalism. As all forms of positivism are based on only empirical data, they are therefore inadequate in explaining lived experience. He argues that the approach of the natural sciences could reduce myriad phenomena and the composition of human lives to natural causal processes, which is a crucial mistake.[11] Husserl's interest was in 'the essences of diverse cognitive or epistemic attitudes (perceiving, remembering, imagining, judging, surmising and so on) that constitute the building blocks of our rational lives as knowers and doers (agents)' (Moran, 2013:41). For Husserl, these epistemic attitudes are based on 'intentionality', which means to orientate towards some object, with intentionality regarded as the crucial element to understand consciousness of lived experience. As Husserl writes:

[t]hose types of lived experience are not a matter of arbitrary special features of an accidental life of consciousness, but rather that terms like 'perception', 'memory', 'expectation' etc., express universal essential structures. (APS 365–6; HUA XI 233, cited in Moran, 2013:42)

A French philosopher, Michel Henry, also criticizes the predominance of naturalism and explores life with a phenomenological approach. His philosophy is based on 'a reflection on the meaning of the lived experience of life' (Davidson and Seyler, 2019:ix). Henry was, however, highly critical of Husserl's analysis of intentionality in terms of its 'ontological monism', which means that 'it reduces all forms of appearing to one type of being' (Davidson and Seyler, 2019:xviii). For Henry, this idea was derived from the dominant idea of Western philosophy that considered an understanding of 'appearing' in the relationship between objects and the self. When perceiving an object, 'it would necessarily entail the distance that separates the subject from itself taken as object' (Davidson and Seyler, 2019:ix). The object should be outside of the self, which is the state of ek-stasis.

In contrast to this, Henry considers that appearing phenomena do not occur in the process of ek-stasis but take place 'in the immediacy of one's relation to one's own living' (Davidson and Seyler, 2019:xix). This is the subjective body which is formed by the self's relation to itself. Yet how can the 'appearing' of the subjective body be perceived by itself? To consider this question, Henry introduces the concept of affectivity which occurs in the pre-intentional state. This can be achieved through *auto-affective processes*.

Henry's phenomenology emphasizes the actuality of 'the self' which is evoked *through* nonobjective and pre-intentional subjective experiences.

Henry argues there are two essentially different modes of phenomenalization: not only intentionality, but also affectivity. Although he distinguishes the two concepts in terms of different modes of appearing, he explains that the foundation of intentionality is grounded in affectivity. This suggests 'the primacy of affectivity insofar as auto-affection is the condition of possibility of all appearing' (Davidson and Seyler, 2019:xii). Hence:

> In order to be affected by something other, subjectivity first has to affect itself. A consciousness without auto-affectivity would not know itself: it would be without ipseity. (Davidson and Seyler, 2019:xii)

This implies that affectivity first takes the fundamental key role in perceiving the self in the transcendental condition of consciousness, and then it works to form a relationship between the self and its environment. It is a vital formation process of world-perception, which is a subjective image of the world.

Through the process of affectivity, (non)consciousness can therefore be able to form actuality, which creates the feeling of 'reality' by sensing the lived experiences. Interestingly, affectivity can also be seen as a similar state to that of *koto*, which only appears in a subjective experience through auto-affectivity. In this light, *affectivity* can be seen as a useful analytical notion with which to explore the dynamism of the conscious–nonconscious perceptive process.

Affect, cognition, and time-consciousness

The notion of 'affect' developed by Deleuze is often used to explore 'questions of the constitution of sensory perception/aesthesis and the specificity of artistic forms of expression' (Angerer et al, 2014:7). In the debate focusing on digital computer graphics technologies, it is often argued that they transformed digital media aesthetics in the moving image into a new type of illusion of reality (actuality) which can produce various kinds of affective effects in cinematic realism. The affective effects are usually designed to elicit spectators' affective responses. Furthermore, the contemporary digitized realities allow spectators to react more actively to moving images than ever before.

This can become particularly intense in interactive computer graphics (such as computer games or virtual reality experiences). In Chapter 6 Bruns addresses computer video games in terms of the relationship between an avatar and a player. The spectators can navigate the virtual space by themselves and enjoy immersive and intense sensations in computer-rendered environments. In this respect, sophistication of the digitized realities can also lead to the extension of our sensory and cognitive worlds.

This assumption, that humans are entwined in media and that media influence human perception, can be seen as an obvious and axiomatic truth. In the era of advanced computational information technology, it can be argued, however, that new forms of digital image production using computing systems and increasingly changing haptic media environments have led to the transformation of the grounds for understanding human perception. This is the central issue the collection attempts to explore. As Hayles (2017) argues, computational media are 'the quintessentially *cognitive* technology' and therefore they have 'special relationships' with the quintessentially cognitive species, *Homo sapiens*. Special relationships between computational media and human cognitive systems can recursively interplay. 'Twenty-first-century media' are capable of gathering data from experience, 'including *our own* experience'. Thus, the data 'literally put us into recursive loops'. This also leads to the situation that Hansen calls 'feed-forward loops' (Hansen, 2015:65). These processes can create new forms of actualities through new forms of affectivities. This implies that the *actuality* which is created by digital media plays an important role in determining our perceptive reality.

'The recursive loops' between trained data and the human experience also suggest that our perception doesn't remain static but instead undergoes changes through time. Husserl offers a phenomenology of the temporality of experience and describes the constitution of the layers of 'time-consciousness' (Bergo, 2021:321) for developing his idea of the 'fundamental "flow" of consciousness' (Bergo, 2021:321). He considers time-consciousness as a 'duration block' (Gallagher, 2017:91) which contains present, past, and future. More precisely, Husserl takes account of the temporal structure of consciousness using three different times: now, no-longer-now, and not-yet-now. In this sense, perceptual presence of consciousness is not just what is happening (now) but occurs in interaction with what happened (no-longer-now) and what is going to happen (not-yet-now). In other words, it is constituted by a 'new now-moment stretching back (as a "retention") and reaching as if "forward" in anticipation of coming events' (as 'protention') (Bergo, 2021:322).

Both Hansen's 'feed-forward loops' and Husserl's phenomenology of the temporality of experience emphasize time stretching back in the past and experience in the past imbued with the future in the present. Cubitt in this collection explores computational and human temporality, focusing on digital data visualization. In doing so, he examines the consequences of future-oriented simulation and highlights the 'crises of time that occur when practices and concepts of time come into contradiction' – chronoclasm.

What is significant here is that 21st-century media create and influence a new experience of temporality.

Affectivity and incomputability

Hence, we can see that digital computational media can no longer simply be conceived as external technological devices for communication, memories, and information. They can now directly influence cognitive processes in the perception of lived realities. As Merleau-Ponty (2002/1945) remarks, 'perceiving as we do with our body, the body is a natural self and, as it were, the subject of perception'. In this rendering, the body becomes the fundamental entity that mediates the relationship between reality and our perception. At this point, the body itself becomes a techno-biological mediated entity.

In this context, some scholars show their ambivalent feelings about the compatibilities between the mechanisms of digital information technologies and human perception. The digitized realities are created by mathematically constructed algorithmic reasoning systems, whereas affective responses are a qualitative mode of human (non)conscious sensation. Therefore, there is an argument that the human affective response cannot be fully measured and represented by complex quantitative calculations, and it is an effectively incomputable property.

For example, Hubert Dreyfus explores 'skillful coping', which is an embodied technique and tacit knowledge for human intelligence, and argues that 'the human brain doesn't work like a heuristically programmed digital computer, applying rules to bits of information' (Dreyfus, 2014:36). For instance, any kind of expert has the capacity to effortlessly and rapidly see the present situation as resembling similar instances that they hold in their memory 'without resorting to time-consuming feature detection and matching' (Dreyfus, 2014:36). The debate about the disjunction between (in)computable affective experiences and computational calculation is discussed by Tamari in Chapter 3, which focuses on human perception in contrasting digital computational and hand-drawn rendered images. Hansen's chapter also addresses the limitations of algorithmic operationality on the internet, which does not fully capture affective and bodily potentialities.

(Non)subjective affectivity and temporality

When it comes to human perception, as mentioned earlier, Michel Henry emphasizes the importance of 'auto-affection' (Davidson and Seyler, 2019:xii) which occurs in one's relation to one's own being.

This process takes place *in* a subjective body. Although computers can engage in 'self-evaluation' to refine their systems with preprogrammed computational algorithms and trained sets of data, it doesn't mean a computer has a subjective body (that is, computer programmes do not have emotions, feelings, and motivations as well as a physical body); it operates with different mechanisms from human subjectivity.

Husserl's phenomenological approach, which emphasizes subjective consciousness and lived experiences, can often be seen as incompatible with the theoretical and empirical analysis of affect, since affect is considered as a pre-intentional, presubjective nonobjective state of consciousness.

As mentioned earlier, Sampson in this collection introduces a different angle to consider the relationship between human perception, moving images, and consciousness. He offers a Whiteheadian nonphenomenological approach by locating percipient experience of movement in the flow of 'the event'. Rather than emphasize subjective perceptual experience, he remarks that it is 'the event itself that becomes the concrete fact of experience' and 'the events decide the subject'. The subject's view on experience belongs to an 'impersonal web' of events. Furthermore, in his analysis of the event perspective, he argues it is particularly important to examine moving images rather than static ones (such as photographs).

Unlike Sampson, Henry's phenomenology of life and his approach are essentially concerned with interpretations of the subjective perception of experience, which is similar to Husserl's claims. Henry's auto-affective approach can, however, occur in the process between presubjective consciousness and subjective intentionality, since 'affectivity provides the condition of possibility for intentional consciousness' (Davidson and Seyler, 2019:xi).

This implies that we need to consider at least two different levels of consciousness in the configuration process of affect.

In the first level, affectivity remains the presubjective consciousness to which the subject's experience, along with its rational and emotional dimensions, has not yet become fully related. Hayles's contribution to this collection explains this level in terms of the complex recursive dynamics between nonconscious cognition and consciousness. For her, nonconscious cognition can integrate affective experiences, which include different kinds of sensory signals, such as audio, visual, and bodily movements, in order to help consciousness to create a coherent body representation and a sense of the world. In this process, nonconsciousness takes about 200 milliseconds to become aware of sensations after the onset of sensory stimuli, which is much faster than that of the process of consciousness (which takes about 500 milliseconds). Furthermore, nonconsciousness also discerns patterns in noisy information in order not to overwhelm consciousness and create an integrated sense of the world. This is the first level of affect, which implies that the subject has not yet fully established its own sense of the world, and so it is still in the process of presubjective consciousness.

The idea of processual consciousness can resonate with Husserl's notion of time-consciousness, in which he sees the flow of consciousness as a construction process of meanings, intentions, and anticipation. He describes the process of time-consciousness by using four technical terms: the empty anticipation; primal impression; retention; and protention. The first and second terms are particularly important to understand a move from presubjective consciousness (the first level) to subjective consciousness (the second level). Husserl conceives that 'first there is an empty expectation, and then there is the point of the primary perception, itself an intentional experience' (Gallagher, 2017:93). This suggests that there is a passage of succession in the construction process of subjective meanings at the advanced level of affect.

This process is also reminiscent of Stengers' remarks on the passage of time. She considers that 'the passage is neutral, and the slippage of the present into the past always comes first, ready to be mobilized in terms of a cause or a reason' (Stengers, 2014:71). This suggests that although the passage is a continuous series, it is not a linear timeline. This is because 'the slippage of the present' can be referred to the past in order to connect to its subjective causalities. This is a process whereby the presubjective consciousness moves into subjective consciousness. At this second level, it might be said that affectivity starts identifying an intentional correlation of subject and its experience. This is a level of 'subjective affect'.

Affectivity can be found in all 'lived' experience. Thus, how we can find 'pure affectivity', which escapes from our everyday life in the social, political, cultural, and biological context, or analysing how complex information about the social 'environment' can be translated into neurological mechanisms, are still open questions. But we can explore how our affectivity and actuality 'appear' and how they are perceived in our everyday life.

In addressing these challenges, this book largely seeks to provide accounts of the phenomenological approach to human perception in digital information technologies, considering both biological determinism and neuroreductionism without 'all or nothing thinking' in order to scrutinize affective effect and response produced by digitized computer-rendered moving images. Hence, this approach requires not only the consideration of the social, political, and cultural perspectives, but also psychological, biological, and neurological ones. This critical engagement, the core aim of the book, still needs to be more fully articulated, especially the potential integration of the fields of animation studies, body studies, media theory, and the digital humanities.

Notes

[1] Audio and sound effects are vital to analyse the affective effects and experience of screen culture, which includes cinema, animation, and videogames. It is fair to say that human perception is not only constituted by the visual, but also by other sensory sensibilities, such as hearing, smell, taste and touch. The body (as a whole) is the fundamental entity which communicates with the environment. In sensory studies and body studies, senses

such as touch or hearing have been extensively discussed (for example, the 2022 special issue of *Body & Society* 28(1–2) on symmetries of touch). Rather than covering multiple sensory approaches, which are too wide to include in a single book, this collection focuses more on the visual capacity and visual representation of moving images. It is worth noting that the book includes visualizing data, maps and photographs that are not always accompanied by sound, since the notion of animation in this collection encompasses not only the cinematic modality, but also broader forms and concepts of 'moving images'.

[2] Despite the rapid growth of MRI, there still is much room for further development in neuroscience research. In fact, medical devices that utilize bioelectric phenomena can only catch and measure brain cells which generate electricity, but recent electrophysiology has discovered there are some cells, such as astrocytes, that do not generate electricity but are still active. This suggests that there are many elements of the brain that have not been completely discovered.

[3] A robotics scholar, Yukie Nagai, has been involved in research that investigates how neural mechanisms work for the development of social cognitive abilities, applied to robots via computational neural network programmes (see Nagai's academic profile at http://developmental-robotics.jp/en/members/yukie_nagai, accessed 10 September 2022). 'Somatic marking' (Damásio, 1994, 1996) and 'embodied appraisals' (Prinz, 2004) were also introduced as other research based on neurocognitive theories of emotion (cited in Pitts-Taylor, 2016:4).

[4] This shift is called the 'neuroscientific turn' (Pitts-Taylor, 2016:3).

[5] These issues include the question of 'how our brain generates a subjective perspective that we can flexibly use and report to others' (Dehaene, 2014:8).

[6] For Pitts-Taylor, bodies are bodies with brains and have three core features: neurobiological bodies with emphasis on nervous and neuron network systems and brain regions; minded bodies, which have material, physical and phenomenological psychic capacities; and social bodies, which play a role in communicating with 'other bodies (and things) with which they coexist' beyond times (evolutionary time as well as the immediate past and present) (Pitts-Taylor, 2016:1).

[7] Bergson defines images as referring to 'a certain existence which is more than that which the idealist calls a representation, but less than that which the realist calls a thing – an existence placed halfway between the "thing' and the "representation"' (Bergson 1908/ 1991:9). We can understand that 'image' can be matter as well as mind. In this light, he argues that the body is an image which is not just matter, but also is mind. This is because the body is not just constituted with various organs, brains, and tissues (matter), but also with perception, emotion, and feeling (mind).

[8] For Deleuze, we find ourselves in 'the set of what appears' ('image') which can be seen as 'the exposition of a world' where 'image = movement' (Deleuze, 1983/2022:65).

[9] A moving image has to be understood as a phenomenon of movement not only in space but also in time. Considering time in relation to cognitive processes is particularly important to understand the interdependent relationship between conscious and nonconscious cognition (see Hayles, 2017:41ff, and this collection). The debate on time (timing) in affect has also been discussed a great deal in the fields of psychology, neuroscience, film theory and media theory, such as Brian Massumi's 'the missing half second' (Massumi, 2002). A number of books, such as *Timing of Affect: Epistemologies, Aesthetics, Politics* (2014), edited by Marie-Luise Angerer et al, and *A Tenth of A Second: A History* (2009), by Jimena Canales, are also important. For the purpose of this paper, I only focus on space and will consider issues in relation to time on a different occasion.

[10] Kimura's notion of reality is obviously different from Deleuze's pure object, but it can be seen as a similar notion to Bergson's things in this context.

[11] Horkheimer criticises Husserl's phenomenology in terms of its ahistorical and undialectical method. Horkheimer argues that it is difficult to establish the absolute validity that is the priority through a concrete situation of a specific cultural and historical moment. Hence, he thinks that Husserl's concept of apriority is undialectical. It is important to note that Husserl never rejected science and argues for the significance of history, which deeply penetrated into spirit of life. He sees history, however, as not a method of science and argues that 'the task of philosophy is to be science, not to be [the] worldview for an age', and that if we consistently resort to sceptical subjectivism, we consequently lose the validity of ideas such as truth, theory and science. He considers that there would be no validity in itself. Hence, he emphasizes the importance of the first-person perspective to reveal lived experience and various phenomena in society (see Türker, 2013:623).

References

Angerer, Marie-Luise (2015) *Desire After Affect*, translated by Nicholas Grindell, London/New York: Rowman & Littlefield.

Angerer, Marie-Luise, Bösel, Bernd and Ott, Michaela (eds) (2014) *Timing of Affect: Epistemologies, Aesthetics, Politics*, Zurich: Diaphanes.

Ash, James, Kitchin, Rob and Leszczynski, Agnieszka (2016) 'Digital turn, digital geographies?', *Progress in Human Geography*, 42(1): 25–43.

Barry, Susan R. (2009) *Fixing My Gaze: A Scientist's Journey into Seeing in Three Dimensions*, New York: Basic Books.

Bazin, Andre (1967) *What is Cinema? Volume 2*, translated by Hugh Gray, Berkeley, CA: University of California Press.

Bergo, Bettina (2021) *Anxiety: A Philosophical History*, Oxford: Oxford University Press.

Bergson, Henri (1908/1991) *Matter and Memory*, translated by N.M. Paul and W.S. Palmer, New York: Zone Books.

Blakeslee, Sandra and Blakeslee, Matthew (2007) *The Body Has a Mind of Its Own*, New York: Random House.

Buchan, Suzanne (2013) 'Introduction: Pervasive Animation', in Suzanne Buchan (ed) *Pervasive Animation*, London: Routledge, pp 1–21.

Clark, David (2005) 'The Discreet Charm of the Digital Image: Animation and New Media', in Chris Gehman and Steve Reinke (eds) *The Sharpest Point: Animation at the End of Cinema*, Toronto: YYZ Books, pp 138–49.

Damásio, António (1994) *Descartes' Error: Emotion, Reason, and the Human Brain*, New York: AVON Books.

Damásio, António (1996) 'The somatic marker hypothesis and the possible functions of the prefrontal cortex', *Philosophical Transactions of the Royal Society B: Biological Sciences*, 351(1346): 1413–20.

Davidson, Scott and Seyler, Frédéric (eds) (2019) *The Michel Henry Reader: Studies in Phenomenology and Existential Philosophy*, Evanston, IL: Northwestern University Press.

Dehaene, Stanislas (2014) *Consciousness and the Brain: Deciphering How the Brain Codes Our Thoughts*, New York: Penguin Books.

Deleuze, Gilles (1983/2022) *Cinema 1: The Movement-Image*, translated by Hugh Tomlinson and Barbara Habberjam, London: Bloomsbury Academic.

Deleuze, Gilles and Parnet, Claire (1983) *Dialogue II* (revised edn), translated by Hugh Tomlinson and Barbara Habberjam, New York: Columbia University Press.

Dreyfus, Hubert L. (2014) *Skillful Coping: Essays on the Phenomenology of Everyday Perception and Action*, edited by Mark A. Wrathall, Oxford: Oxford University Press.

Gallagher, Shaun (2017) 'The Past, Present and Future of Time-Consciousness: From Husserl to Varela and Beyond', *Constructivist Foundations*, 13(1): 91–7.

Geniusas, Saulius (2020) ' "Multiple Realities" Revisited: James and Schutz', *Human Studies*, 43(4): 545–65.

Gregg, Melissa and Seigworth, Gregory J. (eds) (2010) *The Affect Theory Reader,* Durham, NC: Duke University Press.

Hansen, Mark B.N. (2015) *Feed-Forward: On the Future of Twenty-First-Century Media*, Chicago: University of Chicago Press.

Hayles, N. Katherine (2017) *Unthought: The Power of the Cognitive Nonconscious,* Chicago: University of Chicago Press.

Jenkins, Eric S. (2013) 'Another *Punctum*: Animation, Affect, and Ideology', *Critical Inquiry*, 39(3): 575–91.

Jenkins, Eric S. (2014) *Special Affects: Cinema, Animation and the Translation of Consumer Culture*, Edinburgh: Edinburgh University Press.

Kimura, Bin (1963) 'Zur Phänomenologie der Depersonalisation', *Nervenarzt*, 34(9): 391–7.

Kimura, Bin (1982) *Jikan to Jiko (Time and Self)*, Tokyo: Chuo Shinsho.

Kimura, Bin (1994) *Kokoro no Byouiri wo Kangaeru (Considering Mental Pathology)*, Tokyo: Iwanami Shinsho.

Liu, Alan (2012) 'The state of the digital humanities: A report and a critique', *Arts and Humanities in Higher Education*, 11(1–2): 8–41.

Massumi, Brian (2002) *Parables for The Virtual: Movement, Affect, Sensation*, Durham, NC: Duke University Press.

Merleau-Ponty, Maurice (2002/1945) *Phenomenology of Perception*, translated by Colin Smith, London and New York: Routledge.

Moran, Dermot (2013) 'Edmund Husserl and Phenomenology', in Andrew Bailey (ed) *Philosophy of Mind: The Key Thinkers*, London: Bloomsbury, pp 37–58.

Pfeifer, Rolf and Bongard, Josh (2006) *How the Body Shapes the Way We Think: A New View of Intelligence*, Cambridge, MA: MIT Press.

Pitts-Taylor, Victoria (2016) *The Brain's Body: Neuroscience and Corporeal Politics*, Durham, NC: Duke University Press.

Prinz, Jesse (2004) 'Which Emotions Are Basic?', in *Emotion, Evolution, and Rationality*, edited by Dylan Evans and Pierre Cruse, New York: Oxford University Press, pp 69–88.

Sampson, Tony D. (2020) 'Affect, Cognition and the Neurosciences', *Athenea Digital*, 20(2): e2346.

Stengers, Isabelle (2014) *Thinking with Whitehead: A Free and Wild Creation of Concepts*, Cambridge, MA: Harvard University Press.

Stiegler, Bernard (2015) *Symbolic Misery, Volume 2: Catastrophe of the Sensible*, translated by Barnaby Norman, Cambridge: Polity.

Tomoko, Tamari (2021) 'Interview with Samantha Frost on "The Attentive Body": Epigenetic Processes and Self-formative Subjectivity', *Body & Society*, 27(3): 87–101.

Türker, Habip (2013) 'Horkheimer's Criticism of Husserl', *Philosophy & Social Criticism*, 39(7): 619–35.

PART I

Animation and Consciousness

1

Pastures New: Atmospheres, Mud, and Moods

Esther Leslie

Mud mood

An observation on human existence today might benefit from hurtling backwards to some sort of origin, mythic or not. We are golems, mud people, inanimate matter that had life breathed into it, once long ago. We crawled from the mud. We shaped it around us eventually to make a shelter. Now we might think we are elevated above it, have asphalted over it or fenced it off. Mud is from another time, if not another place. Mud is not conceived of as modern, as the stuff that builds up our digital worlds. Mud surrounds us still, but it is not meant to figure in our futurist dreams, our fully automated futures, our clean technologies or shiny screens and interfaces that are all we are meant to desire. The opposite of mud must be the liquid crystal. Mud is opaque, unlike liquids and crystals. Mud is dirty, unlike our dreams of liquids and crystals. Mud is brown and sticky, unlike our flowing liquids, our translucent crystals. Mud must be the contradiction of the liquid crystal environments that illuminate our cities, our homes, our own bodies – greeny, bluey, cool whitish light reflected chin-ward – which are not brown, opaque, sticky, dirty. But sometimes mud floods in on us. We find ourselves stuck in the mud, actually or metaphorically. Landslides, mudslides occur periodically, the result of development, the stripping away of trees, encouraged by extreme weather events. But mud sticks to us in another way, is our inheritance, is what we came from but cannot brush off easily. To start in the mud, mud-bound, in any reflection, is to evoke a primal state before our time, when there was only mud. This mud was a context for life and, indeed, has been found in its kaolinite form to hold traces of the soft, microbial life of 540 million years ago, which did not leave fossils, because it lacked hardness. In time, life hardened, and in time too, mud became clay, became the vessels and objects of something called civilization.

Mud is old, but mud is still present, is still our ground, even if we rarely touch it. To reflect on it allows an acknowledgement of how much there is, in our time, in theory, a love affair developing with matter and materiality, with its capacities, its possible liveliness, its unpredictability, its self-orientations, that can be mobilized *for us*. Mud has been and is always there and speaks anew to a hum or a buzz about materiality. It is ancient and of the moment. Matter, new and anciently old, is 'vital'. Matter possesses 'agency'. Matter matters again, just as it always matters; but now, it matters for now.

Matter has history; or how it comes to matter for us has history. Mud becomes clay becomes digital environment through time. This is not to imply that each of these – from mud to digital infrastructure – is a separate matter. Shannon Mattern has written of the connections that flow from material to material, even as these become apparently immaterial. Mud in its various forms has formed cities, and cities have taken on shape on the basis of material forms within them:

> For millennia mud and its geologic analogs have bound together our media, urban, architectural, and environmental histories. Some of the first writing surfaces, clay and stone, were the same materials used to construct ancient city walls and buildings, whose facades also frequently served as substrates for written texts. The formal properties of those scripts – the shapes they took on their clay (or, eventually, parchment and paper) foundations – were also in some cases reflected in urban form: how the city molded itself from the materials of the landscape. And those written documents have always been central to nearly all cities' operation: their trade, accountancy, governance, and culture. (Mattern, 2017:88)

These written documents, once made as impressions in mud, will become strikes in silicon and expressed in inks of petrol and ground-up polyester. As Mattern puts it:

> our cities have been smart and mediated, and they've been providing spaces for intelligent mediation, for millennia. That intelligence is simultaneously epistemological, technological, and physical; it's codified in our cities' laws and civic knowledges and institutions, hard-wired into their cables and protocols, framed in their streets and architectures and patterns of development. The city mediates between these various materialities of intelligence, between the ether and the

iron ore. Clay and code, dirt and data intermingle here, and they always have. (Mattern, 2017:xii)

Media exist in the city and these media are material. Cities are palimpsests, scribbled on, messy, a tangle of old and new modes, old and new codes, messy with materials, with leftovers, with old ore and new ethers, 'untidy, productively "confused" materialities and temporalities' (Mattern, 2017:156).

Matter is in the process of reinvention in the laboratory, but also in thinking. Matter combines with the digital to make new materials for and of the digital world. Clay itself is reinvented for the digital world. It exists in the extraction sites of rare earth elements across the world. Since the 1990s, the earth's crust has been scooped out to provide the minerals for smartphones, wind turbines, electric vehicles, and other high-tech products that require rare earth elements. To get at these elements, layers of topsoil are removed and placed in a leaching pond to be subjected to the actions of acids that separate out the elements from the clay, soil, and rock. Sometimes, instead, holes are drilled into hills and plastic pipes and rubber hoses flush out the mud and pump it into the leaching ponds. Once the matter has all been extracted or the mining company has collapsed, left behind are concrete leaching ponds and plastic-lined pools for waste water, their contents toxic, precariously held within the dips. The mud threatens to spill out into groundwater, the soil is polluted. Sometimes uranium contaminates the soil and it sits there leaking, a silent bomb. These new muds yield up our touchscreens and liquid crystal environments.

The new muds are surrounding us. They drag us in and we are formed from them again, because we ingest them and we are surrounded by them and they stick to us. New muds are airy forms of muds, or foams, and they are slimes, sludges that draw in the fingers, like the slime of playground crazes, a neon or glittery or creamy sludge that demands the fingers, the knuckles, the balled fist to work and rework it into endless shapes for shaping's sake.

Moving bodies in mud

Who, what, where are we amid the froth of modern technology, the brew of chemicals and the agitated air of particulates and data streams? How are we? A small question – but a hard one. What do our solid bodies, drawn from the mud and now annexed to the liquid crystal device, still have to do around here? What uses us? Our contemporary understanding of physiology, which is a science of the body, is one now predicated on processes that are digital, computational, data-driven and data-generating. The body is quantified. Medical practitioners diagnose not by sight and touch and are far removed from a laying on of hands. They look at the computer read-outs, the graphs and plotted lines, and give a verdict. Each one of us does this as we upload data from our fitness devices and analyse our own performance. A medical health news site reports on recent developments in 2019:

> Smartwatches account for 29.8% of all wearables, and are evolving quickly beyond the simple measurement of heart rate or steps. Built-in algorithms monitor blood oxygen levels, calories burnt and sleep quality. Last year, Apple presented a breakthrough innovation – its Watch Series 4 with ECG had been cleared by the FDA. From that moment on, heart health monitoring in real time became as easy as checking body temperature. With this new feature, the smart watch became a medical device to detect irregular health rhythms. In a broader meaning, medicine started to move away from the hospital to the home. (Olesch, 2019)

The body is information. It floats free as data, but it is also bound into machinery. It is located precisely in time and space. Bodies stream from themselves, like a halo, like aura, like a mist condensing all the time. Bodies emanate a new ether. Not mud, but mud only deep down, repressed, hidden, and present only as something airy, as ether, a matter that is barely one and yet has been everything, alchemical, chemical, mystical, aesthetic, anaesthetic.

If we would wish to predict the future for humans, which may be the purpose of social theory, then we can look to cows, because their bodies are the testing grounds of the new pastures to be engineered out of the dirt–dust. Some cows still spend their days in proximity to mud, nibbling grass. Many are displaced, and increasingly so across the world, into the megafarms: a crammed, industrialized environment, in which livestock in their thousands are held in one place, overseen by digital systems and cybersecurity measures. The US has many mega farms, but they are developing elsewhere. Qatar has produced self-sufficiency in dairy through the construction of air-conditioned sheds for thousands of cows that are kept away from the sometimes sweltering heat, blasted by giant fans and sprayed with a fine mist of water (Whitehead, 2019). In such settings, where digital machinery monitors and logs each part of the herd, every mouthful of milk can be traced to source. A recent report on the Dairymaster website notes of its technologies that it is exporting to Chinese megafarms:

> The MooMonitor+ allows the cow to follow her natural cycle and is bringing wearable technology to the farmyard which as a result is helping to change the face of agriculture. The MooMonitor+ utilises technology from cloud computing, wearable sensing and big data to make health and reproductive monitoring better. They also used technology from rockets and smart phones to give farmers real-time

information about the health and fertility status of each cow in their herd. (Dairymaster, 2018)

All events within the air-conditioned barn are digitally and genetically monitored: insemination, gestation, birth ease, pharmaceutical intervention, udder suitability for robotic milking, lactation. How much milk a cow produces is combined with other data sets: for example, with meteorological data to produce parameters for 'smart grazing'. There is a desire to know more and more, to know how much each cow eats and drinks, if she is lame or her udders inflamed and in need of medical attention, if she is acting in any way strangely. The Irish company Cainthus has developed a digital vision system that gathers information on each animal, in order 'to passively monitor' the farm's cows '24/7 and analyze their well-being, productivity and performance, alerting you when it matters most' (https://www.appeng ine.ai/company/cainthus). This occurs through daily notification to a phone, providing the farmer with detailed analytics.

The application of artificial breeding techniques to improve livestock is now routine in the dairy industry. Given the advances in embryo transfer technology from the 1970s onwards and the development of sexed semen identification in the 1990s, the dairy industry became enmeshed in dairy genetics, carried through artificial insemination or AI. Companies specializing in cattle genetics provide catalogues containing an almost limitless assortment of semen from sires at all pricing points for a worldwide marketplace. There is no longer a need to have live bulls at the dairy. Instead a phial or 'straw' of frozen sperm arrives.

'Artificial breeding', or AI, is aimed at increasing milk yields in cows, specifically through improving udder traits. AI is used as a tool for reproduction efficiencies in herds, which in turn leads to increased profits.

Genetics has been applied to the increasing of milk yields. Milk yield per cow has more than doubled in the last half century: many cows create more than 20,000 kg of milk in each lactation. This increase in milk yield has been accompanied by a decline in the rate of conception for lactating cows. The cow body might make milk, but it produces and sustains fewer calves. It is reported that, 'in the U.S., calving intervals increased from less than 13.0 months to more than 14.5 months and the number of inseminations per conception from 2.0 to greater than 3.5 from 1980 to 2000 in 143 U.S. commercial herds' (Oltenacu and Broom, 2010). In addition, dairy cows suffer from more metabolic diseases such as mastitis, laminitis, and acidosis, difficulties resultant primarily from the rise in stress that attends increased milk production. The cows are exhausted. The dairy industry has, for decades, acknowledged that the average productive life span of a milk cow is less than four lactations. Perhaps, so the hope goes, more data can bring the fix and the weaknesses can be eliminated genetically in the creation of a superbreed that can withstand anything. Bodies digitized are bodies becoming optimized.

We have long looked to animals to augment human fertility and reproduction, using cow's milk, for example, as a proxy to develop human infant milks. Bovine ovulation kits predated the human ones by twenty years. The whole apparatus of genetics and fertility sciences is rehearsed, in particular, on dairy animals. Other animals have been involved in the optimization of human fertility. Dr Serge Voronoff transplanted slices of monkey testicles into ageing men in the 1920s – famously, a former middleweight boxing champion of the world named Frank Klaus announced that he had undergone this operation to boost his failing career. To this day, most commercial HRT and gender reassignment oestrogen is manufactured from the urine of pregnant mares (it is secreted in the name Premarin, pregnant mare's urine). Captured digital and genetic data, and the financialization of that data at the biochemical scale, emerges as a model in the dairy industry, where animals are given 'a net (economic) genetic merit' calculated by their fertility, milk yield, teat suitability for robotic milking, propensity to infection and disease, feed consumption, ease of birthing, and 'sire genetic potential'. Genetic lines are sold via semen, embryo transfer, and IVF. Genetic lines are discontinued when 'genetic merit' cannot be realized. Hormone regulation is developed as an economic pathway, and milk is abstracted as economically valuable medium. Omics are brought to bear on the body of the cow, which becomes a collation of molecules, as computational biology or bioinformatics, the science of managing and analysing biological data using advanced computing techniques, erases old-style physiology: genomics, the study of genes and their function; proteomics, the study of proteins; metabolomics, the study of molecules involved in cellular metabolism; transcriptomics, the study of the mRNA; glycomics, the study of cellular carbohydrates; and lipomics, the study of cellular lipids.

The digital capture of the cow takes another route too, one that leads directly into the realm of affect. Cows are conceived of as emotional beings, and their emotions can be measured through the quantities of cortisol produced. The calmer the cow, the higher the milk yields. Higher cortisol, sign of more stress, leads to less milk, and so productivity plummets. There are technological fixes. If there is stress, new virtual reality headsets, adapted to a cow's flat face, may help, as tested in 2019 in Russia on the Rusmolco research farm near Moscow. The cows are apparently led, through digital animation clamped before their eyes, to believe they are in warm summer fields and not cold wintery ones. This calms them down, reduces their anxiety, and encourages them to produce more milk. 'As for the particular summer environment they were immersed in, the designers gave it a warm and predominantly red color scheme, since studies on cattle vision have shown that cows perceive the red part of the visible spectrum better than others' (Chandler, 2019).

There may be something comedic about a cow wearing VR goggles, at the same time as it is tragic. Tragic too, that our own disenfranchised futures may be modelled here. Recent theories of biomedicine are beginning to countenance the idea that precarity (and specifically precarity under the conditions of late capitalism) is a condition that creates permanent change in the body's reception of insulin, meaning that a stressed body is more prone to obesity and diabetes. Emotions manifest in the body, making of it an index of oppression and exploitation. Stress produces excess cortisol, which is associated with the production of certain types of body fat (Kendrick, 2016). Damage done to the mind, to the sense of well-being, expresses itself on the body. This recognition of a connection between states of mind and states of the body replaces older theories that apportioned obesity to a cultural naiveté in how to cope with plenitude, or, in simpler terms, blamed the populace for their unregulated appetites when living, blessedly, in the land of milk and plenty. We, so it seems, require our cortisol levels to be reduced to remain fit and less of a burden on health systems. In the absence of social changes that might effect chemical ones in the body, animation can step in. Could we be played by the machinery, by the AI, our emotions swayed without us even knowing that we are inside the matrix? What bodies are these bodies whose physiology is meshed with something that is there and not there, deceives the senses, produces affect, has no corners to look around? What lies at the interface between that which is computational and unaffective and the affect produced for a self who cannot see around the edges of the construct? We – perhaps those who are old, rejected, unemployed, redundant – will be deluded into thinking that the world is beautiful, a land of milk and honey, as we interact minimally in our stripped-back care homes, engaging with a pixel world whose delivery will be designed to be cheap, according to some economic rationale. But perhaps more optimistically, this animation will set us free to follow ludicrous lines and confected imagery, to make up our own delirious notebooks in the field of the world, in the new fields of digital dictatorship, frolicking while bound in the pastures that are around us, unreal but inhabited

The cow has become digital, just as its products derived from milk get enmeshed in digital systems. And humans too become digital, right down to the capturing of their emotional states, on a constant basis, in order to hone workplace management and consumer behaviours. Contemporary culture is organized around digital media, including social media, and these social media are generators of affect, reaction, dramatic expression, spaces in which care and abuse are meted out overtly. When this digital environment becomes a virtual, immersive environment that is indistinguishable at a sensory level from the non-digital world, the sense of the mediatized environment as a provoker of affect, as a possession rather than a feeling, becomes an emotion or an all-encompassing atmosphere in which external and internal worlds meet and bind (Döveling, Harju and Sommer, 2018). Emotion becomes a kind of motion, batting back and forwards between subject and system, an input become output, circled back as further stimulus, in a cycle of data.

The cycle is related to breathing – a circuit of gas exchange, a rising and falling of lungs, in input and output of air. The cycle is already integrated into the new pastures in the case of Neon's BreatheVR, a virtual reality application for Gear VR and Oculus Go. A user puts on a headset and is in a bright and colourful animated meadow – perhaps the same one as the cows. There is calming music and the sound of birds chirping. The user is asked to inhale deeply through the nose and to exhale fully through the mouth. The microphone detects the breath as it passes through the mouth and the leaves on the trees in the meadow begin to rise upwards. The user is encouraged to breathe more regularly and more deeply to lift the leaves, in this as-if world. In this way, physical pain and mental anguish are to be mitigated, managed by individuals who suffer chronically. Inside the machinery, in the fake meadow, we are asked to breathe again, as if reborn as digital beings whose pain can be managed internally if we submit enough to the banal rewards of the machinery. As the website for the programme on Oculus Go's website puts it:

> Take a few minutes out of your day and engage in some deep breathing relaxation to promote wellbeing. Taking time and responsibility for your health in today's fast paced society is now more important than ever. (Oculus, 2018)

We are caught in there, living virtual lives, with virtual breath, attention undivided. This fast-paced society does not allow for switching off – sleep in today's world is the temporary state adopted by devices as they wait primed to spring back into action. To remedy this, time after time, a sleepwear company produces kaleidoscopic animations, thrust on a late-night scroller through data harvesting, and these, once they have engaged the attention, trigger sleepiness through the right hemisphere and lull that supposed insomniac into sleep (Ads of Brands, 2020).

To be target of a quest for attention is a significant aspect of what it means to be human today. The field of neuroaesthetics is one of the more recent modes of exploring how attention is captured and held. Through such a framework, aesthetic experience is located as a property of neural systems conceived of as rooted in circuitry. Specific aesthetic experiences are seen to 'activate' things called 'visual motion areas' or 'the place area in the parahippocampal gyrus'. Normative ideas of beauty are assumed, with beautiful faces said to activate 'the fusiform face and adjacent areas' and to trigger 'general reward circuitry' (Wikipedia, nd). Mirror neurons are identified as parts in the brain that react to action, produce embodied responses to visual art, as well as other perceived actions. Bits of the brain light up here and there as universally agreed pretty things are flashed at it. This constitutes science, and it is dubious in the extreme. This does not stop it being operationalized by advertisers, or by Google researchers. In 2019 Google contributed to an exhibition at Milan Design Week, in coordination with scientists from Johns Hopkins University. The aim of the three-room installation, *A Space for Being*, was to show how so-called aesthetic elements can influence mood. Lighting, sounds, scents, and textures act on the visitors' senses in different ways and try to elicit various states of mood. A wristband detects each visitor's physical and physiological responses – heart rate, skin conductivity – to each space: one warm and 'womblike', one bright and playful, one minimalist. At the end of the visit, a computer read-out tells the visitor which room made them feel most comfortable according to the data.

Atomic intelligence

Scientific speculators dream of third nature. Third nature, designed nature, proposes a seemingly magical or nightmarish world that exists only as a result of infrastructures that are highly capitalized. At its more fantastical ends, it provides extraordinary images of the world remade from the atom up according to the digital command. The digital that is entangled with the body scoops down to encompass the atom, if only still in fantasy. In 1965, Ivan Sutherland imagined a room in which 'computers can control the existence of matter' (Sutherland, 1965). A developed version of this vision promotes a concept of the whole world, of each particle in this world, infused by liquid crystal digital prowess. The world's smallest parts can be remade, digitally. The idea of 'radical atoms', such as is promulgated at MIT by Hiroshi Ishii and the Tangible Media Group, proposes a world remade from the bottom up. It is responsive to human command. Physical objects have a limitation, remain too fixed, their properties immutable – they are too solidly crystalline. Liquidity, transformability – or animation, animatedness – needs to be engineered into the very substance that forms them. The liquid crystals that have been for some time the basis of all reproduced images, all digital optics, become the thing itself. The entire world becomes image. The entirety of images become world. Instead of the usual function of liquid crystals, which is to cast images, it seems the world itself might be cast through liquid crystal, that is to say, literally and physically in their image. Atoms, re-engineered into a certain liquid crystallinity, a solidity that can liquefy itself, are brought out of their 'current static and inert states to active and kinetic dimensions', according to the experimenters at MIT. That is to say atoms are to be instilled with properties of liquidity and crystallinity, with a certain sliminess, an ability to move and to move between states, to have form and to deform. They congregate to make entities in materials that can transform their shape, colour, properties, through digital or other stimuli, heat, light, sound. The proposal extends the flatness of pixel painting – in CGI or illusory 3D digital models – into the dimensionality of pixel sculpture, released into the environment. This is a digital clay that can be directly manipulated by human hands, deformed and transformed, which sends back signals to an underlying digital model – the human becomes an input, a physical inputter of information. At the same time, this digital clay can conform in response to a computer directive: solid shape transforms before watching eyes into another shape, changes colour, moves, dances, when the computer demands or when the input – heat, wind, light, and so on – requires it. An umbrella changes form and softness depending on wind direction or amount of rain. A screwdriver senses the screw head shape and readjusts accordingly. When some digital clay is rolled by clumsy human hands into a ball, it snaps into a perfect sphere. Another object comes close, it links to it using Boolean operations (Ishii et al, 2012:47). If it is cut in half, one side can mirror the other. In this futurist scenario, energy from the temperature of the body, from the light of the environment, could be extracted as a power source for devices, a radicalization of its current use within the circuitry of the touch screen device. Our devices would charge as we exist, as we emanate from ourselves, holding them, and they exist then without the tangle of wires, transformers, sockets.

Radical atoms are a dream of pixels released into the environment, pixels made 3D and ubiquitous. Ubiquitous computing, or the screen as pervasive, animation as everywhere, manifests not in terms of the visibility of devices, LCD screens, but rather subtly, faux-magically, an impelling that is barely perceptible but is knowable in the form of an invisible suture between material and computation, on the premise of responsive materials, which transform one type of energy into another. These radical atoms are, as yet, fictional 'digital clay', a knowing mud that can respond and shape itself, like the golem once did. Ubiquity is coexisting or synonymous with each cell of our body, each fluctuation of our body temperature, each shadow we cast or remove. The bleeding edge of technology is the prospect of technology not just on the body, at the fingertips, on the skin, not just on the screens and in the multiple devices around us, but rather integrated into every atom of the world, each atom whose capacities are augmented so that they might account for phases from fixed to flowing, from liquid to crystal. The world has its own screen capacities built into it in each particle. The height of this imagination – a digital interface implanted directly into the eyeball – not only augments the bejewelled surface of what it sees with data feeds: it exerts the ability to shapeshift what it looks at through the energy of thought. Photography melds with seeing, which melds with shaping. Liquid crystal, the sliminess of matter, is mobilized for a vision of a world that is subject to transformation, improvement, beautification in the light of the hi-tech, post-human engagement with nature. When everything that happens, and has scientific significance, operates not on the visible surface but in the realm of the subperceptual, at the atomic level, in the realm of the nanoscale, how quaint it is to speak of vision. The golem was a pile of dust wetted and made into clay, an inanimate thing made animate. The atom too, each atom of each body, each bit of atomic dust is to be reanimated in the light of the liquid crystal, its own liquid crystal intelligence redoubled and subject to and subject of inputs and outputs. They are matter remastered.

Muddy borders

Old muds, the ones that have lingered from ancient times, stick around as the dirt to be either eradicated or excavated and turned into value. These old muds become new in becoming information. Sediments at the floor of the sea, at the floor of a once-was-home for humans, yield information about history. Forms in the muddy slime of the seabed and lake bottoms are catalogued – the phenotypes of bacteria and archaea lodged in the mud that lies in vents within hot springs yield DNA and RNA and allow a full mapping of life, such that it might be made again, anew. A luxury yacht, the Sorcerer II, owned by a venture capitalist called Craig Venter, a 'wealthy maverick geneticist' as *Wired* described him, scooped up the slime in the early 2000s to make a bolus of new life (Shreeve, 2004). There is more life, more animated being in bacteria and microorganisms, an endless and proliferating world of unknown energy and potential product lines. Mud becomes digital becomes value. Venter trapped the DNA of these microorganisms on filter paper and sequenced and analysed it in order to discover hundreds of millions of genes. The quest is an extrapolation of all life on the planet. All animation will be catalogued. Should any gaps be found in the whole universe of forms, then they might be plugged by engineering. New systems of cataloguing develop – DNA-based instead of the conventional taxonomies. The digital mode of cataloguing is far better suited to DNA. Such information can be deployed efficiently – it does not even need 26 letters to record it but just four – A, C, T, G. Sequenced and informatized, the result may be a swift translation from DNA code to bank code. Where there's muck, there's brass is an old saying that does not stop ringing true. Once it is all logged, it can become the parts to make life from scratch. Venter, in 2014, formed a company Human Longevity, Inc., which sought to extend human lifespans through the use of genomics, metabolomics, microbiomics, and proteomics.

This mud at the bottom of the sea, this mud that is dense with rare earth metals, this mud in our world, squashed under concrete buildings or breaking through, rich with recyclable waste or contaminated with unrecyclable waste, it was always there but now newly there, yields much, and eventually, like everything else, transforms into money or value. In becoming value, mud moves from the material to the abstract. It turns spectral, becoming something like its apparent opposite, which might be imagined as air, or, more accurately, a muddied air. This muddy air comes at us, flies at us, as the polluted and clouded air of industrial farming's dirt tracks. This produces a loosening of topsoil, result of reckless modifications in land use, and we move around a world that is becoming everywhere a new Dust Bowl, something like the dust world of devastation in 1930s USA. Dusts appear in our environs as the particulated air of pollution, a turbid, agitated air, thick with matter. This is our environment. Atmosphere, this thing that should be light, aerated, floating, bobbing like utopian art's inflatable structures, stiffens. We exist nowadays in a muddy atmosphere, a dirty world, our bodies' motion mapped, our moods logged, our attention riveted.

References

Ads of Brands (2020) 'Zzzomnia: The first ad designed to make you sleep', Ads of Brands, 17 February [online], Available from: https://adsofbrands. net/en/news/zzzomnia-the-first-ad-designed-to-make-you-sleep/1268 [Accessed 18 February 2022].

Chandler, S. (2019) 'Virtual Reality Used to Relax Cows into Producing More Milk', Forbes, 29 November [online], Available from: www.forbes. com/sites/simonchandler/2019/11/29/virtual-reality-used-to-relax-cows-into-producing-more-milk/ [Accessed 18 February 2022].

Dairymaster (2018) 'Dairymaster technology chosen to build mega farms in China', Dairymaster, 2 August [online], Available from: www.dairymas ter.com/dairymaster-technology-chosen-to-build-mega-farms-in-china/ [Accessed 18 February 2022].

Döveling, K., Harju, A.A. and Sommer, D. (2018) 'From Mediatized Emotion to Digital Affect Cultures: New Technologies and Global Flows of Emotion', Social Media + Society, 4(1). https://doi.org/10.1177/2056305117743141

Hibma, J. (2017) 'The History Behind Artificial Insemination', Farming Magaine [online], Available from: www.farmingmagazine.com/livestock/ artificial-insemination-history [Accessed 18 February 2022].

Ishii, H., Lakatos, D., Bonanni, L. and Labrune, J.-B. (2012) 'Radical Atoms: Beyond Tangible Bits, Toward Tranformable Materials', Interactions, 19(1) [online], Available from: http://web.media.mit.edu/~ishii/RadicalAt oms_ACM_Interactios.pdf [Accessed 18 February 2022].

Kendrick, R. (2016) 'Metabolism as Strategy: Agency, Evolution and Biological Hinterlands', in Emma-Jayne Abbots and Anna Lavis (eds) Why We Eat, How We Eat: Contemporary Encounters between Foods and Bodies, London: Routledge, pp 237–54.

Mattern, S. (2017) *Code and Clay, Data and Dirt: Five Thousand Years of Urban Media*, Minnesota: University of Minnesota Press.

Oculus (2018) 'BreatheVR: A Healthy Mind Has an Easy Breath', Meta Quest, 24 May [online], Available from: https://www.oculus.com/experiences/go/1478011548974390/

Olesch, A. (2019) 'Opinion: How self-tracking biometrics influence patients, medicine and society', MobiHealthNews, 23 May [online], Available from: www.mobihealthnews.com/content/europe/opinion-how-self-tracking-biometrics-influence-patients-medicine-and-society [Accessed 18 February 2022].

Oltenacu, P.A. and Broom, D.M. (2010) 'The impact of genetic selection for increased milk yield on the welfare of dairy cows', *Animal Welfare*, 19(1): 39–49.

Shreeve, J. (2004) 'Craig Venter's Epic Voyage to Redefine the Origin of the Species', Wired, 1 August [online], Available from: www.wired.com/2004/08/venter/ [Accessed 18 February 2022].

Sutherland, I.E. (1965) 'The Ultimate Display', *Proceedings of the Congress of the International Federation of Information Processing (IFIP)*, 2: 506–8.

Whitehead, R. (2019) 'Desert dairy made Qatar self-sufficient in milk production in wake of blockade', Dairy Reporter, 12 June [online], Available from: www.dairyreporter.com/Article/2019/06/12/Desert-dairy-made-Qatar-self-sufficient-in-milk-production-in-wake-of-blockade [Accessed 18 February 2022].

Wikipedia. (nd) 'Neuroesthetics', last edited 30 May 2023, Available at https://en.wikipedia.org/wiki/Neuroesthetics

2

The Neurodynamics of Technically Mediated Motion: Perceptual vs. Conceptual Animation in Artworks of Nam June Paik and Bill Viola

N. Katherine Hayles

Stillness has always been the dark other to animation's motion. From flipbooks to celluloid film, stop-motion animation and on into the digital era, the still image has provided the foundation for motion, achieved through the brain's neurological processing that blurs images into motion when the frame rate reaches or exceeds 24 fps. These facts, well-known for over a century, have recently been given an empirical foundation by neurological research into nonconscious cognition. A deeper understanding of how nonconscious process works together with conscious perception highlights the importance of recursive dynamics to animation's effects and leads to a theoretical framework distinguishing between perceptual and recursive animation. This framework sheds light on the complex recursive dynamics that Nam June Paik explored through several of his artworks.[1] Through the work of video artist Bill Viola, it also opens new ways to understand how stillness and motion may be seen as a continuum rather than a binary either/or perception. Together, these developments suggest that recursive dynamics constitute a relatively unexplored area within animation theory, providing a basis of rethinking the relation of theory and practice in artworks using stillness as well as motion to achieve their effects.

Nonconscious cognition: integrating temporal information

Although experiments with nonconscious cognition were performed in the 1960s, it was not until the late 1990s that the experimental designs were sufficiently rigorous to provide the necessary empirical evidence for this mode of neuronal processing and to identify some of the functions it performs – functions, it turns out, essential for consciousness to operate (Lewicki, Hill and Czyzewska, 1992; Dresp-Langley, 2012). Its importance for consciousness notwithstanding, nonconscious cognition remains forever inaccessible to conscious introspection. In this respect it differs both from broad background awareness of the 'new unconscious' (Hassin, Uleman and Bargh, 2006), which can instantly become available to consciousness when appropriate, and from the Freudian unconscious, postulated to communicate with consciousness through dreams and symptoms.

One of nonconscious cognition's functions is integrating different kinds of sensory signals (for example, audio, visual, and kinesthetic inputs) to create a coherent body representation and a coherent sense of the world (Kouider and Dehaene, 2007; Eagleman, 2012). Within a window of about 100 ms (one-tenth of a second), nonconscious cognition synchs together sensory signals coming from different parts of the brain to create an integrated representation that then becomes available to consciousness. Whereas early electrical engineers in television and film were concerned with synchronizing audio and visual inputs exactly, they soon realized that within this window of 100 ms, the inputs would be synchronized 'automatically' by the brain, or as we now know, by nonconscious cognition.

The magic number for animation – 24 fps – is equivalent to a threshold of 44 ms per frame, precisely in the middle of the time frame within which nonconscious cognition operates upon sensory stimuli. It is therefore likely that the integration of successive stills into smooth analogue motion also occurs through nonconscious cognition. Knowing how nonconscious cognition communicates with consciousness is thus crucial for understanding the neurological basis for animation's motion effects, and consequently for how the thematics of different artworks interact with these neuronal processes to create densely textured multidimensional experiences that speak both to consciousness and to nonconscious perceptions.

Recursive dynamics in models of consciousness

In the 1980 *Autopoiesis and Cognition*, Humberto Maturana and Francisco Varela argued that cognition itself is nothing other than a recursive cycling between structure and organization, with the parts generating the whole, and the whole sustaining the parts. The intuition that recursive dynamics and cognition are deeply linked took centre stage again in the work of Nobel Prize winner neurologist Gerald Edelman and his collaborator, Giulio Tononi. Their model of human cognition gave a central role to neuronal recursivity (2000). Edelman's earlier work had demonstrated that synaptic networks develop in relation to environmental inputs in a process he called 'neural Darwinism,' a kind of survival of the fittest in which networks that get environmental stimulation grow and expand, while those not stimulated shrink and may even disappear (Edelman, 1987). Highlighting the brain's neural plasticity, this process is known as synaptogenesis. While natural selection operates at the species level, this process operates within the brain of an individual, proceeding through a selective process that has the effect of fitting the individual to the environment by literally re-engineering their brain (and, through the individual's effect on the environment, fitting the environment to the individual).

We can appreciate the power of this mechanism by considering what happens to an infant born into a specific environment. In a baby's brain, the number of neurons is of the order of 100 billion cells. Synaptogenetic winnowing makes about 100 trillion connections between cells through their synapses (Ackerman, 1992). If we calculate the possible permutations between these different connections, the result is many orders of magnitude larger than the atoms in the universe, 10 to the 70th power.

One of the distinctive contributions of Tononi and Edelman's work is the discovery of neuronal clusters, in which neurons from different parts of the brain, and different kinds of neurons, interact much more strongly with each other than with other neurons active at the time (1998). These clusters, they argue, are a fundamental basis for cognition. Thus, cognition itself is a distributed function occurring at different brain sites; moreover, it is differentially enacted with neurons of different kinds. In turn, these clusters are themselves recursively interacting with the synaptic connections comprising them, with information flowing up from the networks to the clusters, and down from the clusters to the networks. In addition, each cluster communicates with other clusters, sending and receiving information, so a second level of recursivity emerges from the meta-cluster networks and the clusters themselves.

So massive and interconnected are the resulting information flows that Edelman and Tononi (2000) decided not to use the term 'feedback' and instead devised their own term, 'reentry' or 'reentrant connections', to name these multilevelled recursive processes. In its original context when it emerged as a term in early 20th-century cybernetics, the concept of feedback was linked with the notion of homeostasis, as one of the mechanisms the human body uses to maintain its internal temperature, blood pressure, and other critical variables within the narrow range necessary for health and life. Actually, the idea of feedback is ancient, known to the Greeks through mechanisms that stabilized water flows and other devices. It was only in the early twentieth century, however, that the idea of feedback was joined with new concept of information to create an informatic-theoretic framework (Hayles, 1999). Simple cybernetic mechanisms like the Bedbug (a mechanical device that avoided light) and the Moth (a mechanism drawn to light) were fabricated to demonstrate the effects of positive and negative feedback (Hoggett, 2009).

For Edelman and Tononi, recursion is distinct from feedback not only because it denotes massive information flows, but more importantly because recursive dynamics do far more than merely maintain a steady state. In recursion, information flows operate to change the structures of neuronal circuits, thus enabling the brain to evolve into new states of emergence. These recursive dynamics account for the brain's plasticity and its ability to learn new things, even into old age.[2]

Perhaps the greatest pay-off in their theory about the role that recursion plays in brain dynamics is their claim that it is responsible for the emergence of consciousness itself (2000). They speculate that it is precisely the brain's recursive architecture, with its exponentially huge number of combinations, that enables the human species to achieve symbolic representations including language, qualities that Terrence W. Deacon has argued are the distinctive characteristics separating humans from other conscious mammals (Deacon, 1997). In a talk he gave at IBM, Edelman noted that 'there is no object in the known universe so completely distinguished by reentrant circuitry as the human brain' (2006), a sentiment with which Emily Dickinson would no doubt have agreed.

> The brain is wider than the sky,
> For, put them side by side,
> The one the other will contain
> With ease, and you beside.
> (107, Dickinson, Thomas J. Johnson (ed), 2012)

Forwarding information from nonconscious cognition to consciousness

I turn now to consider how nonconscious cognition forwards the results of its processing to consciousness. Undoubtedly, nonconscious cognition evolved first and consciousness was, so to speak, built on top of it. This progression is consistent with the temporal dynamics at play. Whereas consciousness takes about 500 ms to become aware of sensations (the 'missing half-second,' [Libet, 2005]), nonconscious cognition is much faster, operating at about 200 ms after the onset of sensory stimuli. Thus information is processed first by nonconscious cognition. Moreover, nonconscious cognition has been shown to discern patterns in information too dense and noisy for consciousness to process as anything other than chaos. Nonconscious cognition can also learn through experiences, draw inferences, and guide behaviour (Lewicki, Hill and Czyzewska, 1992; Dresp-Langley, 2012). What it cannot do, by itself, is to initiate voluntary actions (Dehaene, 2009:101).

The temporal dynamics are crucial to understanding this distinction. Starting at about 200 ms, nonconscious cognition begins synaptic processes that create an activation wave through different parts of the brain, peaking at about 400 ms (Edelman and Tononi, 2000). To endure past this point, the activation wave must receive top-down reinforcement signals from consciousness. This implies that context is important to the interactions between consciousness and nonconscious cognition, for only if the context is appropriate will consciousness respond positively to nonconscious cognition's information. We might think of it as akin to nonconscious cognition tugging slightly at consciousness's sleeve. If consciousness turns toward the tug, then the activation wave will continue through the 500 ms threshold. As Stanislas Dehaene puts it, recursive dynamics in the form of reverberating circuits will then result in the ignition of the [brain's] global workspace (Dehaene, Kerszberg and Changeux, 1998; Dehaene, 2015; Dehaene, Sargent and Changeux, 2003), At that point, the thought associated with the activation may continue indefinitely as long as the recursive dynamics are operating. Otherwise, the activation wave coming from nonconscious cognition dies out, and that information never becomes available to consciousness.

Representing cognitive recursivity: Paik's *TV Buddha*

To make connections between these neuronal processes and Paik's artworks, I turn now to Paik's 2014 *TV Buddha*. A statue of Buddha sits facing a closed circuit TV set, on which is displayed an image of the same sitting Buddha.[3] In a meditative pose, the statue seems as if it is regarding its own representation. But this repetition is not merely a copy or reproduction, for technical media have become co-presenters with the statue itself. The kind of cognitive activity that the pose may suggest is now blended with the electrodynamics of the TV circuit and camera. Moreover, since the screen refreshes at something like sixty times per second (60 Hz, the typical rate), the putative interaction between statue, image, and TV circuit can be seen as a continuous dynamic in which the Buddha contemplates its image, which affects its contemplation, which generates a new image, and so forth. Of course, since the Buddha is an inanimate object rather than a living being, this counts as a gesture toward cognitive recursion rather than cognitive dynamics in themselves; which is to say, it is art commenting on life as a recursive cycle of meditation/reflection. When a viewer takes in the artwork, their cognitive functions, operating through the kind of recursive dynamics documented by Edelman and Tononi, instantiate the gesture in a living body, thus animating and completing the cycle.

In contrast to traditional animation achieving motion through the perceptual processing of nonconscious cognition, *TV Buddha* manifests *conceptual* animation.[4] By back formation, the traditional concept may be called *perceptual* animation. As we have seen, in perceptual animation, neuronal processes create the impression of motion at the level of nonconscious cognition. By contrast, conceptual animation involves processes occurring at the level of consciousness and meta-consciousness (that is, consciousness of consciousness) through the kind of reentrant connections described by Edelman and Tononi. In conceptual animation, nonconscious cognition is, of course, also operating, but now its role is fundamentally different. It discerns patterns in dense information streams rather than creates motion out of the succession of still images. Forwarded to consciousness, these patterns work together with higher cognitions to create the impression of motion created when the viewer interacts with the artwork, now emerging at the high level of the massive recursivity of meta-consciousness.

Consequently, both perceptual and conceptual animation can be understood as converting still images into dynamic motion. Moreover, both use recursive dynamics to bring this effect into conscious awareness, but the sites where technical mediation occur are different. Also different are the temporal and neuronal dynamics of how the still images are converted into motion. From a certain perspective, perceptual and conceptual animation can be regarded as mirror images, which of course invert along the left–right axis. Now, however, the inversion occurs along a vertical axis of top–bottom. In perceptual animation, information 'bubbles up' from the nonconscious, while with conceptual animation, it 'filters down' from meta-consciousness to consciousness, and from there to nonconscious cognition and the sensory systems.

A similar example is instantiated in Paik's 1976–78 *TV Rodin*. Head in palm, a small reproduction of Rodin's famous sculpture *The Thinker* resides on a small white cube, staring down into a closed circuit TV displaying his image. The relative sizes here are important; whereas Rodin's seated original was 73 inches high (and thus more than life-size), here the statue is only slightly larger than the small TV (about 24 inches), with both the statue's white cube and the TV posed together on a much larger white cube. Moreover, occupying the same floor space as the large white cube, the closed circuit camera is clearly visible, located on a tripod to bring it up to the statue's level. The spatial arrangement indicates that the statue, TV, and camera are all part of the same circuit, continuously interacting in an imagined space in which *The Thinker* thinks the thoughts that the camera records and the TV displays, which leads to new thoughts, in a recursive cycle that never ends. Already highly mediated as a result of its instantiations in various materials, different sizes, and diverse cultural contexts, *The Thinker* in this version is inextricably bound together with the mediatized commodity it has always already become.

When the viewer perceives the installation, they are incorporated into the conceptual animation that they behold, for their thoughts about the installation instantiate in their body the artwork's animating dynamics, converting its technically mediated recursive images into motion through their *internal* recursive dynamics of consciousness and meta-consciousness (see Torre, 2014 for an account of this dynamics from a process-based perspective). Obviously, it is not by chance that *The Thinker* and the meditating Buddha are chosen as the objects of technical mediation, for their associations with consciousness and meditation, respectively, already suggest how still images and conceptual recursion may dynamically interact, a process reflexively mirrored in the viewer's own neuronal processes.

At this point the sceptical reader may ask if conceptual animation is 'real' animation. The answer, of course, depends on how one defines animation. A better question: what is gained, theoretically and conceptually, by introducing the term and linking it with perceptual animation? The advantages, I would argue, are multiple. First, it draws attention to the relevant neurological processes in ways that go well beyond the common knowledge about 24 fps. Second, it expands the scope of animation studies to include artworks in which recursive dynamics happen at higher levels of neuronal processing than nonconscious cognition. Finally, it sharpens through contrast the multidimensional ways in which still and moving images interrelate, an especially important consideration with the development of HD video and other technical mediations which exceed the boundaries of conventional animation, as the examples of Bill Viola's work discussed below illustrate.

Recursivity in systems theory

A final recursion through Paik's artworks will prepare for the discussion of Viola's installations. Another major site where recursivity plays a critical role, in addition to models of consciousness, is systems theory. Dating from Ludwig Bertalanffy's formulation of general systems theory in the 1930s (Bertalanffy, 1969), through to Niklas Luhmann's theory of social systems in the 1980s and 1990s (Luhmann, 1996), systems theories in general posit that systems exist in the context of environments. For Luhmann (working from the framework created by Spencer-Brown (1979 [1969]) in *Laws of Form*), the first operation in analysing a system is making a cut (as Luhmann calls it) that distinguishes between the system and its environment (Hayles, 1995). Another founding principle of any systems theory is that all the components of a system interact with one another, typically exchanging information and communication as well as energetic and material resources. Bertalanffy primarily applied systems theory to individuals; he thought it had applications to social systems as well, but his work in this direction did not go very far because of the complex issues involved.

Building on Bertalanffy's research but also going beyond it, Luhmann developed a theory of social systems that Bertalanffy merely gestured towards. Luhmann began his analysis from the premise that a system is operationally closed, an idea he adopted from Maturana and Varela's work on cognition, mentioned earlier (Luhmann, 1996). Maturana and Varela were well aware of the classic article, 'What the Frog's Eye Tells the Frog's Brain' (Lettvin et al, 1959; Maturana was a co-author). This research showed that any information the frog's brain receives has already been highly processed by its sensory and neuronal systems. Hence Maturana and Varela, in *Autopoiesis and Cognition*, refer to the environment as *triggering* informational responses, rather than transmitting information itself.

Working from this premise, Luhmann posited a model in which a system is situated within an environment much more complex than the system itself (think of an individual walking through a forest, where many different plant and animal species reside, all with their own ecologies and interactions with the environment and each other). Confronted with this complexity, the system (closed to informational input but open to energy and material exchanges) strives to recreate within itself some of this complexity to avoid being overwhelmed and breaking down. As a result, the environmental complexity has the effect of stimulating an increase in the system's internal complexity.

This effect, however, is indirect. It is precisely because the system strives to keep its boundaries intact, thus preserving its informational closure, that it ratchets up into increasing complexity. The mechanisms for accomplishing this increasing complexity, according to Luhmann, are multilevelled acts of differentiation that divide its interior space into subsystems which in turn divide into more subsystems, each of which interacts with components on its level as well as with components above and below its level. Similar to the recursive complexity that Maturana and Varela envisioned, the resulting dynamics can be modelled as part/whole relations in which the whole interacts with the parts, while simultaneously the parts interact with and constitute the whole. With a focus on social systems such as law, the welfare state, politics, and so forth, Luhmann's systems theory barely takes note of individuals at all (Luhmann, 1996).

The kind of recursive dynamics at work here resembles, albeit on a radically different scale, the dynamics responsible for the generation of consciousness in Edelman and Tononi's model. There too, the recursive dynamics of reentrant connections emerges through interactions with the environment, which always has a complexity much greater than the individual organism. Thus the brain's development of synaptic networks and neuronal clusters can be seen as responses by the cortical/sensory system to deal with this greater complexity by recreating, in a different mode, some of that complexity within its internal structure.

These comments set the stage for an analysis of Paik's 1995 *Electronic Superhighway: Continental U.S., Alaska, Hawaii,* an installation in which perceptual and conceptual animation interact to create an extremely complex viewing experience. *Electronic Superhighway* is perhaps the most technologically elaborate of Paik's installations, comprising 51 channel videos, custom electronics, steel and wood underlying structures, and accompanying audio. Standing a monumental 15 feet high, 40 feet wide, and 4 feet deep, the artwork is in the shape of a US map, with state boundaries outlined in glowing white light. Within each state perimeter, multiple video screens play clips from historically and politically significant moments, in addition to others blaring out banalities typical of broadcast TV. The first impression of a viewer standing before it is enormous complexity. If we think of this artwork as a system, it can be understood of reproducing within itself a reflection of the greater complexity of the US as its exterior environment, an impression that includes the cacophony of sound created as each monitor plays its accompanying audio. Moreover, the TV clips provide a window onto the invisible electromagnetic waves mediating their contents, a perception underscored by the work's title.

One advantage of a systems theory perspective is that one can always change what counts as the system and environment, thus creating new insights into the systemic dynamics.[5] Performing such a reversal, we can consider the work as the environment observed by the viewer, who now counts as the system. The installation as a whole can be considered a still image, in the sense that its outlines do not change and its general structure remains constant. Within this structural stillness, however, motion abounds in the video clips, where on a smaller scale, perceptual animation converts successive images into impressions of motion. Within the viewer, nonconscious cognition performs multiple roles, for at the same time it is creating motion, it is also interpreting the dense information streams and perceiving patterns in them.

One of the patterns occurring at the level of conceptual animation is a dynamic alternation between complexity and simplification. The viewer sees a very complex installation containing videos in which complexities are flattened into the sound bites typical of broadcast TV. As William Burroughs observed of heroin, 'The junk merchant doesn't sell his product to the consumer, he sells the consumer to his product. He does not improve and simplify his merchandise. He degrades and simplifies the client' (Burroughs, 1959:119). In similar fashion, broadcast TV can be said to simplify the viewer so that the viewer will be more likely to become addicted to TV's simplifications. Incorporating this dynamic into its larger complexities, the installation reverses this procedure, building complexities within the viewer's cognitions via the multiple recursive processes through which the active viewer interacts with the work. Here, perceptual and conceptual animation work together to create cascading and interpenetrating dynamics at multiple levels of temporality and neuronal processes, all interacting to produce dense networks of meaning and significance.

Given the relatively early date of the work (1995), most viewers seeing the work in the mid 1990s would probably have only a vague sense of what the term 'electronic superhighway' might mean. (The first website, available on CERN's network and made by Tim Berners-Lee, was published on 20 December 1990. On 6 August 1991, Berners-Lee posted a public invitation for collaboration on the web project on internet news groups.) It would have been difficult to predict then how the internet would explode exponentially over the next two decades to become a major technological force within the emerging global culture that it was largely responsible for creating. In its prescient vision, *Electronic Superhighway* prepares the viewer for this future, seeking to create internal complexities adequate to cope with the issues of control, surveillance, and freedom that inevitably arise as technical mediation grows more intense, sophisticated, and pervasive.

Merging perceptual and conceptual animation: Bill Viola's *Passions* artworks

During the 1970s, Bill Viola was influenced by Paik's video art, particularly Paik's embrace of Cage's chance operations, so there is some continuity between the artists. By the late 1990s, Viola had developed his own style and was well established in the art world. As the millennium approached, Viola recounts in an interview with Hans Belting, he began making visits to the desert and filming whatever he saw there, with little sense of how that might enter into his art (Viola and Belting, 2:189–90). This fallow period reached a climax with his mother's death, a momentous event in his personal life. The turning point, he recounted, came when he took the personal videos he had made of her during her final days into his studio and became focused on them, an examination that culminated in a renewed interest in the emotions (Viola and Belting, 2003:190–1). John G. Hanhardt, commenting on this period, remarks 'in the 1990s Viola makes a definitive turn to the treatment of the human body through the representation of emotions […] linked […] by his treatment of time' (Hanhardt, 2015:163). In his notebooks during this period, Viola writes:

Breakdown – breakthrough. Reach the peak of physical existence – It is no longer possible to be in the Body. The pressure is unbearable. The load unsustainable. […] All emotions condense at a single point, a unity, and then race outward, splintering into shards and fragments flying off in all directions. The aftermath of this harrowing journey through the narrowest of apertures is both a release from suffering and the manifestation of that suffering – Joy and Sorrow, Exhaustion and Strength. Breakdown and Breakthrough. (Walsh, 2003a:166–7)

Shortly thereafter, he began work on *The Greeting* (1998), inspired by the Pontormo painting *Visitation* (c.1528) depicting the Virgin Mary, pregnant with Jesus, meeting her older cousin Elizabeth, pregnant with John (the Baptist), with the two women confiding their conditions to each other. Viola used a 35 mm high-speed camera, capable of shooting at 300 fps, to film professional actors enacting a similar encounter between two women while a third looks on. Filmed for only 40 seconds (which consumed 12,000 frames of film), the work as shown at 24 fps stretches to 8 minutes, with the result that actions are slowed almost to immobility. In effect, this technique gives a much more fine-grained experience of time than is normally the case. 'I knew from experience,' Viola commented in an interview with Hanhardt, 'that slow motion could actually make visible the events that were unconscious and could bring things right up front, which is ultimately what I was after' (Galansino and Perov, 2017:163).

Here I continue my discussion of nonconscious cognition by referring to the work of Antonio Damasio on emotions (2000). In Damasio's terminology, 'emotions' refer to physical processes that begin in the sensory systems and are processed nonconsciously, with information flowing back into the central and peripheral nervous systems, where it initiates physiological reactions such as neck hair standing on end, adrenaline flowing into the organs from the endocrine system, and so forth (Parvizi and Damasio, 2001). Only then is the information forwarded to consciousness, where it evokes the psychological correlates of emotions, which Damasio calls 'feelings.' According to this schema, the body knows what is happening and reacts accordingly many milliseconds before consciousness becomes aware of threats, dangers, sources of joy or sorrow. Nonconscious cognition (which Damasio calls the protoself), with its faster response time and more extensive capabilities to process dense information, is closer to what is happening on the ground, so to speak, a phenomenon manifested in the documented ability of humans to avoid stepping on snakes before they even become consciously aware that a snake is present (Kawai and He, 2016). Moreover, consciousness tends to confabulate, inventing stories to explain what it does not understand; for example, someone who has an uneasy feeling about a situation may nevertheless convince himself it is safe to proceed, when information coming from the nonconscious clearly indicates otherwise.

Through the extreme slow motion made possible by filming with the high-speed camera, *The Greeting* in effect brings into conscious awareness subtle nuances of gesture, facial expression, and consequently emotions as they are processed by the nonconscious but that are not normally forwarded to consciousness in this rich detail. Commenting in 1989, Viola said, 'I have come to realize that the most important place where my work exists is not in the museum gallery, or in the screening room, or on television, and not even on the video screen itself, but in the mind of the viewer who has seen it' (Hanhardt, 2015:163). The critic Donald Kuspit, commenting on Viola's *The Passing* (1992), remarks that his 'poetics of light and time' conveys 'a radical state of consciousness inseparable from the awareness of mystical personal sensation. They seem not just to alter one's consciousness but to uproot one's being' (Kuspit, 1993). In effect, consciousness in these works is confronted with a density of information similar to what nonconscious cognition processes, slowed down so that consciousness, with its belated cognitions and more limited information processing ability, can grasp emotions in all their subtleties and nuances. Through this technique, then, perceptual animation (which normally takes place in nonconscious cognition) fuses with conceptual animation (enacted in consciousness through recursive dynamics), a union made possible through the temporalities created by new kinds of technical mediations.

Kira Perov, Viola's close collaborator (and spouse), wrote about the technical demands of creating *The Greeting*.

> We hired a full technical crew, with producer (Peter Kirby), director of photography (Harry Dawson [...]), set designer (Dennis Knightley), wardrobe stylists, and the usual crew of grips, lighting specialists, set painters, and production assistants [...] [the high-speed camera] meant that one thousand feet of film flew by in about sixty seconds [...] each second would expand to ten seconds of viewing time, and had to be counted out while shooting. We called this method 'micro-directing' – when every second mattered. When the work was recorded on 35 mm film it was transferred to standard definition video for editing and preparation. (Perov, 2017:179)

Her description makes clear the scrupulous preparation required, not to mention the substantial expenses involved.

For the *Passions* works created between 2000 and 2002, a high-speed camera was again used, as well as a full crew and professional lighting. There was, however, a difference in their presentation. Perov remarks that such portraits as the 2001 *Man of Sorrows*, showing in slow motion a single actor expressing deep sadness, 'were made possible by the new video flat panels that revolutionized the moving image world' (Perov, 2017:179). Displayed on these screens, the work measures only 19″ × 15″.[6] Perov continues:

> These plasma and LCD screens could be made to look like photographs by striping the casing to add a custom metal frame and mounting them vertically on the wall [...] the 35 mm film was transferred to

high-definition video, also quite new, and thus we entered the digital world. (Perov, 2017:159–60)

Viola recalled his impression of seeing an LCD flat panel for the first time in 1988.

> I knew that I was seeing a new step in the evolution of the moving image. It had none of the characteristics of the television monitor, the old CRT (cathode-ray tube). There were no scan lines, no electronic colors, or harsh edges. The image had a soft, satin-like quality because there was no glass in front of the picture. It was photographic but it also had a texture, a really unique physical appearance more like the page of a book than an electronic screen. [...] I found myself falling into the image, getting lost in its aura, and it was only 16 inches wide! (Viola and Belting, 2003:203)

As electronics improved, the effect was paradoxically to make the technical mediation less visible and more reminiscent of older media such as books, photographs, or paintings.

In neurological terms, this effect strengthened the connection between perceptual and conceptual animation. It was as if the conscious mind was connecting directly with the nonconscious, seeing with the nonconscious perceptual eye but with the full force of conscious awareness. Given Viola's focus on emotion, this also meant that consciousness was seeming to see bodily emotions at the moment of their creation, something that could never happen in reality. As the re-enactments performed by actors were slowed by a factor of ten, the viewer's consciousness could witness the actor's body registering, through the smallest gestures and expressions, the flow of information from patterns created by the nonconscious upward to consciousness, where the feelings associated with the bodily emotions would emerge. Of course, since these were actions performed according to a script, the information originated with the actor's consciousness, but it was the body and the nonconscious that largely determined the precise physical expression these would take. (Good actors know that these actions are best left to nonconscious mechanisms, because if directed in detail by consciousness, they will seem forced and artificial). From the viewer's perspective, feelings such as fear, anger, joy, and sorrow, normally experienced many hundreds of milliseconds later than the corresponding bodily emotions, could now be linked directly with nonconscious affect because those milliseconds were no longer 'missing' but rather recorded on the film as it flew by at one frame every 3 ms.

Similar techniques were used in group compositions, such as *Quintet of the Astonished* (2000), inspired by the Hieronymus Bosch painting

Christ Mocked (The Crowning of Thorn), c.1490–1500.[7] As Viola describes the work, the five actors were to express 'the rising emotional energy independently, with little acknowledgement or direct interaction with their companions [...] the extreme slow motion makes visible the smallest of details and subtle nuances of expression, and creates a subjective, psychological space where time is suspended for both performers and viewers alike' (Hanhardt, 2015:184). Each group of five in the *Quintet* series was 'framed half-length, placed against a dark background, and lighted from a source at the upper left.' Rear-projected and viewed in an enclosed, darkened space, the performers' expressions 'move from neural to sorrow, pain, anger, fear, rapture' (Walsh, 2003b in Walsh, 2003a:36). Later pieces in this series were edited to be displayed on a pair of large upright plasma screens. Viola comments, 'I realized that these pieces had to be shot as single takes with no editing, since the movement was created by the emotion itself, and the medium for this emotion, its constant base, was the person. Any kind of editing would disrupt this relationship' (Viola and Belting, 2003:200).

The extreme example of this technique is where one minute of filming is stretched to eighty-two minutes of playing time (see Perov in Galasino, 2017). For this work, Viola identified four primary emotions – joy, sorrow, anger, and fear – and instructed the three actors, filmed separately, to create similar emotional trajectories expressing all four during the one minute filming time. 'I was most interested in opening up the spaces *between* the emotions,' Viola comments. 'I wanted to focus on gradual transitions – the idea of emotional expression as a continuous fluid motion. This meant that the transitions, the ambiguous time when you shift from being happy to sad, is just as important as the main emotion itself' (Viola and Belting, 2003:200). Elsewhere he refers to this in-betweenness as 'what the old masters didn't paint' (Walsh, 2003b in Walsh, 2003a:36).

The three portraits, two females and one male, are displayed as a triptych, following similar trajectories but with many individual differences. Peter Sellers, describing his experience of the work, calls it as 'an astonishing meeting of stillness and motion' (Sellers, 2003:180). He continues:

> You see what you take to be three commercial portrait photographs of three friendly people. Again, what you don't notice right away is that they are breathing. Watching a smile break across the face of Henrietta Brouwers over three minutes, feeling the upwelling of pleasure and well-being from the very center of her heart, watching the light of happiness enter her eyes – and feeling all of this before she feels it, seeing all of this before she herself is aware of it – is to share some of the privileged information of the Knower of Hearts'. (Sellers, 2003:181)

his picturesque name for what I have been calling nonconscious cognition (Hayles, 2012). 'Eternity plays out in an instant,' he comments, 'and every instant opens into an eternity' (Sellers, 2003:181), concisely summing up the interpenetration of stillness and motion in this work, as well as the merging of perceptual with conceptual animation.

In comments about video (and film as well), Viola remarks:

> The essence of the medium is time. The 'time-form' of a work is intangible but real. It's a visceral thing, a backbone that comes into being anytime you create moving images. It has a unique shape for every situation, and it is unconsciously perceived by the viewer – felt more than seen. It is on the level of the time-form that a work usually fails or succeeds. (Viola and Belting, 2003:199)

His insight suggests that even in works where perceptual animation seemingly dominates, the work's temporal patterns and rhythms are also being perceived nonconsciously and deeply affect the viewer's experience, either cohering into an aesthetically powerful pattern, or not. In this perspective, perceptual and conceptual animation are *always* in play, working together in aesthetic experiences even when the filming is not modified beyond 24 fps and recursive dynamics are not thematically central to the artwork.

Implications for animation studies

Since animation is deeply tied in with human perceptions of time, research in neuroscience, cognitive science, cognitive psychology and related fields may contribute richly to discussions of aesthetic effects in film and video. Dan Torre (2014) makes an excellent start with his concept of cognitive animation theory, relating the construction of motion in animation to visual processing as well as to process philosophy, but much more can and should be done. Moreover, in artworks such as Nam June Paik's and Bill Viola's that specifically draw upon conceptual as well as perceptual animation, expanding the theoretical resources and associated vocabulary of the field can result in insights that open the works to deeper and more inclusive understanding.

In creating technologies that exteriorize cognition, including computational media, electronic circuits, LCD screens, and high-speed cameras, humans have vastly extended the techno-biological circuits in which contemporary societies are immersed. A larger implication, and therefore more difficult to grasp as the scale increases exponentially, is animation's role in re-engineering human cognition. A wealth of evidence points to the neurological effects of constant exposure to digital streams of information (Dehaene, 2009; Carr, 2010). Because of the brain's plasticity, discussed earlier, environmental effects can create new kinds of synaptic connections that, in effect, rewire the brain in ways that make it more adaptive for its environment.

For example, it is common knowledge in the film industry that the time it takes audiences to recognize quickly flashed images has decreased significantly since the 1950s. In addition, storytelling techniques in television have become significantly more complex during the same period, for a variety of factors (Mitchell, 2015). Then there is the Flynn effect, the rise in IQ from the later twentieth century to the present (Flynn, 2012). Finally, as I have argued elsewhere (Hayles, 2010), there is a cognitive shift in developed societies from deep to hyper attention, most noticeable in children and young people where brain plasticity is the greatest. These changes occur through culturally transmitted mechanisms rather than through genetic transmission, so from an anthropologist's viewpoint, they are often seen as ephemeral. But if built environments such as computationally dense infrastructures replicate similar conditions over decades, the effects may not be short-lived but continue across generations. Moreover, there is every indication that information flows will continue to increase and intensify (short of environmental collapse or cultural apocalypse), so there is reason to be concerned about their long-term consequences.

Of course, there is an upside to these changes, as Mitchell, Flynn, and others contend, because these trends can be seen as preparing people for more dense information environments. But there is a price as well, paid for in the coin of deep attention. As distracted moments multiply and as people increasingly switch quickly between different information streams, the tendency is to want more and more distraction. Humans are infovores, and once the cycle of distraction has begun, it becomes more difficult to sustain attention on a single source, whether a long novel, a difficult mathematical theorem, or a complex philosophical argument. Critics such as Nicholas Carr (2010) and Bernard Stiegler (2010) have warned that the 'programming industries,' as Stiegler calls them, are destroying the ability of young people (and older folks too) to engage for sustained periods of time with cultural materials that do not immediately deliver rewards or quick satisfaction.

This is the context in which the interplay between still and moving images assume larger cultural significance. Works such as Nam June Paik's *TV Buddha* and *TV Rodin* and Bill Viola's *Passions* series present viewers with the opportunity to slow down, to absorb fully and completely rather than quickly and superficially, and to readjust the ways in which the nonconscious and consciousness interact. Significantly, some critics viewing *Anima* and similar works in the *Passions* series expressed frustration with their incremental changes, saying that they wished they had a fast-forward button. But that is precisely the point – to escape from the cycle of distraction and focus fully and completely on the artwork, letting it work its slow magic on the all the complex synaptic connections that enable nonconscious cognition and conscious awareness to function. The flourishing of animation theory in the last few years has opened many promising new avenues for interpretation and analysis (Beckman, 2014; Bukatman, 2012; Crafton, 2012). These can fruitfully be expanded further by adding more capacious vocabulary such as perceptual and conceptual animation, a larger toolbox of resources including neurodynamics and neuroscience research, and increased attention to stillness as well as motion.

Notes

[1] I am grateful to Sooyoung Lee and the Nam June Paik Art Center to allow some ideas to be adapted from 'Inside Out, Outside In: Recursive Dynamics in Posthumanism and in Nam June Paik's Artworks', translated into Korean by Seong Eun Kim et al (2017) *NJP Reader #7 'Coevolution: Cybernetics to Posthuman'*, Nam June Paik Art Center, pp 399–413.

[2] The brain's recursive potential is clearly on display in the case of stroke victims, who over time can partially recover part of their lost functionality with carefully directed physical therapy. In these instances, the brain is using the power of recursion to develop new neuronal pathways to perform some of the functions previously done by the damaged pathways.

[3] See https://explore.namjunepaik.sg/artwork-archival-highlights/tv-buddha/)

[4] The definition given here of conceptual animation is very different from how the term is conventionally used in design, where it functions somewhat analogously to 'conceptual art.' For an example of this kind of usage, see Yalanska and Yerokhin (2018) https://blog.tubikstudio.com/conceptual-animation-making-ui-design-stand-out/. By contrast, the distinguishing characteristic in how I define the term is not just that is is 'arty' but rather that it incorporates in specific ways the recursive dynamics characteristic of human consciousness.

[5] Niklas Luhmann, the father of social systems theory, identified the first necessary move in creating a system to make a distinction between system and environment. In this he was following the lead of George Spenser-Brown in *Laws of Form* (1979), (Luhmann, 1996). If another kind of distinction is made, it generates a different system.

[6] See video at https://www.youtube.com/watch?v=H_X40FqFQsw.

[7] For an excerpt from *Quintet* performance, see https://www.youtube.com/watch?v=MR9av-I35ME.

References

Ackerman, S. (1992) 'The Development and Shaping of the Brain', in *Discovering the Brain*, Washington, DC: National Academies Press. Available from: www.ncbi.nlm.nih.gov/books/NBK234146.

Beckman, K. (ed) (2014) *Animating Film Theory*, Durham, NC: Duke University Press.

Bertalanffy, Ludwig von. (1969) *General Systems Theory: Foundations, Development, Application* (revised edn), New York: Penguin/George Braziller, Inc.

Burroughs, W.S. (1959) *Naked Lunch*, Paris: Olympic Press.

Bukatman, S. (2012) *The Poetics of Slumberland: Animated Spirits and the Animating Spirit*, Oakland, CA: University of California Press.

Carr, N. (2010) *The Shallows: What the Internet is Doing to Our Brains*, New York: W.W. Norton.

Crafton, D. (2012) *Shadow of a Mouse: Performance, Belief, and World-Making in Animation*, Oakland, CA: University of California Press.

Damasio, A. (2000) *The Feeling of What Happens: Body and Emotion in the Making of Consciousness*, New York: Mariner Books.

Deacon, Terrence G. (1997) *The Symbolic Species: The Co-Evolution of Language and the Brain*, New York: W.W. Norton.

Dehaene, S. (2009) *Reading in the Brain: The Science and Evolution of a Human Invention*, New York: Viking.

Dehaene, S. (2015) *Consciousness and the Brain: Deciphering How the Brain Codes Our Thoughts*, New York: Viking.

Dehaene, S., C. Sergent, and J.-P. Changeux. (2003) 'A Neuronal Network Model Linking Subjective Reports and Objective Physiological Data During Conscious Perception', *Proceedings of the National Academy of Sciences* 100(14): 8520–5. https://doi.org/10.1073/pnas.1332574100.

Dehaene, S., M. Kerszberg and J.-P. Changeux. (1998) 'A Neuronal Model of a Global Workspace in Effortful Cognitive Tasks', *Proceedings of the National Academies of Sciences* 95(24): 14529–34.

Dresp-Langley, B. (2012) 'Why the Brain Knows More than We Do: Non-Conscious Representations and Their Role in the Construction of Conscious Experience', *Brain Sciences* 2(1): 1–21.

Eagleman, D. (2012) *Incognito: The Secret Lives of the Brain*. New York: Vintage.

Edelman, G. (1987) *Neural Darwinism: The Theory of Neuronal Group Selection*. New York: Basic Books.

Edelman, G. (2006) 'From Brain Dynamics to Consciousness: A Prelude to the Future of Brain-Based Devices', IBM Research, Almaden Institute conference on cognitive computing, 10 May. Available from: https://www.youtube.com/watch?v=8mvHQ6hLTLs.

Edelman, G. and G. Tononi. (2000) *A Universe of Consciousness: How Matter Becomes Imagination*. New York: Basic Books.

Flynn, J. (2012) *Are We Getting Smarter? Rising IQ in the Twenty-First Century*, Cambridge: Cambridge University Press.

Galansino, A. and K. Perov. (eds) (2017) *Bill Viola: Electronic Renaissance*, Florence: Giunti.

Hanhardt, J. (2015) *Bill Viola*, edited by K. Perov, London: Thames and Hudson.

Hassin, R.R., J.S. Uleman and J.A. Bargh. (eds) (2006) *The New Unconscious*. Oxford: Oxford University Press.

Hayles, N.K. (1995) 'Theory of a Different Order: A Conversation with Niklas Luhmann and Katherine Hayles', *Cultural Critique* 31: 7–37.

Hayles, N.K. (1999) *How We Became Posthuman: Virtual Bodies in Cybernetics, Literature, and Informatics*, Chicago: University of Chicago Press.

Hayles, N.K. (2010) 'How We Read: Close, Hyper, Machine,' *ADE Bulletin* 150: 62–79. https://www.maps.mla.org/content/download/155872/file/ade.150.62.pdf.

Hayles, N.K. (2012) *How We Think: Digital Media and Contemporary Technogenesis*. Chicago: University of Chicago Press.

Hoggett, R. (2009) 'Wiener's Moth "Palomilla" – Wiener/Wiesner/Singleton', Cybernetic Zoo, 19 September [online], updated January 2010. Available from: http://cyberneticzoo.com/tag/norbert-wiener/.

Johnson, Thomas H. (2012). *The Poems of Emily Dickinson*. New York. Start Publishing ebook.

Kawai, N. and H. He. (2016) 'Breaking Snake Camouflage: Humans Detect Snakes More Accurately than Other Animals under Less Discernible Visual Conditions', *PloS ONE* 11(10) e0164342. Available from: https://journals.plos.org/plosone/article?id=10.137/journal.pone.0164342.

Kouider, S. and S. Dehaene. (2007) 'Levels of processing during non-conscious perception: A critical review of visual masking', *Philosophical Transactions of the Royal Society B* 362(1481): 857–75.

Kuspit, D. (1993) 'Bill Viola: The Passing', Artforum 32(1) (September), [online], Available from: https://www.artforum.com/features/bill-violas-the-passing-204274/.

Lettvin, J.Y., H.R. Maturana, W.S. McCulloch and W.H. Pitts. (1959) 'What the Frog's Eye Tells the Frog's Brain', *Proceedings of the Insitute of Radio Engineers* 47: 1940–51.

Lewicki, P., T. Hill and M. Czyzewska. (1992) 'Nonconscious acquisition of information', *American Psychologist* 47(6): 796–801.

Libet, B. (2005) *Mind Time: The Temporal Factor in Consciousness*, Cambridge, MA: Harvard University Press.

Luhmann, N. (1996) *Social Systems*, translated by J. Bednarz, Jr. with D. Baecker, Stanford: Stanford University Press.

Maturana, H. and F. Varela. 1980. *Autopoiesis and Cognition: The Realization of the Living*. Dordrecht: D. Reidel Publishing Co.

Mitchell, J. (2015) *Complex TV: The Poetics of Contemporary Television Storytelling*, New York: New York University Press.

Parvizi, J. and A. Damasio. (2001) 'Consciousness and the Brainstem', *Cognition* 79(1–2): 135–60.

Perov, K. (2017) 'The Creative Process: Making the Invisible Visible," in A. Galansino and K. Perov (eds) *Bill Viola: Electronic Renasissance*, Florence: Giunti, pp 168–99.

Sellers, P. (2003) 'Bodies of Light', in J. Walsh (ed) *Bill Viola: The Passions*. Los Angeles/London: J Paul Getty Museum and The National Gallery, pp 158–88.

Spencer-Brown, G. (1979 [1969]) *Laws of Form*, New York: E.P. Dutton.

Stiegler, B. (2010) *Taking Care of Youth and the Generations*, translated by S. Barker, Stanford: Stanford University Press.

Tononi, G. and G.M. Edelman. (1998) 'Consciousness and Complexity', *Science* 282 (4 December): 1846–51. Available from: http://idealab.ucda vis.edu/IST/ISTF08/readings/tononi_science_282_1846_98.pdf

Torre, D. (2014) 'Cognitive Animation Theory: A Process-Based Reading of Animation and Human Cognition', *Animation* 9(1): 47–64.

Viola, B. and H. Belting. (2003) 'A Conversation,' in J. Walsh (ed) *Bill Viola: The Passions*. Los Angeles/London: J Paul Getty Museum and The National Gallery, pp 189–223.

Walsh, J. (ed) (2003a) *Bill Viola: The Passions*. Los Angeles/London: J Paul Getty Museum and The National Gallery.

Walsh, J. (2003b) 'Emotions in Extreme Time: Bill Viola's Passions Project', in J. Walsh (ed) *Bill Viola: The Passions*. Los Angeles/London: J Paul Getty Museum and The National Gallery, pp 25–64.

Yalanska, M. and K. Yerokhin (2018) 'Conceptual Animation: Making UI Design Stand Out', Tubik blog, 10 April [online], Available from: https://blog.tubikstudio.com/conceptual-animation-making-ui-design-stand-out/

3

Moving Images and Human Perception: Affect in Hand-Drawn Animation and Computer-Generated Imagery

Tomoko Tamari

Introduction

The chapter attempts to examine the (human) reception of moving images by considering the role of 'affect' – 'the affective psycho-sensory complex' – which people simply *feel* but find difficult to articulate in language. The paper focuses on the differences between digital aesthetics created by computer animation and analogue aesthetics in hand-drawn animation.[1] Both are different ways to provide representations of reality. The development of 3D computer animation has sought to produce photorealistic images and brought about broader possibilities for creating verisimilar naturalistic films. In contrast, analogue animation, especially 'conventional' hand-drawn animation, depends on expressive form. The aim is not to duplicate or produce photographic reality, rather to appeal to our emotions, sensation, memory, imagination, and fantasy.

Recently, computer-generated imagery has become a part of the fabric of social life, from computer games to medical data images, from military training simulation to stock market data visualizations, from various advertisements to private photoshopping. Contemporary society is unable to escape the continuous flows of millions of computer-generated images that appear on ubiquitous screens. These images restlessly stimulate and influence our perception. The prime question here is the extent to which machine-generated images influence human embodied practices and feelings, such as experiences, emotion, sensation, and judgement.

The animation industry has often been characterized as a central part of the 'fantasy factory' since its emergence, with this feature further emphasized today through the use of advanced computer technologies. Yet hand-drawn animation still attracts a considerable audience and is often appraised as an art form that involves a sophisticated capacity to express human emotions and senses. Here, attention will focus on the influential Japanese animator Hayao Miyazaki.

Conventional animation depends on an ordered sequence: hand-drawing images on cells; placing the set of image cells under the camera; and shooting a whole sequence of frames. With computer-generated imagery (CGI), the rendering process involves pixels and mathematical calculations for lighting, staging, framing, performance, and camera movements. Digital figures do not need to have a substantial form in the real world, relying on pixels and mathematical formulas for their existence. All these processes 'are carried out within the computer' (Furniss, 2007:174).

Despite the increasing development of CGI technologies, there are still some difficulties in creating natural motion in images, or producing certain types of images – such as humans – because, although the human body is a very familiar and common optical object, each body is individual and singular.[2] Bodies are also almost always in motion. The variations in an individual character (such as walking styles) can be considered an 'imperfection', since they are 'non-standard elements' within the computational system (Furniss, 2007:188). In this system, the human body can be identified as 'the absolute imperfection of living things' (Parisi, 1995, cited in Furness, 2007:188). The challenge of CGI today is still the same as it has always been: how to create 'organic' feelings by the depiction of moving living beings that are absolutely 'perfect' for the real world (for human perception) but 'imperfect' in digital space. Accordingly, Carolyn L. Kane (2014) considers that today's computational system leads to a new optical situation – we are losing our optical images. She argues that human perception and experience are increasingly shaped and structured by the logic of informatics. This new cultural domination, that she calls 'algorithmic visualization', leads to the reduction of 'optical images'. This is because digital images are always an adjunct to the algorithmic operation, which is constituted by the logic of informatics that relies on a huge but still 'limited' standard element of data.

If we follow the idea of 'algorithmic visualization' with replication of a sense of the liveliness and the real in animation, the key issue is not just to consider how to create the feeling of organic life, but also how human perception captures these images. This chapter, therefore, considers the relationship between human perception and 'affective effects', which can be understood as physio-psychological effects in the process of cognition and emotional constitution. Perception can be understood as part of the process of human cognition that has complex dynamics to constitute our view of the world. Hence the question can be how human cognition is constituted in (non)consciousness in order to make sense of the world we experience. To address this question, the chapter explores the significance of 'noise' (incompleteness and ambiguity), 'abstraction' (selectivity), and 'recursivity' in the dynamics of human perception, and analyses the nature of biological and technical cognitive systems to conceptualize the interaction between the machine and human perception in moving images.

Completeness and incompleteness

Motion capture has become one of the most common digital computational technologies. It is a technique for the digital recording of the movement of objects and human actors. It has been used not only for filmmaking and videogames, but also in medical and sports technologies, robotics, and various forms of entertainment. Markers are attached to various parts of the actor's body and are photographed by hundreds of cameras (optical-based method). The collected data is digitized, then transmitted to computers. The data is captured by computer software in order to track a specific moment of the sequence of motion.

Motion capture was largely used for the 3D CGI film *Avatar*, directed by James Cameron and released in 2009, which was acclaimed as a new milestone in digital cinematic technology.[3] *Avatar* was produced via the principle of basic verisimilar naturalism by combinations of both advanced digitally generated images and orthodox filming of motion pictures. According to Cameron, the new methods enable full performance capture, including facial expressions, and allow the filmmakers to transfer 100 per cent of the actor's physical performances to their digital counterparts.[4] In his statement, it is clear that 100 per cent suggests 'perfection' and 'completeness' (see Kaufman, 2009).

In contrast to the production process of 3D CGI film with motion capture, hand-drawn animation never pursues a 100 per cent perfect photographic image of reality, but attempts to express how we could be affected by or feel the reality we experience in nature.

Pat Power states:

> Generally, illusionistic 3D attempts mimesis of an external (or cinematic) reality whereas [hand-drawn] expressive styles play more with the nature of mind and of perception, emotion, memory, and imagination. (Power, 2009:109)

Kostas Terzidis elaborates on this:

the expressive [hand-drawn animation], has many advantages *over the realistic* and [...] the computer-graphic quest for realism is essentially about *completeness*. (2003:58 cited in Power, 2009:109, emphasis added)

Terzidis (2003:58) suggests the expressive has many advantages over the realistic and, whereas the computer-graphic quest for realism is essentially about completeness, 'notions of incompleteness, imperfection, and subjectivity' invite interactive participation and have an expressive value that can surpass this explicitness.

In this context, clearly, the mention of an advantage 'over the realistic' does not mean 'hyper-reality', 'super-reality', or 'virtual reality'. Rather, it is closely associated with human perception – how we 'see' the moving image – which is constituted by a complex dynamism of our/human sensitivities. I will elaborate this issue later in the discussion of the human–machine information processing in cognitive (non)consciousness. Here, we need to consider the question: if the expressive style (with incompleteness) is able to create an advantage 'over the realistic', how can it be created and work successfully? To address this question, it can be useful to compare the production processes of cinematic reality (including 3D live-action film) and conventional hand-drawn animation.

Abstraction and contrived unreality

In a discussion of the differences between cinema and animation, William Schaffer states that what differentiates animation from cinema is the fact that the animator needs to physically produce each frame's content and manually control the interval between successive frames, which should be set to express part of a whole movement (Schaffer, 2007:461). In other words, animators have to have 'the degree of control in the creation of moving-images – the need to decide and provide the content of each individual frame and manipulate the relation between all of them' (Schaffer, 2007:461).

Hence, it can be said that animation is constructed by a number of frames deliberately chosen from a sequence of movements that are selected as key moments in the movement. Then each frame is arranged and put together using the sense of timing of animators – the sense of timing of human perception.

In the process, it is necessary to *abstract* a specific moment from the original movement. In other words, animators must find and abstract/ extract and engender a specific moment that can inspire the sense of a whole sequence of movements (see Torre, 2014:52). Interestingly, such an abstract scheme is significant for both hand-drawn and motion capture technology. The abstraction is a selection from the realm of possibilities, and ultimately each movement is mutually related to create an extensive movement image. Although the abstract scheme as a production process can be seen as a common method for both the analogue and the digital, the technical method itself can be different. Motion capture or CGI is created by encoding, recording, and decoding movements by algorithmic computer programmes. This is a cinematographic editing method based on the production machinery of automatic filming. The hand-drawing animators have to encode each abstracted motion, relying on the animator's human, sensory, haptic knowledge, experience, and memory.

Here, Hayao Miyazaki's animation perfectly exemplifies this feature of hand-drawn moving images. Miyazaki is one of the most celebrated anime filmmakers both in Japan and worldwide. He has become famous since his much acclaimed *Spirited Away* (2001) won the 52nd Berlin International Film Festival Golden Bear prize in February 2002, and a Hollywood Academy Award in 2003. It is also worth noting that this was the first time that Japanese anime was appreciated and appraised as an art form. Miyazaki still favours the hand-drawing method to produce his work. He always attempts to minimize the use of CGI and creates the majority of frames by hand-drawing.[5] His work is still today globally much-admired and characterized by his distinguished talent to express sensation, emotion, imagination, and fantasy in the animation form.[6]

French comic artist Jean Giraud, aka Mœbius, who is regarded as the most influential *bandes dessinées* artist, was one of many who acclaimed Miyazaki's work. In a conversation with Miyazaki on the subject of drawing, Mœbius commented that the quality of Miyazaki's drawings stems from his emphasis on 'his perception' rather than drawing technique. Miyazaki responded by saying that technique *is* perception (Bigelow, 2009:68). In other words, technique is how animators can create animation that corresponds well with the complex sensitivities of human perception. Hence, his drawing conveys the narrative not in photorealistic imagery but through a 'contrived unreality' (Levi, 1996:22, cited in Bigelow, 2009:68). Miyazaki insists that *animation should be a deceptive means*. This suggests that 'the more "real" the imitation, the more fraudulent it becomes' (Davis, 1999, cited in Power, 2009:109). Accordingly, we can see that the world of animation is *deception*, but the human perception of animation is the *actual*. Miyazaki knows that humans are not always able to capture the 'real' nature of the world; rather, we are trying to make sense of 'our' natural world only through 'our' perception.

Mimesis and affect

Miyazaki believes that 'bodily-perceptual orientation' (Carman, 2008:30) is indispensable for understanding both the world we live in and for drawing moving images. Miyazaki explains that creating 'contrived unreality' (by applying 'deceptive means') requires a set of talents for the animator: a sense of gravity, a sense of the moment of inertia, the feeling of elasticity, the law of fluidity, the method of perspective, an acute sense of timing, and also the ability to calculate and dissolve a motion into 24 moments per second.

The production process of hand-drawn animation, with its 24 movements per second, is unlike the machinery production system of cinema; each consecutive movement is usually 'unevenly distributed' in filming time and space. All these multisensory adaptation skills are important in order to produce each frame and to rearrange the frames to create a sequence of motion. Therefore, the scene created by animators does not always make sense in terms of the laws of the natural or the real world. This is why, for Miyazaki, it is important for the animators to have the capacity to feel and perceive 'something real' through their 'six senses' and integrate 'bodily feelings, psychological, and even unconscious states'.[7]

The most important factor for creating contrived unreality is to not pursue the simulation of the real world, but to make up moving images that are adaptable for human perception. Animators require tuning appropriately to human perception, which is a reflection of multiple human sensitivities. This shows also that animators – more precisely, their perceptions – have a capacity of interaction with moving images and reconfigure synaptic networks to connect to embodied knowledge, memories, and experiences in order to create representations of moving images that perfectly adapt to our kinaesthesia (Ingold, 2013:98).[8] Miyazaki also insists that animators should try to 'become a character in the story' or 'to possess a character' (Miyazaki, 1996:106). This is an important process: 'The animator finds himself reanimated in turn by the characters he animates and feels himself becoming a cartoon' (Schaffer, 2007:462).

This is a process of 'making oneself similar to an Other' (Puetz, 2002:np). The process can also be described by using the term mimesis.[9] Michael Taussig (1993) explains that the mimetic faculty is 'to copy, imitate, make models, explore difference, yield into and become other' (Taussig, 1993:xiii, in Puetz, 2002:np). Hence, through mimesis (such as a child imitating a dog), 'the distinction between the self and other becomes flexible' (Puetz, 2002:np). Subject and object are not fixed but, rather, pliable. Paradoxically, this can only be possible where there is a subject that can identify with the other. 'Observing subjects thus assimilate themselves to the objective world' by mimetic imitation (Puetz, 2002:np). Through imitation/mimesis, animators can acquire creativities and techniques which entail both embodying and detaching/externalizing skills to envision the characters they create. This is an important aspect of the animator's capacity to 'be affected' (embodied/subjectified), at the same time as they can create an 'affective effect' (through the externalized/objectified) in the characters.

With regard to mimesis, it could be useful to elaborate how affective effects emerge and work in our perception by examining the field of neuroscience.

A fascinating development in the field of neurophysiology was the mirror neuron, discovered by Giacomo Rizzolatti and his co-workers at the University of Parma in the early 1990s. They remarked that the subject responded not only when they performed a given action, but also when the subject observed someone else performing that same action (Rizzolatti and Sinigaglia, 2008).

V.S. Ramachandran also assures us that:

> It's as if anytime you want to make a judgment about someone else's movements, you have to run a virtual-reality simulation of the corresponding movements in your own brain. And without mirror neurons you cannot do this. (Ramachandran, 2011:123)

We could have 'pictorial' depictions of the behaviour of others without a mirror mechanism, but we would not understand the intentions, expectations, or motivations of others. However, thanks to the mirror neuron system, we are able to understand these immediately without any reasoning (Rizzolatti and Sinigaglia, 2008).[10]

Rizzolatti (2008) explained:

> Emotions, like actions, are immediately shared; the perception of pain or grief, or of disgust experienced by others, activates the same areas of the cerebral cortex that are involved when we experience these emotions ourselves. (Rizzolatti and Sinigaglia, 2008: Preface xii)

Emotions such as affection involve 'an initial fast, unconscious, but coarse *affective* appraisal of the immediate environment, involving low-level neural circuits, particularly the amygdala' (Power, 2009:112).[11]

Deleuze also states that 'affection' is a (sub)component of perception, which is an attenuated or short-circuited perception (Hansen, 2003:210). Robinson's 'low-level neural circuits' (amygdala) (cited in Power, 2009) and Deleuze's 'short-circuited perception' also imply there is a mechanism that is a process involving 'affect' that can be shared between the self and others. This also suggests that mirror neurons in the brain as a biological cognition system serve as essential parts of the interrelation between perception and comprehension.

In other words, thanks to the way mirror neurons act as a mechanism for sharing our perception, we can share the same or similar feelings, emotions, and bodily senses (even intentions). Here, we can suggest that mirror neurons' attributes can lead to '(affective) emotional attunement'. Hence, we can understand that in the grounded biological view, the mirror neurons could be part of the mechanisms to apprehend the initial stage of perception, which can be described as 'unstructured non-conscious experiences' (Featherstone, 2010:199). With this in mind, we can see that animation can work as a medium/interface between the animator and the audience. The mirror neurons in this process help foster the mutual appreciation of immediate intensive sensibilities such as affect between animators and audience. This process can be called 'affective trans-subjectivity'. Here, affect can be referred to as a communicative implication which arises in the initial stage of perception, a preformation of perceptive processes in nonconscious cognition, and immediate intensive sensibilities which develop in a process of the configuration of human perspective in seeing animation – moving images.[12]

If the mirror neurons can help in sharing our perception such as (affective) emotional attunement, this property of mirror neurons could equally influence our perception of both CGI and hand-drawn animation. However, as mentioned earlier, some scholars and animators believe that an expressive style of hand-drawn animation, which produces contrived unreality, can work to enhance 'affective effects'. It could be that hand-drawn animation works better to create affective effects than CGI. Although this view is intriguing, it needs further examination to better understand how the machine and the human-made 'affective effects' respectively can be produced.[13] If human perception plays an important role in creating affective effects, it is equally important to consider how machine 'perception' can produce them. To consider this issue, it might be useful to examine human and machine perception in terms of their formation processes and mechanisms.

Perception, cognition, and consciousness

To elaborate human and machine perceptions, it could be useful to scrutinize potential mechanisms or systems of (initial stage) perception in relation to cognition, since cognition 'is often defined as an "act of knowing" that includes "perception and judgment"' ('Cognition', in *Encyclopedia Britannica*, www.britannica.com/topic/cognition-thought-process, cited in Hayles, 2017:15).[14]

We should also be aware of the close relationship between cognition and consciousness. Hayles explains that whereas consciousness helps make sense of our lives and supports our view of the world's coherence, cognition has a much wider capacity of consciousnesses and extends into issues around neurological brain processes as well as computational systems. Although she admits 'cognitive capacity that exists beyond consciousness goes by various names', she prefers the term 'nonconscious cognition' for her attempt to unpack the complex interdependency between consciousness and nonconsciousness 'at a level of neuronal processing inaccessible to the modes of awareness, but nevertheless performing functions essential to consciousness' (Hayles, 2017:9–10).

Hayles explores how human nonconscious cognition forwards the results of its processing to consciousness. Beginning by introducing Edelman's theory of neuronal group selection, which emphasizes neuronal recursivity in the brain (for more detail, see Hayles's piece in this collection: Chapter 2), Edelman and Tononi proposed that neural clusters (groups) expand their network through recursive 'reentrant connections' (Edelman, 1987: 45–50, especially 45, cited in Hayles, 2017:47). They also explain that the human brain's recursive architecture makes it possible to deal with the neuron's massive possible connections. This creates a human's highly sophisticated consciousness.

The brain's recursive property is important in understanding the 'dynamics' of the information flow between conscious and nonconscious cognition. It is generally accepted that nonconscious cognition starts to work first, before consciousness activates. Hayles illustrates this process in more detail: nonconscious cognition has the ability to reduce the millions of units of information and discern patterns so that conscious processing does not suffer an overwhelming overload of information from complex sensory stimuli in the surrounding environment. These processes involve scanning, choosing, and editing information and, therefore, making possible interpretation of meaning. This process between nonconscious and conscious cognition recursively continues, unless incoming information is relevant for consciousness. Hence, nonconscious and conscious cognition are a mutually supportive and entwined process of information processing (Hayles, 2017:55–6; this collection, Chapter 2).

This process and the role of nonconsciousness also resonate with Simondon's 'technical mentality'. 'Technical mentality always offers coherent and usable schemas for a cognitive interpretation' (Simondon, 2009:19). It is 'coherent, positive, productive in the domain of the cognitive schemas, but incomplete and in conflict with itself in the domain of affective categories because it has not yet properly emerged' (Simondon, 2009:17). The nonconscious works before constructing coherent, positive, and productive information in the formation process of conscious cognition. As Brassett further elaborates, '[a]t the boundary between coherence and conflict, technical mentality is always about to emerge when considering the range of affective relationship in which it is nested: there is forever more to come' (Brassett, 2016:166).[15] The most significant point Hayles makes is that structural and functional similarities can be found in 'cognition' in both biological organisms and technical systems, such as computational media (Hayles, 2017:13).[16]

For her, technical devices such as

> [m]edical diagnostic system[s], automated satellite imagery identification, ship navigation systems, weather prediction programs and a host of other nonconscious cognitive devices, interpret ambiguous or conflicting information to arrive at conclusions that rarely if ever are completely certain. Something of this kind also happens with the cognitive nonconscious in humans. (Hayles, 2017:24)

What I would like to underline here is that human and technical nonconscious cognitions share the same attributions of selecting, editing, and interpreting information, and connecting that data with meanings. All the information in technical devices, such as computers, is encoded as 'bits' which are represented in the form of zeros and ones. This is the main digital operation which 'plays a unique and crucial role as the tool of abstraction, the digital's chief technique' (Evens, 2015:9).

The power of abstraction is a crucial property of digital computation, but it can also be found in the process of human nonconscious cognition, which selects and transforms all information from the various stimuli in the environment to avoid overloading the information process at the early stage of conscious cognition. This means, as Hayles remarks, that 'humans can abstract from specific situation into formal representations; virtually all of mathematics depend on these operations' (Hayles, 2017:12).

Biosemiotics and affect

> Abstraction achieves in the bit an apotheosis. [...] With no meaning of its own, the bit readily adopts to any information need, offers itself to any articulable meaning. (Evens, 2015:9)

This means that the abstraction of the bits as 'a universal language of the digital' (Evens, 2015:5) makes possible 'any information' to be defined by datafication undertaken by the digital technology.

Affect theories have been developed with science, especially neuroscience, and information theories and question the assumption of the body-as-organism. Rather, they claim, bodies are beyond the distinction between organic and nonorganic and matter should be conceived of as informational (Clough et al, 2007:62). The brain, too, as part of the body, is regarded as an informational entity. The relevant question it raises for this chapter is the (un)measurability of the brain: more precisely, the (un)measurability of affect (which is the sensuous dimension of human perception) in nonconscious cognition. In other words, affect in the brain could be (in)computable. To consider this question, Hayles's understanding of the computational brain could be useful. She conceives that there is no scientific evidence to explain 'the hypothesis that the brain manipulates symbols to accomplish its tasks' and argues there is no reference to 'what the brain actually has to work with, namely the body, extended nervous system outside the brain, organs such as skin and viscera, etc' (Hayles and Sampson, 2018:62). Furthermore, whereas biological organisms have intrinsic imperatives to survive, computational media do not. Therefore 'computers do not evolve, but are designed for purposes' (Hayles and Sampson, 2018:63).

She also emphasizes the similarity of computational media and biological organisms in their meaning-making formation though sign-exchange processes. For computational media, operations are driven by 'signs which may be "indexical" rather than symbolic' and 'signs require an interpretant, the "someone" for whom the sign signifies something of consequence' (Hayles and Sampson, 2018:66). The signs work to signify something to the cell in the biological organisms too. This is why, in her view, 'biosemiotics' is helpful.

If affective responses can be created at the stage of 'nonconscious cognition', there can be a process of meaning-making through its selection and interpretation of a massive number of signs. But this selection is subjective orientation. As Hayles explains, biosemiotics originates with Jakob von Uexküll's concept of *Umwelt*, which refers to the idea that 'all that a subject perceives becomes his perceptual world [*Merkwelt*] and all that he does, his effector world [*Wirkwelt*]. Perceptual and effector worlds together form a closed unit, the *Umwelt*' (von Uexküll, 1934/2010:6, cited in Bueno-Guerra, 2018:np).

Hence, we can see that biosemiotics supports the subjective view of the concrete framework of the meaning-making process. This suggests that the biosemiotics approach is fundamentally different from the logic of the digital. The biological meaning-making process cannot be represented by computational media, which seeks for the greatest and the least difference. The selection process in biosemiotics is not a universal but an exclusively subjective orientation.[17]

The logic of the digital and computational media must operate in its environment to fulfil its preprogrammed purpose. It is always programmed to make a decision which is an anticipation of future consequences and to achieve a result through communication with a pre-given *environment*. 'The environment includes its [pre-given] data set, the operative system, sensors, actuators present in the system, and other affordances' (Hayles and Sampson, 2018:63). In particular, the nature of content and the way of producing the data set should not be overlooked, since a pre-given data set is the only reference (pre-given environment) to calculate and achieve a result. To recreate affective effects, the data set should be constituted by *all* the information which is abstracted through 'affect' (human perception). However, it is not possible to generate a *full* set of data in order to create affect as a result. This is because 'the logic of the digital' (universal) means it is never possible to *fully* encode affect (subjectivity) into signs.[18]

If we do not have a *completed* set for the data set of affect, it is thus impossible to recreate *perfect/absolute* human perception. This is because there is only an existing *incomplete* pre-given data set as a reference. Eventually, the lack of a full set of pre-given environment data may cause a failure of the recreation of affective human perception. Hence, we can now understand that the affective effects of moving images produced by the hand-drawing of the human animator could produce different qualities from the affective effects of computational generation, since the constitution of the given data sets and associated environments are different.

Neuronal selectivity

Although affect is not fully able to be encoded by computational media, it is important not to forget that digital affective effects are always received by human perceivers. Hence, digitally encoded affect will be again decoded through human perception. Such participation of human perceivers can be therefore seen as part of the 'cognitive assemblage' (Hayles, 2017:115). Further consideration about the reception of image processing in human perception is important.

It could be helpful to draw on Ramachandran's neuroaesthetic concept of 'nine laws of aesthetics' to address this issue. One of the concepts in particular – *isolation* – can bring us fascinating insights about human perception. The law of isolation indicates one single visual modality (a perceived image), which automatically excludes others in the dynamics of perception (Ramachandran, 2011:221). This suggests that the neural activities and networks in the brain have a limited capacity; therefore, they constantly select information of images for restricted attentional resources. As Ramachandran continues, 'this seems initially counterintuitive, since one would expect that the richer the cues available in the object the stronger the recognition signal and associated limbic activation' (Ramachandran and Hirstein, 1999:24). This is the reason, Ramachandran believes, that 'an outline drawing or sketch (as "art") is more effective than a full colour photograph' (Ramachandran and Hirstein, 1999:24).

Although how human perception 'automatically' chooses a single perceived image from the others and its mechanism are still not fully understood, it is a significant finding which suggests that there might be a process of selectivity in image information processing. This idea of selectivity in human perception clearly has similar features to Hayles's understanding of the information processing processes between nonconsciousness and consciousness, as discussed earlier.

Additional evidence of this view comes from the Japanese neuroscientist Keiji Tanaka's discovery of neuronal selectivity. In the research on the neural code for objects, Tanaka and his colleagues found that there is an 'image simplification process' in the temporal cortex and that the brain's multimodal neuronal activities are selective. These neurons initially produce 'a rough categorization of image and single out its details' (Dehaene, 2009:135).

Dehaene further elaborates this 'image simplification process' by remarking that when we perceive objects, our neurons detect their contours, searching for characteristic configurations, such as the shape T, Y, or F.[19] These fragments of shapes are known as the 'non-accidental properties' of visual scenes (Dehaene, 2009:138), found at the places where several edges of an object meet: 'when one of these shapes appears on the retina, the brain can safely assume that it corresponds to the contour of an object present in the outside world' (Dehaene, 2009:138). They are invariant but key factors to determine an object's shape. Consequently, they characterize an object's sharp corners and their orientation.

According to Dehaene (2010:138): 'our primate nervous system seems to have discovered this invariant [non-accidental] property and used it to encode shapes'.

To make it clear, Dahaene introduces the psychologist Irving Biederman's hypothesis that we extract a sketch of non-accidental properties from the object, and this extraction allows us to reconstitute the elementary stage of the object's three-dimensional structure and then to assemble it into a whole representation of the object's shape (Dehaene, 2009).

Biederman provides examples to support this hypothesis, along with further explanation. Biederman writes (1987, cited in Dahaene, 2009:140):

> Complex objects are recognized through the configurations of their contours. At the places where they join, there contours from reproducible configurations shaped as T, L, Y, or F. If these junctions are erased, the images become much more difficult to recognize, whereas deletion of an equivalent amount of contour that spares the junctions causes much less difficulty. (see the simple cube diagram 'non-accidental properties' in Dehaene, 2009:140)

Hence, it seems that we do not need perfect or fully available information to reconstruct images of the object. It is safe to say that the same mechanism of human perception could apply to both hand-drawn and CGI animation.

Noise

In this context we need to address another interesting angle to better understand human perception of images with rich information and poor noise ratio, as Power explains: 'realistic imagery has a poor signal-to-noise ratio that can distract attention' (Power, 2009:115). If we follow this assumption of 'less is more' (less information and more noise enhance attention) or 'more is less' (more information and less noise is distractive for attention), this can lead to the idea that the perfection and completeness of CGI, as film director Cameron conceives it, does not always play the key role in enhancing the creative activities of the brain.

This is because in the process of the brain's complex dynamic neuron system, neuron networking activities can be more stimulated and activated by ambiguity. Hayles also introduces Edelman and Tononi's discovery which proposes that in the synaptic networks, 'neurons from different parts of the brain, and different kinds of neurons, interact much more strongly with each other than with other neurons active at the time' (Hayles, Chapter 2 in this collection). This can be understood as a situation in which these neurons are fired by different (not similar or closely related) information and stimuli, which can make the brain more active than with less ambiguous information and stimuli. The more ambiguity and the more noise it creates, the more actively the brain works. Hayles writes, with reference to Claude Shannon and Michel Serres, of 'formal results within information theory that demonstrated noise in a communication channel need not always destructively interfere with the message, but rather could itself become part of the message' (cited in Krapp, 2011:x).

It can be said that noise, which can induce 'imperfectness', seems to be an important factor in activating the complex dynamic neuron systems in the brain. Eventually, the 'creative' ambiguity' of information processing in the neuron systems can enhance the viewer's imagination and meaning-construction processes. Hence, we can understand, as aforementioned, in terms of neuroscience and psychological debates, human perception could be largely influenced by part of the brain's plasticity, such as its reconstructive, selective, creative, and imaginative attributes.

This reminds us of Miyazaki's suggestive statement about noise, or the gap, in terms of the relationship between moving images and human perception. What is fascinating is that Miyazaki assumes that 'perforation' (the holes in either side of the filmstrip) could play an key role in producing a good quality of animation (Miyazaki and Yorō, 1999:61). Perforation is a kind of limitation of technical engineering; however, this downside of technique actually acts as an important factor in making animation lively. Perforation is a cause of 'blur' that arises from the tiny 'unintentional' gaps of the filmstrip in the projector. This microsecond is an absence of information: that is, 'noise', which is supposed to not carry any meaning. Ironically, these tiny unintentional gaps help to make animation's 'liveliness' happen. This factor could support Power's assumption that 'less is more' and 'more is less', mentioned earlier.

In a dialogue with a Japanese anatomist, physician, and critic, Takeshi Yorō, Miyazaki also explains how 'mathematically calculated moving images are far different from human perception, as they always fail to express lively sensations'. For Miyazaki, 'human perception cannot engage or reflect on so much information' (e.g. 48 frames per second – which is twice the speed and carries much more information than the standard number of 24 frames per second) which means it fails to correspond or tune with human optical perception (see Miyazaki and Yorō, 1999:62). Miyazaki therefore emphasizes that '[A] nimation largely relies on deceptive means that use the nature of the brain and human perception' (Miyazaki and Yorō, 1999:61).

Responding to Miyazaki's statements indicating differences between human optical senses and a machine's, Yorō gives a further neurophysiological explanation of the optical system: when you look at a cup on the table and you suddenly move your head (and eyes) to see another object, say an ashtray, you still see the ashtray without seeing its background changing. This is because our brain can compensate to adjust our mobilizing view (Miyazaki and Yorō, 1999:59).[20] This implies that the information processing in the brain can work not only by abstracting and selecting the information but also actively adjusting to changing environments so that we can make sense of the world. The complex mechanism of neurophysiological human perception does not work in the same way as the 'camera' view. In other words, to grasp moving images, human perception doesn't need to have much information. It also doesn't acquire moving images in the machine (scientific) way, which captures a photographic real image in line with natural and physical laws.

Miyazaki goes on to assure us that CGI doesn't help him to create lively 'scenery' (Miyazaki and Yorō, 1999:61). He also shows he is suspicious about 'super high-definition' technology (Miyazaki and Yorō, 1999:61). This is because human perception does not correspond well with super high-definition technologies that are supposed to be the (almost) perfect accurate replication of 'naturalistic' vision. Human perception, however, could work better with the noise, gaps, and ambiguity of moving images. Miyazaki's animations are thus produced through human-perception-oriented design and calculation, created by his embodied 'craftmanship' and tacit knowledge.

Knowledge formation

To make this point further, I draw on the philosophies of technology of Simondon and Stiegler to consider the social implications of knowledge formation in advanced computational information society. Both philosophers address *alienation*, which is evident in the shifting relationship between knowledge and humans in the developing processes of technological society.

For Simondon, knowledge formation in human life with technological development needs to be articulated through the human relationship with machines. Simondon explains that mechanization of production led to an alienation of knowledge for both producers and users (consumers). As opposed to craftsmen in pre-industrial societies, factory workers or capitalists no longer needed to know every aspect of production processes when the machines were brought in.[21] Eventually, consumers also lost their chance to learn about practical production processes and tacit knowledge of their products.

In a similar way, when he writes about alienation in computational capitalism, Stiegler also argues that the digitalization and computerization of technical fields have led to the externalization of knowledge (for example, know-how or practical knowledge, memory, and experience), through 'the inscription of binary code into central processing units composed of silicon' (Stiegler 2018:20, cited in Alombert, 2019:322). Hence, he warns that digital computation destroys the knowledge of ways of living and replaces it with algorithmic calculations, which no longer require humans to do manual or physical activities in everyday life. Consequently, humans lose the ability to understand how things work, since we do not understand how the machine works. This is what he calls 'generalized proletarianisation' (Alombert, 2019:316).

We now can turn back to the discussion of the impossibility of computerization or datafication of affective effects and Miyazaki's animation grounded in his craftmanship and tacit knowledge. Miyazaki's skills and competence cannot be translated and transferred into computer data sets through algorithmic calculations. This means that his 'embodied' knowledge seems to be always evident in developing and producing *inventions*: creativities that depend on his own unique auto-affectivity, something that cannot be replaced by CGI (that is, machines). Hence, it is fair to say that he is not totally alienated from the production process of animation. His is not 'a closed system' in which technical knowledge, memory, and experience are conserved and repeated within embodied/habituated technical schema. For Miyazaki, 'openness' to potential is vital.

This resonates with Simondon's notion of 'margin of indeterminacy',[22] which refers to the crucial capacity to be open and sensitive to outside information for creating an *invention* (Simondon, 2017:51, cited in Voss, 2019:281).[23] The attitude of openness towards outside environments can imply continuities and limitless expansion of the information sources (data sets). At the same time, the openness enables Miyazaki as a subject to interpret, translate, transfer information, and also select, accumulate, classify, and save. His creative activities could be seen as fighting against 'symbolic misery' (Stiegler, 2015:23). These qualities enhance subjective embodied memory and tacit knowledge, some of which cannot be coded in line with the logic of digital computational media.

In this view, maintaining and expanding embodied memory and tacit knowledge through actual and direct experiences are indispensable for hand-drawn animation. For example, Miyazaki notes that the younger generation of animators has had little direct experience of seeing 'fire-flames'. They do not have a *memory* of 'real' fire-flames, since it is very rare to see 'fire-flames' in contemporary urban life. Hence they can only draw fire-flames by technically learning 'animated-drawing of fire-flames'. Consequently, he thinks they often produce over-technically driven animation as they have no personal understanding of how to express the vitality of fire as a moving image. Because they don't know how to capture the sense of nature's subtle motions and rhythms through their own perception, this means that they can only know and produce 'virtual' fire-flames.[24] This also indicates that the younger animators' 'virtual' experiences, which are most likely to have been produced by computer algorithms (technical cognition), could well be incorporated into their 'tacit knowledge' which helps them to construct 'an actuality'. The actuality they construct has already been mediated by technical and non-human perception. On the one hand, we might say that we suffer from a new form of alienation and difficulty in perceiving the 'real'. On the other hand, we can also think that these virtual experiences become part of their knowledge environment and 'data set' which can influence a new way of constructing reality (notwithstanding the animator's production of affective effects). This is a recursive interconnection between the trained data set (experience) and cognition. Consequently, it can also influence the construction process of (non)conscious cognition. This could then be helping to evolve a 'new' form of human perception.

Conclusion: cognitive assemblages and digital cultural intermediaries

Katherine Hayles emphasizes the importance of cognition and describes these complex interactions between human and nonhuman cognizers (including all biological life forms and many technical systems) as 'cognitive assemblage' (Hayles 2017:115). She writes:

> Because humans and technical systems in a cognitive assemblage are interconnected, the cognitive decisions of each affect the others, with interactions occurring across the full range of human cognition, including consciousness/unconscious, the cognitive nonconscious, and the sensory/perceptual system that send signals to the central nervous system. (Hayles, 2017:118)

Addressing cognitive assemblage, her goal is actually much wider than simply considering the interpenetration of technical cognition into human cognition. She insists that cognitive assemblage enables us to consider how the deep recursive interconnection of human and non-human life forms and technical cognizers in 'larger' cognitive assemblages can transform the planet's environment. In her view, we now live in a world that depends on the symbiotic relationship between humans and technical systems. Given that these systematic transformations are profoundly changing planetary cognitive ecologies, the humanities should endeavour to understand the implications (Hayles, 2017:216).

The above discussion has highlighted the ways in which human perception of moving images can be viewed as just one specific case in a vast array of cognitive assemblages. It is, however, a key example which illuminates the complex interpenetration of human and technical systems and reveals the similarities and limitations of human and technical cognition in terms of creating affective effects. Speculating about the neuropsychological dynamics of production and analysing the reception of the affective effects of moving images can provide us with a new approach for theorizing recursive information flows that highlights the interdependencies between consciousness and nonconscious cognition in both humans and technical systems.[25]

To further elaborate the relationship between technical systems and humans in new cognitive environments, it could be useful to consider Simondon's mechanologist (mechanologue) where he seeks a mutual understanding between machines and humans, and to 'represent technical beings to those who elaborate culture in order to favour the integration or the incorporation of technical schemes into *culture*' (Simondon, 1958:207, emphasis added, cited in Alombert, 2019:319). While I would acknowledge Simondon's suggestion to consider the vital social roles of the mechanologist, questions such as who they are, how they autonomously conduct their responsibilities (as part of cognitive assemblages), and their location in social milieus in the era of the massively expanding and deeply intertwined contemporary computational network society are in need of further elaboration. What we could learn from his suggestion is, however, that the integration of technical and human cognition into 'culture' requires new types of actors who have the ability to understand both changing technical systems and humans. Although they could face the challenges of all the same questions raised about Simondon's mechanologists (and hence this needs further theoretical and practical exploration), it could be worth considering the role of those we might call 'digital cultural intermediaries' – either people or systems which have been required to develop a highly sophisticated capacity for 'a new media literacy'.

As 'cognitive assemblages' continuously expand, computers and their ways of thinking could well become part of our consciousness and influence our perception of the world. Hence, the future implications of the symbiotic relationship between humans and technical systems in the bio–technosphere and planetary cognitive ecologies remain a persistent challenge we need to address.

Notes

1 Aesthetics in this chapter carries a broader sense than the traditional sense of beauty in philosophy and art. The focus is more on physio–sensory emotional affects than outer appearance.

2 From the animator's viewpoint, objects that exist in nature and are familiar to us can be more difficult to draw than objects that do not exist and are unfamiliar to us.

3 *Avatar* was nominated for Best Picture and Best Director, and won Best Cinematography, Best Visual Effects, and Best Art Direction in the 82nd Academy awards, 2010.

4 In the production of *Avatar*, a facial expression capture device was used. Each actor wears a head-cap with a small camera in front of the actor's face. The collected digital information of facial expressions is encoded in computers for the animators to create virtual images.

5 In 2008 *Ponyo on the Cliff by the Sea* was released. Miyazaki attempted to minimize the use of CGI and created the majority of frames by hand-drawing.

6 John Lasseter, the former chief creative officer at Pixar, Walt Disney Animation Studios, and Disney Toon Studios, remarked that Miyazaki had had a profound effect on his work and life (see Noh, 2014).

7 He mentioned that in the process of the production of animation, his ideas come from numerous fragmented and chaotic images, and an even deeper level of the unconscious (Nakajima and Kawamura, 2006:71).

8 Ingold introduced Sheets-Johnstone's 'thinking in movement', which is 'not to think by means of movement, or to have our thoughts transcribed into movement, rather the thinking is the movement: "To think is to be caught up in a dynamic flow; thinking is, by its very nature, kinetic"' (Sheets-Johnson, 1998:486, cited in Ingold, 2013:98).

9 The term mimesis is predicated on the Greek *mīmēsis*, which means to imitate and is often defined as imitating the manner, gesture, speech, or mode of actions and persons, or superficial characteristics of a thing and artistic expression (see Puetz, 2002).

10 Isoda remarks that 'the mirror neuron system in humans is involved not only in the recognition of the goal and intention of actions, but also in imitation, empathy, facial expression recognition, and other social cognition functions' (Isoda et al, 2016:1).

11 The distinction between affect and emotion is still debated in the field of media and communication. Lünenborg and Maier mention that 'affect is described as intensity (Massumi, 2002) or a dynamic, relational occurrence through which bodies are connected to each other (see, for example, Röttger-Rössler and Slaby, 2018), while emotion is understood as a complex, socially formed interplay of thoughts and feelings, as outlined over 30 years ago by Hochschild (1983)' (Lünenborg and Maier, 2018:2).

12 I would argue that there might be two stages of the process in affect: the presubjective stage in the initial stage, followed by the conscious stage. Please refer to the introduction of this book.

13 Although sound effects and other sensorial impacts can also be significant factors that create affective effects, this essay focuses more on the visuality of moving images, since human sensory capacities can be rather complex mechanisms that are too broad to be covered in this chapter.

[14] Hayles defines cognition as 'a process that interprets information within contexts that connect it with meaning' (Hayles, 2017:22).

[15] Hayles also emphasizes 'temporal dynamics', which is a micro-duration of the recursive information process between nonconscious and conscious cognition (see Chapter 2 in this collection).

[16] She claims: 'Notwithstanding the profound differences in contexts, nonconscious cognitions in biological organisms and technical systems share certain structural and functional similarities, specifically in building up layers of interactions from low-level choices, and consequently very simple cognitions, to higher cognitions and interpretations' (Hayles, 2017:13).

[17] This view can also resonate with Lazzarato's discussion of the 'semiotic operator'. He discusses the distinct regimes of the sign between machinic enslavement and social subjection from a semiotic perspective. He conceives that machinic enslavement works based on 'asignifying semiotics' (for example, computer languages) which do not have *subject reference* (Lazzarato, 2014:39).

[18] Although affect can subjectively emerge first at this stage, owing to the mirror neuron it will then be shared with others. Therefore, the production process of affect is subjective, but the appreciation of affect can be communicative. Affect is by no means universal.

[19] Shape detectors apply not just to Western letters, such as T, F ,Y, or O, but Tanaka has observed that some neurons code for a black dot on a white background and other neurons are sensitive to hand or finger shapes (Dehaene, 2009:139).

[20] This is called the vestibulo-ocular reflex. Barry provides an example to understand this compensatory system between head orientation and eye movement: 'The average video camera does not have a built-in vestibulo-ocular reflex, so when it moves up and down as a cameraman walks, it takes frames from many different angles' (Barry, 2009:76–7).

[21] In the process of concretization, Simondon argues, the parts are 'like workers, they cooperate without knowing exactly what the others are actually doing' in the initial stages (Simondon, 1989:21, cited in Schmidgen, 2005:14–15). Yet when technical objects are concretized, the parts are related in a manner of a 'pure functional scheme' (functionally related to each other without losing their own potential).

[22] A similar reflection on this idea can also be found in contemporary soft robotics. In their research on artificial evolution, robot scientists have been developing 'selection schemes' which supposedly can affect the evolutionary process. One popular scheme is known as the 'roulette wheel' in which individuals have a certain probability, proportional to their fitness, of being selected for reproduction. It is important not only to select the best individuals but also to include less fit ones in order to keep the diversity in the population'. (Pfeifer and Bongard, 2007:180).

[23] Another notion Simondon insists on is 'operative solidarity', which assumes 'the threshold to *invention* depends on the potentialization of the elements presently in place as [a] function of their future' (Massumi, 2009:40, emphasis added). This process is encapsulated in Simondon's emphasis on concretization, which is a process of 'operative solidarity of the coupled multifunctionalities of the formerly disparate energetic field of the different element[s]' (for example, oil and water) (see in more detail in Massumi, 2009:40).

[24] Miyazaki felt that none of the Ghibli animators could successfully draw the character Calcifer (a fire demon) in *Howl's Moving Castle*. https://matome.naver.jp/odai/21542081 29448860501 (accessed August 2019). This original link unfortunately has recently been removed. There is an alternative Japanese link [https://batque.com/feature/272] that explains the vital points Miyazaki makes about drawing the Calcifer fire-flame character. Miyazaki was disappointed with the younger animators' limited drawing skill and inability to capture the fire-flame.

25 Animation in the cultural industries can also be a prime field to discuss the socio-economic and political implications of computational technology, and that makes us consider that the 'cognitive assemblage' itself cannot be conceived as independent from cultural, economic, and political matters in any technical development. This is why it provides us with the opportunity to consider the role of power in the evolution of computational technologies in their intersection with capitalism. These issues cannot be fully discussed in this chapter but are significant points to be taken up in further analysis.

References

Alombert, Anne (2019) 'How Can Culture and Technics Be Reconciled in the Digital Milieu and Automatic Societies? Political Implications of the Philosophies of Technology of Simondon and Stiegler', *Culture, Theory and Critique*, 60(3–4): 315–26.

Barry, Susan R. (2009) *Fixing My Gaze: A Scientist's Journey into Seeing in Three Dimensions*, New York: Basic Books.

Biederman, Irving (1987) 'Recognition-by-components: A Theory of Human Image Understanding', *Psychological Review*, 94(2): 115–47.

Bigelow, Susan J. (2009) 'Technologies of Perception: Miyazaki in Theory and Practice', *Animation*, 4(1): 55–75.

Brassett, Jamie (2016) 'Speculative Machines and Technical Mentalities: A Philosophical Approach to Designing the Future', *Digital Creativity*, 27(2):163–76.

Bueno-Guerra, Nereida (2018) 'How to Apply the Concept of *Umwelt* in the Evolutionary Study of Cognition', *Frontiers in Psychology*, 9:2001, https://doi.org/10.3389/fpsyg.2018.02001.

Carman, Taylor (2008) *Merleau-Ponty*, London: Routledge.

Clough, P.T., Goldberg, G., Schiff, R., Weeks, A. and Willse, C. (2007) 'Notes Towards a Theory of Affect-Itself', *ephemera*, 7(1): 60–77.

Davis, Michael (1999) *The Poetry of Philosophy: On Aristotle's Poetics*, South Bend, IN: St Augustine's Press.

Dehaene, Stanislas (2009) *Reading in the Brain: The New Science of How We Read*, New York: Penguin Books.

Edelman, Gerald M. (1987) *Neural Darwinism: The Theory of Neuronal Group Selection*, New York: Basic Books.

Evens, Aden (2015) *Logic of the Digital*, London: Bloomsbury.

Featherstone, Mike (2010) 'Body, Image and Affect in Consumer Culture', *Body & Society* 16(1): 193–221.

Furniss, Maureen (2007) *Art in Motion: Animation Aesthetics* (revised edn), Eastleigh: John Libbey Publishing.

Hansen, Mark B.N. (2003) 'Affect as Medium, or the "Digital-Facial-Image"', *Journal of Visual Culture*, 2(2): 205–28.

Hayles, N. Katherine (2017) *Unthought: The Power of the Cognitive Nonconscious*, Chicago: University of Chicago Press.

Hayles, N. Katherine and Sampson, Tony D. (2018) 'Unthought Meets the Assemblage Brain', *Capacious: Journal for Emerging Affect Inquiry*, 1(2): 60–84.

Hochschild, A.R (1983) *The Managed Heart: Commercialization of Human Feeling*, Berkeley, CA: University of California Press.

Ingold, Tim (2013) *Making: Anthropology, Archaeology, Art and Architecture*, London: Routledge.

Isoda, K., Sueyoshi, K., Ikeda, Y., Nishimura, Y. Hisanaga, I., Orlic, S., Kim, Y.-K. and Higuchi, S. (2016) 'Effect of the Hand-Omitted Tool Motion on mu Rhythm Suppression', *Frontiers in Human Neuroscience*, 10: 266. https://doi.org/10.3389/fnhum.2016.00266.

Kane, Carolyn L. (2014) *Chromatic Algorithms: Synthetic Color, Computer Art, and Aesthetics after Code*, Chicago: University of Chicago Press.

Kaufman, Amy (2009) 'Jackson, Cameron Saddened by State of Film Industry (Video)', *The Wrap*, 25 July [online], Available from: www.thewrap.com/jackson-cameron-saddened-state-film-industry-video-4578/ [Accessed 18 July 2020].

Krapp, Peter (2011) *Noise Channels: Glitch and Error in Digital Culture*, Minneapolis: University of Minnesota Press.

Lazzarato, Maurizio (2014) *Signs and Machines: Capitalism and the Production of Subjectivity*, translated by Joshua David Jordan, Los Angeles: Semiotext(e).

Levi, Antonia (1996) *Samurai from Outer Space: Understanding Japanese Animation*, Chicago: Open Court.

Lünenborg, Margreth and Maier, Tanja (2018) 'The Turn to Affect and Emotion in Media Studies', *Media and Communication*, 6(3): 1–4.

Massumi, Brian (2002) *Parables for the Virtual: Movement, Affect, Sensation*, Durham, NC: Duke University Press.

Massumi, Brian (2009) '"Technical Mentality" Revisited: Brian Massumi on Gilbert Simondon, with Arne De Boever, Alex Murray and Jon Roffe', *Parrhesia*, 7: 36–45.

Miyazaki, Hayao (1996) *Starting Point 1979–1996 (Shuttpatsu ten 1979–1996)*, Tokyo: Tokuma Shoten.

Miyazaki, Hayao and Takashi Yorō (1999) 'Dialogue, Miyazaki Hayao vs Yorō Takashi', in *Kenejyun Muttku, Filmmakers 6, Hayao Miyazaki*, edited by Takashi Yorō, Tokyo: Kinema Jyunposha, pp 56–77.

Nakajima, Yukari and Kawamura, Takashi (eds) (2006) *Ghibli Museum, Mitaka Catalogue* (revised and enlarged edn), Tokyo: Tokuma Memorial Cultural Foundation for Animation.

Noh, Jean (2014) 'John Lasseter talks about Japanese inspirations', *Screen Daily*, 27 October [online], Available from: https://www.screendaily.com/news/john-lasseter-talks-about-japanese-inspirations/5079059.article [Accessed 20 August 2019].

Parisi, Paula (1995) 'The New Hollywood', *Wired*, 3(12), 1 December [online], Available from: https://www.wired.com/1995/12/new-hollywood/ [Accessed August 2019].

Pfeifer, Rolf and Bongard, Josh (2007) *How the Body Shapes the Way We Think: A New View of Intelligence*, Cambridge, MA: MIT Press.

Power, Pat (2009) 'Animated Expressions: Expressive Style in 3D Computer Graphic Narrative Animation', *Animation*, 4(2): 107–29.

Puetz, Michelle (2002) 'Mimesis', The University of Chicago, Theories of Media, Keywords Glossary, [online], Available from: https://csmt.uchicago.edu/glossary2004/mimesis.htm [Accessed 15 June 2019].

Ramachandran, V.S. (2011) *The Tell-Tale Brain: A Neuroscientist's Quest for What Makes Us Human*, New York: Norton.

Ramachandran, V.S. and Hirsten, William (1999) 'The Science of Art: A Neurological Theory of Aesthetic Experience', *Journal of Consciousness Studies*, 6(6–7): 15–51. https://www.ingentaconnect.com/contentone/imp/jcs/1999/00000006/f0020006/949

Rizzolatti, Giacomo and Sinigaglia, Corrado (2008) *Mirrors in the Brain: How Our Minds Share Actions and Emotions*, translated by F. Anderson, New York: Oxford University Press.

Röttger-Rössler, B. and Slaby, J. (eds) (2018) *Affect in Relation: Families, Places, Technologies*, New York: Routledge.

Schaffer, W. (2007) 'Animation 1: The Control Image', in A. Cholodenko (ed) *The Illusion of Life 2: More Essays on Animation*, Sydney: Power Publications, pp 456–85.

Sheets-Johnstone, M. (1998) *The Primacy of Movement*, Amsterdam: John Benjamins.

Schmidgen, Henning (2005) 'Thinking Technological and Biological Beings: Gilbert Simondon's Philosophy of Machines', *Revista do Departamento de Psicologia UFF* 17(2): 11–18.

Simondon, Gilbert (1958/1989) *Du mode d'existence des objets techniques*, Paris: Aubier.

Simondon, Gilbert (1958/2017) *On the Mode of Existence of Technical Objects*, translated by Cecile Malaspina and John Rogove. Minneapolis, MN: Univocal Publishing.

Simondon, Gilbert (2009) 'Technical Mentality', translated by Arne De Boever, *Parrhesia*, 7: 17–27.

Stiegler, Bernard (2015) *Symbolic Misery, Volume 2: Catastrophe of the Sensible*, translated by Barnaby Norman, Cambridge: Polity Press.

Taussig, Michael (1993) *Mimesis and Alterity: A Particular History of the Senses*, New York: Routledge.

Terzidis, Kostas (2003) *Expressive Form: A Conceptual Approach to Computational Design*, New York: Spon Press.

Torre, Dan (2014) 'Cognitive Animation Theory: A Process-Based Reading of Animation and Human Cognition', *Animation*, 9(1): 47–64.

von Uexküll, J. (1934/2010) *A Foray into the Worlds of Animals and Humans, with a Theory of Meaning*, translated by Joseph D. O'Neil, Minneapolis, MN: University of Minnesota Press.

Voss, Daniela (2019) 'Invention and Capture: A Critique of Simondon', *Culture, Theory and Critique*, 60(3–4): 279–99.

4

New Punctums, Proto-Perceptions, and Animated Entanglements

Tony D. Sampson

Is another punctum possible?

In this article I will take up Eric S. Jenkins' (2013) suggestion that we need to learn from, but ultimately go beyond, Roland Barthes's concept of the *punctum* to describe a new kind of impersonal affective experience of animation. A new punctum needs to be a novel concept that grasps how animated images produce an illusion of movement by affecting perception and an ideological level of comprehension or miscomprehension. To achieve this aim we need to start, as Jenkins does, with Barthes's analysis of the photographic image. To understand how he arrived at the punctum, we need to imagine Barthes sitting at his writing desk, fixing his attention on an image, possibly with a blanket over his head, so as to block out any interference (Figure 4.1).

As he gazes deeply into the photograph, Barthes experiences something that goes beyond the subject of the image. His immersion in it is penetrated by the punctum. This is, as Jenkins points out, part of a now renowned distinction Barthes makes between the *studium* (the subject of the photo) on one hand, and the way the photo itself *pierces* the viewer's observation of the photo and in doing so transforms their perception of the image on the other. This rupture in the experience of the still image is considered, in Barthes's poststructuralist terms, as part of the language of the image: a punctuation in the speech images use to communicate with their audiences.

What is astute about Jenkins referencing of the punctum is his grasping of the opportunities Barthes seems to offer to go beyond a linguistic reading of still images, and address, as such, affective experiences, which might similarly pierce the perception and influence comprehension. This is a

Figure 4.1: *Barthes's Punctum* by Mikey B. Georgeson

Source: Permission granted by the artist.

complex theoretical move, since although Barthes explicitly points to a media experience based on *intensity* rather than just *detail* (p 575), he distances his analysis from moving images. Indeed, as Jenkins notes, Barthes argues that the experience of photography is not at all like that of a moving image (p 576). In fact, one gets the impression that this distancing has something to do with Barthes's concern for the eventual death of the photographic image. It is certainly a mournful Barthes that we encounter here since he suggests that it is the new technology of movement that threatens the old punctum. Which is to say, the essence of the photographic experience beyond the studium becomes lost, Barthes contends, in all this movement (p 576).

So it is that the old punctum seems somehow stuck in the death and detail of Barthes's experience of the still image. His contrast between still and moving image is indeed plain in this sense. On one hand, Barthes's old photos are punctuated by a sombre reminder that while the lives of the subjects pictured in the image are frozen, these subjects are most probably long dead. It is this experience of death in the detail that, one assumes, ruptures the viewer's perception of human mortality captured in the still images. The moving image is, on the other hand, always alive! There is no pause for death or detail since the image keeps moving (p 577). Barthes has a point, perhaps. As Jenkins argues, at 24 fps the moving image leaves 'little time for contemplation' (p 578). As will be discussed later, there are others, like Gilles Deleuze (2005 [1985]), who similarly discusses how the movement image challenges the privileged instants of the photograph.

Jenkins' aim is not, however, as mournful as Barthes's. He does not try to kill off the old punctum, but rather considers how another punctum is possible; a punctum about life, rather than Barthes's obsession with death and detail (p 576). There are evidently reference points littered throughout the history of moving images that provide a possible route to another kind of punctum. This is where structuralist and post-structuralist film theory has generally located its punctuation mark in the form of the filmstrip. As many animators, makers of montage and film editors will contend, it is not the privileged image that provides the liveliness of movement. It is rather the gaps in between each image that supposedly animate. It is this gap or *the cut* that potentially ruptures the perceptual experience. More significantly, it is in this gap that the illusory and ideological effects of moving image experience potentially come alive in the phenomenal mind of the viewer.

What is both fascinating and valuable about Jenkins' approach is that he looks outside of this linguistic frame of reference to locate his new punctum in a 'theory of ideology based on affect' (p 576). This is an exciting move because we no longer get stuck with a purely symbolic mark of punctuation. The reader is invited to break out of the old structuralist accounts of film form couched in language. In fact, we are no longer simply looking at the effect the codified object of the image has on the perceiving subject, experiencing the punctuation. Instead, drawing on affect theory, Jenkins notes the importance of presubjective experiences of animation (p 579). Again, this is a sharp move since Jenkins' analysis of animation does not mourn, as one might assume, the death of subjectivity. On the contrary, he introduces an important three-way distinction made in new materialist affect theory, between (a) the primacy of a presubjective intensity of affect; (b) the felt experience of affect (the sensation); and (c) the experiencer's emotional cognition. This is an important distinction because it recognizes how Barthes's notion of a piercing of experience can be adapted to realize affect not in the direct effects of the punctum on the conscious cognition of the experiencer (experienced emotionally or hidden under blankets), but instead considers the somatic, temporal registering of experience, occurring outside cognizant perception. As follows, a Spinozan affect theory formula kicks into action, which notes the capacity of the punctum to animate the body and the body's capacity to animate the photo in a prepersonal zone of affective experience (p 580).

The realisation of an affective punctum at work in animation requires some careful theoretical moves that maintain the above tripart distinction throughout. To be sure, we cannot confuse affect, feeling, and emotion as the same thing. The new punctum cannot be about 'moving' the subject on an emotional level alone. On the contrary, Jenkins is not interested in the 'emotional identification' or subjective response to the movement of the image (p 586). Along these lines, then, our analysis of animation needs to similarly begin by substituting the symbolic, cognitive consumption of the old punctum for a process wherein it is the presubjective experience that readies the way for the potential of a movement event to trigger subjective responses. Profoundly, then, it is in the primacy of this presubjective experience of the new punctum that the temporal hallucination of animation, as a kind experience of real movement, might be realized (p 583). It could be the case, therefore, that the affective registering of the image helps us to grasp how the ideological tricks of Barthes's mythologies of the moving image work their magical influence on experience beyond symbolic ideas-in-form. The point is: the new punctum does not present a phenomenological relation established between the form of the image (still or moving) and the cognitive mind, but instead offers a nonphenomenological experience of a material relation.

Animated materiality

So as to develop on Jenkins' discussion, I will now turn to address specific ways in which the ideological and illusory trickery of the moving image experience have been expressed in theories of media materiality, broadly understood. To begin with, we must note that what seems to be amiss in Barthes's mournful nostalgia for the fading punctum of the photograph is a satisfactory explanation of how its historical disappearance relates to the emerging materiality of moving images. Following Barthes's logic, the punctum of the photograph seems to be *lost to mind* in the experience of movement. But how can this be? Surely, even if the old punctum appears to die, the materiality of the movement image does not simply perish in its wake? The material penetration of perception does not, similarly, pass away either! On the contrary, as I will argue, the material relation between the image and the brain is very much alive. However, to properly grasp this material liveliness we need to escape the old situating syntax of the punctum and conjure with a new account of experience based on affective intensity.

Contrary to Barthes, this chapter will argue that the strange death of the punctum is not attributable to a defined point in media history where static photographs give way to movement. Which is to say, we need to see how animation has itself become caught up in a somewhat fictitious linear historical trajectory of the image: a trajectory in which the primacy of the perceptive instants of photography have become erroneously privileged over an inferior movement of images. To be sure, on reflection, Barthes's death of the punctum is probably not the best starting place to grasp a theory of the animated image. Its demise might instead be better understood as an impasse or blockage in the desire to make images move from the very beginning of image-making. In this context, animation is not an evolution of the still image. This notion ignores the pre-echoic moving images created by the early animators of Palaeolithic art. According to Azéma and Rivére (2012:318), for example, long before the inventions of Niépce, Muybridge, or Disney, Palaeolithic artists seem to have developed two processes for breaking down movement. These proto-animation techniques meant artists could *superimpose* and *juxtapose* successive images to render movement possible. Looking rapidly from one cave drawing to the next, the viewer can indeed see a tail flick or a leg move. Of course, without going back this far, we can see how movement has always been a part of ancient and modern image-making, whether it is expressed in a line, a brushstroke, or sculptural gesture. Certainly, efforts made to reproduce life as still were challenged by Duchamp's intention (inspired by Étienne-Jules Marey's images of motion) to take the reclining, passive figure of the painterly nude and animate it up a staircase.

We encounter the same sense of linear historical ruptures in the Japanese history of animation. Along these lines, in Yuriko Furuhata's (2011) article, 'Rethinking Plasticity: The Politics and Production of the Animated Image', we find a series of transformative ruptures between drawn images, optical toys, and post-Muybridge celluloid animation. Following such a historical trajectory, the animation of photographic moving images can no longer be grasped like a cartoon that is hypothetically drawn, Furuhata argues. Cell animation becomes a series of images that have become actualized. Certainly, this actualization of movement is endemic to a tendency to historicize images and is reflected in other contemporary debates on the use of, for example, motion capture (mocap) in filmmaking. Mocap has been described as a kind of animation that moves beyond being a mere quality of the profilmic event (what is staged in front of the camera) to an animated movement, grasped in itself as inherently profilmic (see, for example, Ng, 2012).

Significantly, however, what is often missing from these linear histories of media disruption is a consideration of a continuous material relation established between the experience of images and the movement-events in which all images are apprehended. In other words, what is missing in the death of the punctum thesis is a mode of perception caught in the entanglement of mind, matter, and movement. Caught up in its structuralist framework, Barthes's perception of the punctum seems to have magically bifurcated from this material entanglement. For how long was he really stuck under his protective blanket, staring at just one image, before he noticed the lights had changed? To put this another way, Barthes seems to be frozen in a static, phenomenal space of representation, which may well seem like a perceptive command post, capturing the punctuated details of an image, but without allowing for any sense of its temporality or duration. We might say that Barthes's punctum is well and truly stuck in the *here and now* of phenomenal experience. His images have no event to speak of. They are, as such, images marked by a kind of lifeless punctuation that deals only in marking out symbolic spatial meanings that are fixed in the past and ignore a present/future syntax that designates the temporal movement of events. These are images which were *over there* before they are experienced here *and* now, and eventually slipping off into the future-past. The punctum is, as such, not a perceptual command post; it is a mere foothold in the movement event.

Arguably, what is needed is a grasping of images, not defined by a historical rupture between still and moving image, but instead, an analytical transition from the problematics of phenomenological *thinking in forms* to an affective mode of movement event that might occur outside of thought. Along these lines, the analytical focus moves away linguistic forms in the mind or secondary phenomenal zones of experience, toward the primacy of the material intensities of the movement event, registered prior to personal cognitive consciousness. Such an approach will eventually allow us to grasp how still and moving images are intimately related to each other in the sense that neither can be reduced to a transcendental elevation of a privileged or instantaneous moment over the events in which they are experienced. On the contrary, all images (static or moving) occur as image-events. Yet before this shift in focus can happen, we need to map out various ways in which the ideological illusions of the animated image have already been linked to materiality, particularly with regard to brain plasticity. Because it is here, in the very matter of the brain, that we might grasp animated images, not as an extension of form, but instead as a new kind of intensive piercing of proto-perception. Along these lines, then, leaning on historical dialectics, Furuhata's (2011) work on Disney suggestively promises to move 'beyond the phenomenological *perception* of the image to material process of *producing* the image' (p 26). The materiality of animation is, as follows, directly related to the material labour of production registered in the brain.

What is primarily significant about Furuhata's move to the materiality of production is that it differs from the archetypal Frankfurt School ideological analysis of Disney. In contrast to the critique of Disney as a regimental Fordist model of production, characterized by a passive disempowering massification of consumer culture, Furuhata uncovers a differently oriented material relation. Her analytical focus moves away from the Frankfurt School, toward grasping (and making political) a kind of plasticity in the material *appearance* of moving images, similar to a concept originally described by Sergei Eisenstein as *plasmaticness*. Eisenstein's concept notes the 'protean' nature of Disney's animated creations that can 'stretch, squash or twist into impossible contortions,' resisting the 'laws of nature' (p 26). Indeed, Furuhata remarks how Japanese critics saw Eisenstein's plasmaticness as a kind of ideological illusion of escape from the regimental Fordist model of work in which Disney animators mass-produced their drawings.

What is also important to grasp at this point is that Furuhata locates the illusion of animation directly in the synaptic matter of the brain. Referring to Catherine Malabou's (2008) notable account of brain plasticity, Furuhata updates the material history of animation labour from the hypothetical to the actual movement of cells as a kind of dialectical formula moving from malleability to flexibility. Along these lines, the plasticity of the synaptic brain enters into a post-Fordist material relation to animation in which we find a newly configured ideological trap. Herein, the capacity for brain plasticity to be free from the rigidity of genetic determinism becomes ensnared in a post-Fordist cybernetic model of labour that purposefully confuses plasticity with flexibility in the workplace. Indeed, following Malabou, on one hand, we need not be concerned about genetically determined forms of perception because the plastic brain provides a 'possible margin of improvisation' between the synapse and the biological encoding of genetic necessity (p 27). Today, Malabou states, 'it is no longer chance versus necessity, but chance, necessity, and plasticity – which is neither the one nor the other' (p 28). On the other hand, the illusion of movement should no longer be understood as an ideological massification that works on perception. Instead, contrary to the Frankfurt School, the illusion becomes something more akin to what Malabou calls ideological avatars. These avatars act on the material brain at the level of the synapse. This is not a distortion or mythologizing of form, but rather the obscuring of what it really means for a plastic brain to be free.

In many ways, Furuhata's use of Malabou's ideological avatars points toward the development of a synaptic model of proto-perception that precedes phenomenological perception. So how can this model help us to get any closer to Jenkins' impersonal affective punctum? Will these considerations of the emergent properties of synaptic plasticity provide a new punctum that is all about affect and intensity rather than death and detail? It would seem that by focusing on regions of the brain as the experience of moving images occurs, we might gain potential insights into the material sensations felt by the viewer. Again, following Malabou, this felt experience appears to happen at a level of liberated plasticity that can know and modify its own experiences as well as fend off the threat posed to freedom by ideological avatars. This mode of plasticity is what Malabou importantly draws attention to when she asks the question of what we should do with our brains so that we can truly know the material freedom they possess.

Nonetheless, as a theory of proto-perception that is supposed to precede or go beyond phenomenological experience, the emergence of synaptic self-awareness or consciousness has a series of significant limitations. Mainly, although the synaptic self theoretically emerges from a material improvisation between gene power and variability, what emerges does so via a series of neuronal prototypes of personality. What we find in the synapse is a proto-self which effectively develops into phenomenological perception by way of moving up through a series of processes leading to self-awareness. In other words, what emerges from the synapse is a mode of perception grasped by Malabou as a dialectical 'synthesis of all the plastic processes at work in the brain,' allowing the organism to 'hold together and unify the cartography of networks' (p 29). Indeed, according to the synaptic self hypothesis, the emergence of stable thoughts, emotions, and motivations becomes necessary for survival of a coherent and rational neuronal personality; otherwise, irrationality would cast these thoughts out into the wilderness, and emotions and motivations would be scattered in all directions like some unruly mob (p 30). In effect, what emerges from the synaptic self is a phenomenal world in which the 'I' of the person can think and feel itself as *whole*. The emergent self is, as such, a sum total of the parts that lead to consciousness. What is arguably missing from a synaptic self thesis of this kind, which is based ultimately on the emergence of personal experience, is a sense of how multiple proto-perceptions are primarily entangled in the material world without becoming whole. Which is to say, how do we account for prepersonal experiences that do not become conscious yet are clearly affected and affect the world in which they live?

Brains that trigger together, think together

There is some attempt in the various offshoots of neuroscience to overcome the limits of personal phenomenality and explore synaptic entanglements by way of observations of multiple brains exposed to moving image experiences (Hasson et al, 2008). As an extension of the kind of neurocultures Malabou conjures with, neurocinematics, for example, is an attempt to converge cognitive neuroscience and film studies to focus on intersubject correlations. This latest in a long line of neurodisciplines is interested in a mode of perception that is supposedly traceable to neurocorrelates between brain matter and the phenomenal mental grasping of moving image experiences. In a nutshell, what happens in brain matter (sensations) is assumed to correlate with shared mental experiences, like attention, memories, perceptions, and conceptualizations common to a viewing audience. Along these lines, neurocinematic researchers use functional magnetic resonance imaging (fMRI) and other cognitive technologies to observe neural activity and attention according to intensities detected by increased blood flow in certain brain regions, across a sample audience.

Perhaps the connection between neuroscience and the study of moving images is an obvious one to make. In many ways, neurocinematics links to conventional film studies since both work within a similar cognitive frame of reference. For example, central to the neurocinematic approach is a notion of how different aspects of moving image production can *control* a mind. Like this, Hasson et al (2008:1) make the claim that film theorists have always assumed that the moving image has a 'tight grip' on the mind of the viewer; yet, with the 'advent of non-invasive neuro imaging methods' it now possible to 'penetrate a viewer's mind and record his or her mental states while watching a movie'. More direct comparisons can be made with cognitive film theory, which similarly links the illusionary effects of film on cognitive processes, like perception, attention, and memory, to mind control via subtle changes made to cinematography, *mise en scène*, sound, editing, narration. In effect, neurocinematics attempts to turn the immaterial connections made in film studies into the tangible variable relations typical of positivistic scientific methods.

The neurocinematic method compares the illusionary perception of change engendered by the moving image with real-life perceptions of movement. In this sense, the focus falls on the work the moving image does on behalf of the eye, by initially tracing attention to cinematic events through eye-tracking technology. The tracking of attention allows researchers to follow what content audiences are actually focusing on in each frame of a film and therefore analyse misapprehended perceptual responses to movement according to the assumed psychological grip it has on viewers. There is nothing particularly new in this interest in the relation between what the eye sees and the mind thinks when experiencing illusions. As Maria Poulaki (2014:41) notes, film makers intuitively tend to take advantage of certain

'flaws' of natural perception, such as change blindness, use editing in such a way so as to aid the spectator's construction of a fluent and believable diegetic space.

However, according to neurocinematics, exercising mind control over an audience is not just about measuring attention. In order to qualify the extent to which brain responses are controlled by the moving image, neurocinematic researchers make links between audience attention and intelligibility. Which is to say, the research focuses on how viewers comprehend and make sense of the intentions of the filmmaker alongside the observation of controlled brain responses across viewers evident to comparable intensities mapped in fMRI brain images. In other words, we might say that the mantra of neurocinematics is that brains that trigger together, think together.

The neurocinematic assertion that the latest advances in neurotechnology, specifically fMRI, open up the mind to scrutiny has, nevertheless, attracted much criticism. What amounts to a neurocentric methodology based on a neuron-eye-mind hypothesis is critiqued for its assumption that there is a rather crude correlation between blood flow in the matter of the brain and what is supposed to be occurring in the minds of an audience (Sampson, 2017). In short, it is an example of a wide-ranging locationist neurocognitive research programme, often repeated in neuroaesthetics and neuromarketing. By turning her attention to the discursive formations of these programmes, Poulaki (2014:44) challenges similar problematic claims made in neurocinematics by arguing that it presupposes a reliable and predictable series of neural states can be evoked by moving images and correlated to other brains experiencing the same movie. Such an approach is thus based on a version of mind control founded on neural predictability and cognitive triggers assumed to be measurable by often restrictive fMRI practices.

Neurocinematics presents a theory of mind control that not only ignores much of the noise and complexity apparent in a brain's relation to moving images, but also strips away much of the criticality developed in film theory. This is not to say that the approach does not register the powerful influence of illusion. As Poulaki points out, neurocinematics claims to present empirical evidence for 'the long-lasting distinction in film theory between films that remain faithful as much as possible to reality and those that seek to control or distort it' (p 45). Furthermore, the approach flags up a tradition in film production of 'controlled aesthetics and message manipulation through highly structured editing' (p 46). However, the feeling of being held captive in the fictional world of a movie or animation is not really considered as ideologically manipulative or part of a dream factory of illusion. On the contrary, the illusion of the moving image provides the 'most important sources of viewing pleasure' (p 42) for the moving image audience. Indeed, the tracing of this pleasure to particular and predictable brain regions is subsequently intended to provide 'a valuable method for the film industry to better assess [and improve] its products' (Hasson et al, 2008:1).

Poulaki concludes her critique by moving away from the crudity of these cognitive effect models to suggest more value may be found in developing a complexity model that considers an interrelated relation between the brains of an audience and moving images. Along these lines, the illusions of the filmmaker's 'textual system' and the triggered brains of an audience are regarded as something Franco Varela called 'structurally-coupled systems' (p 49) It is this interlocked system, engaged, as such, in open, nonlinear, dynamical cinematic experiences, which cannot be simply detected in the linear neurocorrelates neurocinematics attempts to establish between brain matter (blood flow), tracked visual attention, and evidence of mind control.

In the second part of this article I want to begin to sketch out a mode of stripped-out perception that builds on certain aspects of Furuhata's aspiration to go beyond phenomenological notions of the experience of animated film. By doing so I want to further grasp the illusory experiences of animation in matter itself. Which is to say, the discussion will expand beyond the synapse to consider wider assemblages of materiality and expressivity. The resulting nonphenomenological approach will therefore require a different focus to that expressed in Malabou's notion of how ideological avatars work on the plasticity of the synaptic self. Along these lines, the focus is primarily on Henri Bergson's (1912) *Matter and Memory*, and henceforth traced forward to Gilles Deleuze's (2005) Bergson-inspired three theses on the moving image. Finally, the discussion brings in A.N. Whitehead to conclude with a potential fourth thesis on the new punctum.

Ideological avatars versus Bergson's brain

Before a nonphenomenological approach can be established, we need to initially consider Malabou's (2008) acknowledgement that the dialectical movement of ideological avatars clashes with Bergson's nonrepresentational position in *Matter and Memory*. Which is to say, Malabou's dialectical approach does not sit easily with Bergson's question concerning what constitutes the journey between matter and the illusionary image-event. As Malabou argues, there is, contrary to Bergson's claim, a self-representation of the brain: an auto-representation of cerebral structures that coincides with the auto-representation of the organism. This internal capacity for representation, inherent in neuronal activity (from prototype to fully emerged self-awareness), constitutes a prototypical form of symbolic activity. Everything happens as if the very connectivity of the connections – their structure of reference, in other words, their semiotic nature in general – represents itself, 'maps' itself, and permits a blurring of the borders between the functioning of brain matter and emergent psyche (Malabou, 2008:59–60).

It is this significant disparity between the semiotic nature of Malabou's synaptic self and Bergson's nonrepresentational brain that requires closer inspection in the context of our discussion here. To better understand it, we need to grasp Bergson's delicate philosophical positioning in *Matter and Memory*, wherein the concept of the virtual, or movement image, famously exceeds what the idealists would call a *representation*, while at the same time not altogether siding with what realists would call a *thing* (Bergson, 1912:9). The virtual image is placed halfway between the thing and the representation. For example, when we encounter a novel object, Bergson contends, we are not experiencing it as a representation already stored in the brain, and likewise, if we have encountered the same object a thousand times before in the past, our experience of it does not become a representation stored in memory. In contrast, for Bergson, the memory of things becomes a mechanical habit passing from the original stimulus to the brain without the 'miraculous power of changing itself into a representation of things' (p 29). Conscious processes, such as those experienced in recollecting the past, but also, arguably, these seemingly totalized experiences of self and identity, are not preserved in the brain. They are preserved in themselves – in their *duration*. Bergson's matter therefore becomes an aggregate of images, or the intermediary existence (an endurance) of the thing itself and the representation (p 9). Importantly, then, cognitive processes are not the outcome of a parallelism between matter and mind – the latter emerging from the former – but as an event of the 'intersection of mind and matter' (p 13).

For Bergson, there seems to be no permanent synthesis of subjectivity, no emergent fixed whole consciousness that supervenes the synaptic sum of parts! Unlike Malabou, then, who counters Bergson's movement image by tracing the politics of plasticity to a dialectical movement that produces a synthesis of emergent identity, the Bergsonian brain never becomes One. In short, Bergson's subjectivity in the making always has the capacity to breakout of habitual modes (repeated actions and so on) as well as break from the illusory sense of 'who and what we are' in terms of how we are often badly represented (O'Sullivan, 2013:166). Taking this into account, it is indeed curious that Bergson's creative evolution is drawn on by Malabou to explain the contradictory forces of energy that lead to the formation of the sum total of who we are. To be sure, for Bergson, dialectical movements are impossible movements. He prefers notions of creative explosions, bursts, discharges, and thresholds that transform nature into freedom. These creative evolutions do not arguably mix well with a 'dialectical play of the emergence and annihilation of form' (Malabou, 2008:71). Bergson's multiple processes of subjectification seem to be a manifestation of a different kind of relational energy than that produced by the 'primary and natural economy of contradiction' (Malabou, 2008:71). Malabou's point is that there must be a conflict between two kinds of energy: one seemingly inside, the other outside. For Bergson, the difference between inside and outside is indistinct. We cannot separate inside from outside, just as we cannot divide perception from materiality or, indeed, a thing from its representation.

In contrast to Malabou's ideological avatars, Bergson (1912) presents a stripped-out perception of reality, the latter of which is far too complex to capture in any dialectical movement or indeed emergent conscious phenomenal awareness. To grasp this point, his *Matter and Memory* thesis sets about answering two thought experiments. Firstly, he asks what it would be like if we could disconnect our conscious awareness from the experience of matter. His answer is that matter itself would free itself from the divisible spaces of perception. It would become resolved into numberless vibrations. Matter would become a ceaseless continuum 'traveling in every direction like shivers' (p 276). This is not a relation between matter and a storehouse version of memory. It is a memory of matter, which is, again, persevered in pure duration. Such a disconnection 'would obtain a vision of matter that is perhaps fatiguing for [the] imagination' (pp 276–7), but nevertheless it would provide a pure and stripped-out perception compared to conscious experience. Furthermore, Bergson contends that when we reconnect with consciousness, we return to the divisible spaces with their 'internal history of things', 'quasi-instantaneous views' – a pictorial condensation of the 'infinity of repetitions and elementary changes' of pure duration (p 277). As follows, the distance travelled between the conscious appearance of a representation and the reality of the things observed is something like an animated series of images that sketch out thousands of successive positions of, for example, a person running in 'one sole symbolic attitude' (p 209).

In his second thought experiment, Bergson asks us to imagine a kind of prophetic brain-imaging technology that can directly penetrate brain matter so that neuroscientists can observe the sketch work the animator produces and therefore capture its pure duration. What would this animation look like in the very matter of the brain? To begin with, Bergson contends that the brain state would indicate 'only a very small part of the mental state' (p 13). That is to say, the parts of the brain that translate pure duration into the animation are not identifiable by locating them in specific regions. To be sure, we would not see the representation itself inside the brain. There is no whole flick book containing each sketch in the brain! Any images of movement are emergent. There is no moving image in consciousness 'without some foreshadowing, in the form of a sketch or a tendency, of the movements'(p xvii). So, what would the operators of Bergson's brain-imaging technology actually observe? They may well observe the details of these sketches of movement somewhere in the matter of the brain, as a trace of some kind, but, Bergson contends, such flickers would reveal nothing of any journey between physiology and psychology realms. The brain image captures nothing of the association between matter and consciousness, any more than 'we should know of a play from the comings and goings of the actors upon the stage'(pp xvii–xviii).

Three theses of the movement image

Not unsurprisingly perhaps, the strange materiality of Bergson's instantaneous, pictorial condensations, which are neither representation nor the real thing, prompts a comparison of the experience of real movement to that of illusory moving images. Is not the illusion of reality, and reality itself, the same illusory experience? Well, this is what Bergson appears to say, but this comparison is only really a starting point in a search for a nonphenomenological approach. Indeed, Gilles Deleuze's (2005 [1985]) Bergson-inspired work on cinema (with its brief mentions of animation) is useful here since its posing of three theses asks some probing questions about the experience of the real and illusionary movement of images.

To begin with, Deleuze's first thesis investigates the notion that cinema and real movement are both examples of Bergson's false illusion of movement. To be sure, reading Bergson one would assume that the illusion of movement is what already happens in our perception of nature (p 2). In effect, then, Deleuze further notes how Bergson's delicate positioning of representation (idea) and reality (thing) differs from phenomenological approaches. Significantly though, for Deleuze, the cinematic image cannot be the same as nature. On the contrary, he argues that the movement image does the work of the eye, and in order to do so, it must break with 'the conditions of natural perception' (p 2). This is not because the movement image is the same as the eye, but since cinema is 'forced to imitate natural perception' (p 2). Although appearing to differ with Bergson, this is not really a drastic break from *Matter and Memory*, since in both cases the novelty of life always seems to imitate the liveliness of matter.

Thesis two advances on Bergson's illusory movement image to address two different kinds of illusion. The reader of this article will already be familiar with the distinction Deleuze makes between these illusions, since in effect we return to the distinction made earlier between the old and the new punctum. On one hand, then, ever since Plato, philosophers have looked for their illusions hidden away in forms or ideas. Like Barthes's mythologies, these illusions can move between reality and ideology. On the other hand, though, considered as examples of a stripped-out perception, illusions of continuity, for example, have nothing to do with form. Continuity does not float over or above matter, but is instead immanent to its own animated materiality. In practice, then, an animator does not produce an illusion in the one image that rises above itself before leading to another image, and so on. Likewise, a film editor does not hide the illusion of continuity in the cut between one form and another. Instead, they will create a succession of instances that do the continuity work of the eye. The moving image is thus an expression of movement between 'equidistant instants' that leaves an 'impression of continuity' (p 5). Along these lines, Deleuze's study moves on to focus on the movement image, grasped as *the shot* – in which filmic movement is not 'a figure described in a unique moment, but the continuity of the movement which describes the figure' (p 5). In short, the shot captures all instants in one movement image.

So, does animation function like film? Does it not privilege instants, or hide its illusions in these instants? Or else, are these illusions contained in a continuous matter flow of what Deleuze calls the *whatever-instants*? Some theorists have used this second thesis to argue for a special case for cellular animation. In his development (and critique) of Deleuze's seeming insistence that animation is concretely related to cinema, Schaffer (2005), for example, argues that unlike the shot, the animated sequence has two temporalities. Which is to say, animation is an exception in which both the composition of cells (individual drawings) and the automatic sequence (the playback of the 'whole' shot) occur.

Perhaps another answer to the question is found in Deleuze's third thesis, which is, essentially, all about the movement image itself. This thesis is best understood through the distinction Deleuze makes between phenomenological approaches to perception and Bergson's movement images. On one hand, then, in phenomenology movement is not simply about forms or *ideas in form* actualized in a content. On the contrary, the phenomenologist presents a kind of form that 'organizes the perceptive field as a function of a situated intentional consciousness' (p 57). We might say that phenomenologists establish consciousness as a command post in this perceptive field, or they give a privilege to natural [human] perception, even if this perception does not have access to all things. As a consequence, moving images can never be faithful to the conditions of natural perception. This is the illusion of the movement image as experienced by the phenomenal mind. On the other hand, though, Bergson questions the power of the phenomenological command post as a marker of natural perception. So, although questioning the falsity of moving images, Deleuze makes the point that any misconception of movement cannot be judged next to a model of natural perception constructed phenomenologically. To be sure, the phenomenological command post cannot be the model, because perception is not a vantage point! It has, as such, 'no point of anchorage' (p 57). In contrast, Bergson's stripped-out perception has a mere foothold in the constant change and matter flow of the movement image.

Is it, perhaps, at this point of perceptual disadvantage that the illusory power of the movement image overrides natural perception? Which is to say, is the experience of illusion and ideology in movement hidden away in certain language games. But let's not confuse these conflicting notions of footholds and command posts with the death of Barthes's punctum. In a nonphenomenological approach, the illusion cannot simply be about the matter flow of a movement image surpassing the command post's capacity to read the punctum, since such an approach continues to privilege human perception We need to therefore develop a fourth thesis which expands on A.N. Whitehead's nonphenomenology by locating percipient experience in the matter flow of the event. To be sure, the percipient experience of movement is not a temporal hallucination defined by a loss of mind. It is rather a felt experience of the intensity of the event that is not outside of mind, bifurcated from matter, but instead, wherein mind is in the event and, effectively, nonbifurcated.

Thesis four: freeing experience from the syntax trap

In order to develop a fourth thesis of the movement image we need to test the limits of the phenomenal language games that brought about the first punctum. Arguably, the problem with language is that its syntax has developed by way of a bifurcation between mind and nature. Language of this kind is really only useful when applied to a static world in which subjects experience objects; such is the case when Barthes gazes at his photographs. This syntax fails to express the dynamics and liveliness of an immanent material reality that has not bifurcated from mind (Urban, 1951:304). Along these lines, language presents a crude distinction between, on one hand, the

Figure 4.2: *Thrum II* by William Bishop-Stephens

Source: Photo by Andrew Moller. Permission granted.

real thing, and on the other, the experience of a representation or idea of the thing. A fourth thesis will thus require a radical rethink, which can, like the tools of physics, better probe the dynamics of moving images without putting this syntax at the centre of experience.

In his endeavour to refuse the bifurcation between mind and nature, Whitehead criticized the orthodox linguistic concept of having an experience of a thing, since it is erroneously determined by the mould of the subject–predicate (Lowe, 1951:106). That is to say, the subject (the knower) is always situated by the experience of the thing (the known). As Victor Lowe (p 106) argues, the subject–predicate mould is 'stamped on the face of experience' so that the experient is always the subject who is qualified by the sensations of the objective world. This is how phenomenal language traps experience in the unidirectional relation between the private subject and the public object. As follows, it is the experient who supposedly becomes trapped in the illusory experience of the language of moving images.

A Whiteheadian intervention into the trappings of language is of use here, since we encounter in its wake a viable alternative to these familiar phenomenological trajectories that lead to Barthes's punctum. In contrast to the situated intentional perceptions of a person observing an image, Whitehead's experience is said to be 'the self-enjoyment of being one among many, and of being one arising out of the composition of the many' (Whitehead, 1985 [1929]:145). This arising is not a self-satisfying moment in time beginning with a human brain, mind, or body. A Whiteheadian would not say, for example, that an image is in mind or to hand. Whitehead's experience is evidently associated with human experiences, but it cannot be decoupled from the interlocking assemblages that relate brains, minds, bodies, and images to a lively rendition of matter. In lieu of the intentional perceptions of a person observing an image (a subject-predicated object) we find in Whitehead a much deeper entanglement with the event of nature in which the brain is continuous with the body, and the body is continuous with the image. Whitehead describes such an entanglement as follows:

> [W]e cannot determine with what molecules the brain begins and the rest of the body ends. Further, we cannot tell with what molecules the body ends and the external world begins. The truth is that the brain is continuous with the body, and the body is continuous with the rest of the natural world. Human experience is an act of self-origination including the whole of nature, limited to the perspective of a focal region, located within the body, but not necessarily persisting in any fixed coordination with a definite part of the brain. (Whitehead cited in Dewey, 1951:644)

Clearly, unlike neurocinematics, this entanglement does not limit experience to any privileged region in a sense organ (the brain or the sensation of a body) or a higher level of consciousness (the all-perceiving mind with the capacity for language). Although Whitehead concedes that human consciousness may well be an exhibit of the 'most intense form of the plasticity of nature' (Whitehead, 1967 [1933]:78), there is no dichotomy between the human and what is experienced, and ultimately, in this nonbifurcated entanglement, nature is closed to mind.

Whitehead borrows from William James's concept of pure experience to make a significant contra-Cartesian move (p 70), which does not regard mind or body as the centrepiece of experience, but rather draws attention to how both are composed in a passage of events. Here we see a distinct difference with Malabou's notion of plasticity! The I of the mind (and the body from which it seems to belong) does not determine who we are, since, in the duration of events, both body and mind are swept up in the present before slipping into the past. Therefore, unlike Descartes's dualism, the mind does not determine who we are. Again, this is not the command post of experience we find in phenomenology. It is also not a cognitive command post that judges movement by way of a kind of form that hovers above the movement event. To be sure, the mind always comes after the event! The experience of the illusion of the moving image or animation does not, therefore, belong to the mind. The mind's perceptual judgements, as well as its apparent capacity for memory and attention, can only testify to the passage of events from a percipient foothold – in the duration of events (Stengers, 2014:75).

From an events perspective, then, we can begin to look at the perception of the movement image in a very different light to that of a phenomenological subject's experience grasped in abstract points in time and space on a static grid. Barthes's notion of a punctum that pierces perception needs to be reapproached, not by way of what is real or represented on this grid, but by way of what is in passage: in what Whitehead calls a percipient event (Whitehead, 2004 [1920]:107–8). Therefore, unlike the phenomenal mind of Barthes, who puts the old punctum to death in mental space, it is the event itself that becomes the concrete fact of experience.

Is this percipient foothold in the event our new punctum? Well, there would be no things to perceive, no mindfulness of things, without the passing of these concrete events. The thing perceived is not, therefore, what is concrete or what brings about the abstractions of consciousness (those floating forms, representations or abstract properties of colour, for example). Whiteheadian things are not concrete substances from which abstract properties arise; on the contrary, like the layers atop Bergson's stripped-out perception, things are abstractions (Stengers, 2014:90–1). Along these lines, W. Mays (1952:115) nicely captures why Whitehead wanted to challenge a classificatory nature of abstraction that rendered things according to 'a bundle of disconnected fragmentary qualities'. He was instead interested in an account of the 'essential relatedness of things-that every event in the universe enters into relationship with every other event' (p 115). It is these 'patterns of connections', what we might now call assemblages, that constitute 'the realm of complete and absolute abstraction' (p 115). Moreover, in an events analysis of animation, it is not enough to say here is the thing, since any thing must be perceived in a complex array of related abstract things. Abstract things are not experienced merely in the now either. They provide a uniqueness and continuity of events that pass by; there is the image, and there it is again! It is not, as such, an image in a given space (as it was experienced on Barthes's writing desk). It is an image event or pattern of images that produce the spatiotemporal subjective reality of the image. Ontologically, then, the illusion of the moving image is not hidden from consciousness, but it is declared in the percipient encounter with events (Stengers, 2014:46). To put this another way, it is not the abstract properties of the concrete thing that declares the image (its form, representation, properties or, indeed, punctum), but rather the image is an abstract thing in itself and perceived of in the unified concrescence of the events that declare it. In short, then, the declaration of the movement image offers a potentially false (and illusory) sense of concreteness or, more loosely, an illusion of continuity.

It is important to add that the subject who perceives the movement image is not the author of the image event, or the author of the many variations in image events. However, we must not simply replace subject/object with object/event relations. Following Whitehead, it is necessary to rethink our relation to moving images as a kind of society or a nexus of events in passage that provide *ingression* to things. Which is to say, the thing is expressed in the event, and the event is expressed in the thing (Whitehead, 2004:144–52). As Stengers (2014:52) puts it, every duration of an event 'contains other durations and is contained in other durations'. This is the relational temporal thickness of Whitehead's event, which again, cannot be grasped in individual instants in time or space since events are always in passage.

The idea of a Whiteheadian relational temporal thickness is well captured in the animated sculptural work of William Bishop-Stephens. In *Thrum II* (see Figure 4.2) and *Thrum III* (see Figures 4.3 and 4.4), for example, the artist introduces different scales of animated events, ranging from the mechanical movement of barely perceptible human–nature assemblages to moving images projected on the big screen. This work is *ingressed* in the Whiteheadian sense since Bishop-Stephens considers multiple durations in his work. The movement events at the lower scales are always in passage with those durations more conventionally animated on the big screen. Both pieces are intentionally evocative of early moving image technologies, like the zoetrope or Kaiserpanorama, but to theorize these animations as the mere illusion of movement misses the way the artist presents the movement of things as occurring as multiple percipient events. This work is not animation imitating natural movement, nor is it animation doing the work of the eye to grasp the movement of things. On the contrary, these animations explore how things in events can become misplaced abstractions. The aesthetic appeal of *Thrum II* and *III* is found in the access these works provide to scales, durations, and the relatedness of events that often dip below

Figure 4.3: *Thrum III* by William Bishop-Stephens

Source: Photo by Andrew Moller. Permission granted.

the cognitive processing of movement. But these animations do not offer a command post for conscious perception to grasp or become overwhelmed by movement. Instead, the artist explores the mere foothold a mind has in the duration of events.

To conclude, then, in this article I began to elude to the significance of a kind of experience of animated images deemed to be presubjective and experienced through brain-body-technology entanglements. There are important alignments to be noted here between such entanglements

Figure 4.4: Detail of *Thrum III* by William Bishop-Stephens

Source: Photo by Andrew Moller. Permission granted.

(or relational assemblages) and Jenkins' innovative proposal for a new impersonal affective punctum. Like Jenkins, the discussion here made a claim that the experience of images needs to be explained outside of language. Which is to say, the whole linguistic basis of the punctum – the punctuation of form – or the gap or *the cut* that potentially ruptures the perception experience, lacks what Jenkins grasps as this impersonal, somatic, temporal registering of experience, occurring outside of cognizant perception. So whereas structuralist film theory has generally located its punctuation mark in the form of the filmstrip, for example, Jenkins innovation is to instead look to affect. Although supportive of the theory of ideology based on affect that emerges from Jenkins' thesis, I have made an additional claim that what is missing from the punctum is not just affect but also the event. Indeed, more than that, the event actually undermines the whole notion of a punctum arising from a studium, insofar as it proposes a more general theory of illusion based on a percipient event of a movement image in which what is assumed to be concrete is actually abstract.

It might seem to be the case that there are alignments here between Barthes's mournful death of the author in the production of moving images, and the illusory aspects of the percipient event of a movement image. However, we need to recall that making the subject the author of this kind of image event reintroduces the kind of bifurcation of mind and matter that prompted Barthes's punctum in the first place. Certainly, the human mind (however exceptional its plasticity in nature) cannot experience the whole event. The subject does not decide on events (whether they are here or not here) as such. The events decide the subject. The subject's point of view (this percipient window on experience) belongs to an 'impersonal web' of events (Stengers, 2014:65). To put it another way, events are not some privileged conscious instants an audience experience. They are not like the old punctum. An audience may well occupy the here, but it is their relation to the now that sweeps perception up in a complex matter flow of events. Caught in this flow, it is possible to confuse the observational present for something that exceeds the mere foothold the mind has in all this temporal thickness. Is this not the illusion of concrete experience one encounters in the abstractions of the movement image?

References

Azéma, M. and F. Rivère. (2012) 'Animation in Palaeolithic art: a pre-echo of cinema', *Antiquity*, 86(332): 316–24.

Bergson, H. (1912) *Matter and Memory*, translated by Nancy Margaret Paul and W. Scott Palmer, London: G. Allen & Co Ltd.

Deleuze, G. (2005 [1985]) *Cinema 2: The Time-Image*, translated by Hugh Tomlinson, London: Continuum.

Dewey, J. (1951) 'The philosophy of Whitehead', in P.A. Schilpp (ed) *The Philosophy of Alfred North Whitehead*, New York: Tudor Publishing Company, 641–700.

Furuhata, Y. (2011) 'Rethinking Plasticity: The Politics and Production of the Animated Image', *Animation*, 6(1): 25–38.

Hasson, U., O. Landesman, B. Knappmeyer, I. Vallines, N. Rubin and D.J. Heeger. (2008) 'Neurocinematics: The Neuroscience of Film', *Projections* 2(1): 1–26.

Jenkins, E.S. (2013) 'Another *Punctum*: Animation, Affect, and Ideology', *Critical Inquiry*, 39(3): 575–91.

Lowe, V. (1951) 'The development of Whitehead's philosophy', in P.A. Schilpp (ed) *The Philosophy of Alfred North Whitehead*, New York: Tudor Publishing Company, 15–124.

Malabou, C. (2008) *What Should We do with Our Brain?*, translated by Sebastian Rand, New York: Fordham University Press.

Mays, W. (1952) 'Whitehead's theory of abstraction', *Proceedings of the Aristotelian Society*, 52(1): 95–118.

Ng, J. (2012) 'Seeing Movement: On Motion Capture Animation and James Cameron's Avatar', *Animation*, 7(3): 273–86.

O'Sullivan, S. (2013) 'A Diagram of the Finite–Infinite Relation: Towards a Bergsonian Production of Subjectivity', in J.Ó Maoilearca and C. De Mille (eds) *Bergson and the Art of Immanence: Painting, Photography, Film*, Edinburgh: Edinburgh University Press, 165–87.

Poulaki, M. (2014) 'Neurocinematics and the Discourse of Control: Towards a Critical Neurofilmology', *Cinema & Cie*, 14(22–23): 39–51.

Sampson, T.D. (2017) *The Assemblage Brain: Sense Making in Neuroculture*, Minneapolis: University of Minnesota Press.

Schaffer, B. (2005) 'Cinema Three? Re-Animating Deleuze', *Pli: The Warwick Journal of Philosophy*, 16: 79–100.

Stengers, I. (2014) *Thinking with Whitehead: A Free and Wild Creation of Concepts*, translated by Michael Chase, Cambridge, MA: Harvard University Press.

Urban, W.M. (1951) 'Whitehead's Philosophy of Language and Its Relation to His Metaphysics', in P.A. Schilpp (ed) *The Philosophy of Alfred North Whitehead* (2nd edn), New York: Tudor Publishing Company, 301–28.

Whitehead, A.N. (1967 [1933]) *Adventures of Ideas*, New York: Free Press.

Whitehead, A.N. (1985 [1929]) *Process and Reality: An Essay in Cosmology*, New York: Free Press.

Whitehead A.N. (2004 [1920]) *The Concept of Nature*, New York: Dover.

PART II

Affective Experience and Expression

On Pixar's Marvellous Astonishment: When Synthetic Bodies Meet Photorealistic Worlds

Eric S. Jenkins

Animation is an art of affect, and not only in the human register of enticing feelings of nostalgia, marvel, or wonder but in the nonhuman or more-than-human one as well, because animation experiments in practices of affecting and being affected, of pen to paper, ink to celluloid, hand to clay, photo to projector, light to shadow, colour to colour, and, today, line of code to line of code, or digital model to 3D simulated environment. Each of these relations of affecting and being affected pose implicit questions. How might light and shadow be related such as to convey a sense of three- dimensionality? How might figures be drawn that enable an illusion of movement and even life? How might photographs be taken to enable flat drawings to appear as if a moving figure occupies the foreground of a more distant background? The evolution of animation is the discovery of different answers: shading, squash and stretch, the multiplane camera.

Although CG animation borrows many techniques and practices from the history of hand-drawn and stop-motion animation, it also introduces new questions. Indeed, CG animation presents Spinoza's famous question in stark relief: what can a body do? CG animators must ask, first, how can a digital body (model) be rigged? What are its potential relations of movement and rest, to invoke the 'longitudinal' aspect of bodies understood as modes outlined by Deleuze (1988) via Spinoza? Second, how might these digital bodies relate to the three-dimensional simulated environments? What are the capacities to affect and be affected that constitute the 'latitude' of modal relations? The spectacular power of CG animation rests in the breadth of potential answers to these questions, in the fact that relations of movement-rest and affective capacities are less limited by the laws of physics because the animator works in the realm of the virtual, first constructing potentials that will become actualized by the rendering of computer software. Whereas drawn and stop-motion animation begin from the actual (character sketches, material objects), CG animators begin with the virtual, modelling a range of potential movements and crafting rules of affection that will serve as the physics within which the characters and animators work. Analogue animators, in contrast, must work with rather than craft the laws of physics, bound as they are to material actualities. Analogue animation, it may be said, begins with the actual to construct the virtual. CG animation begins with the virtual to construct the actual.

The complexity of CG animation also stems from this reversal, from the breadth of potential answers to the longitudinal and latitudinal questions. Every constructed potential, every virtual movement and capacity poses possible difficulties or interferences when actualized. What movements seem to work in the abstract grid space of the modelling screen might look different when actualized (rendered) in a CG world of contoured cars, buildings, trees, roads, rocks, and other models. Because the 'camera' can show perfect dimensionality from any point of view, how do animators avoid characters looking too pristine, too perfect and hence uncanny or unreal? How, in short, can digital models seem to inhabit simulated environments when the model and environment are not distinct entities but made from the same stuff (lines of code). As William Schaffer (2004:82) writes in his groundbreaking essay on the Pixar feel, 'Academics, popular commentators, and practitioners have appropriately drawn attention to the intrinsic difficulties faced in making the volumetric realism of CGI subservient to the demands of full animation-style characterization. A digital quality of excessive pristineness, plasticness, or soullessness threatens to defeat possibilities of characterization in advance'.

Schaffer correctly recognizes the centrality, for CG animation, of this implicit question about relating model and world, and it is the purpose of this chapter to elaborate on the Pixar feel, which Schaffer sees as a key reason for Pixar's success. Schaffer depicts the Pixar feel as the feeling of being plastic, perhaps due to the early date of his article (2004). Schaffer (2004:85) focuses mostly on *Toy Story*, but he also contends that Pixar in general (including *A Bugs Life* and *Monsters, Inc.*) resonates 'with the *feel* of plastic. The world it opens up for our imaginations is not just one where some plastic things happen to exist: it is a universe seen from the perspective of plastic beings, experienced in plastic terms'. Schaffer (2004:84) contends that this plastic feel makes sense both technically and thematically, since 'digitally rendered shapes naturally resemble plastic' and plastic and the digital alike promise 'the realization of the very *idea* of design as the intelligent forming of docile matter' since both materials offer a bountiful diversity of sculpting possibilities. With this conclusion, Schaffer focuses too much on the content of particular films instead of keeping the analysis oriented around the central question of affect posed by computer animation. For instance, in *The Incredibles* and *Incredibles 2* (which is the focus of the analysis here), the substance of the human characters appears more like rubber than plastic, posing a different answer to the question of the relation between world and model, a question that remains across the films Schaffer analyses as well as more contemporary Pixar films.

This chapters show how the question of the affective relation of character body and world has presented problems for Pixar specifically and computer animation generally, and how Pixar's 'feel' stems from their unique solution. Pixar's solution has consistently been to construct photorealistic worlds inhabited by synthetic characters (whether that synthetic material be rubber, plastic, metal, or faux fur). These synthetic materials enable Pixar to continue animation's heritage of 'protean plasmaticness' identified a century ago by Sergei Eisenstein (1986), and it is this particular relation of 'impossibility and verisimilitude' behind the Pixar feel, that 'specific sense of magic' many viewers experience (Schaffer, 2004:87). In my first book, I called such feelings or sensations 'special affects', illustrating how the emergence of live action cinema, early animation, and then classical Disney animation enabled new human affects often expressed as wonderful, astonishing, marvellous, and fantastic (Jenkins, 2014). Here, I call Pixar's special affect, its 'feel', the *marvellous astonishment*: a term that, drawing on my prior work, indicates the combination of astonishing photorealism with marvellous, morphing animation. Pixar's solution to CG animation's implicit question is to relate photorealistic worlds with synthetic digital models, and this relation potentially generates a feeling of marvellous astonishment.

This relation, as well as the germ of marvellous astonishment, can be found most directly in 'impact images', which are those filmic moments where the synthetic characters collide with or otherwise contact the photorealistic world. *Incredibles 2* features a large number of such images. Indeed, the movie oscillates between placid images of mostly domestic life in which characters inhabit but do not significantly contact their world and frantic, loud, even explosive impact images in which characters collide with, crash into, and impact (and are impacted by) that world. During these moments, characters' synthetic substances bend and flex in distinctly non-photorealistic ways, even characters besides Elastigirl, whose power to stretch like elastic could provide a narrative explanation for such movements. Pixar over-animates all of the digital bodies' response to the impact and accompanies the collision with bursts of light, colour, sound, or other effects. It is in these moments that the shared substance of world and character possibly becomes visible, since the relation of model and world makes the two touching a consistent problem. As a solution, Pixar over-animates these moments, crafting 'impact images' to disguise these imprecisions and difficulties as well as add dramatic flair.

This special affect, as Schaffer notes, accounts for Pixar's commercial success, yet this chapter concludes by illustrating how it also constitutes an ideological *expression*, in Brian Massumi's (2002) sense. Beyond selling CGI and Disney products, Pixar's solution to CG animation's implicit question represents an ideological translation fit for control society. By relating fixed, hard, 'realistic' worlds to rubbery characters with an impressive ability to bounce back from any impact, *Incredibles 2* suggests that individuals must be or should be flexible and adaptable to the unchangeable socio-economic systems they find themselves inhabiting. Such a view resonates with a neoliberal understanding of the subject stressing individualism and adaptability under economic precarity and thereby masks the ongoing construction of dividual models by the culture industries within controlled digital platforms. Computer animators are not alone in the culture industries in conceiving and constructing models that redound onto actual bodies (think of Facebook's algorithms), and these practices of modelling and then channelling consumers epitomize capitalism in control society, a condition which Pixar's solution expresses even as they engage in such modelling and channelling practices.

From drawing to computer model: the problem of touch

The similarities between the work of 3D computer animators and Deleuze's Spinozist understanding of a body are remarkable. In Deleuze's (1988:123) view, a body consists of two aspects: a longitude, which is 'the relations of motion and rest, of speed and slowness' between the particles that compose a body; and a latitude which is a 'capacity for affecting and being affected that also defines a body in its individuality'. This understanding of the body comes from two of Spinoza's propositions, a kinetic proposition and a dynamic proposition. The kinetic proposition tells us that a body is not a set form or function but that those forms and functions derive from the relations of motion and rest between the parts. Take a human hand. A hand's form and function stem from the range of motion of the fingers and wrist, their relative mobility in relation to the stability of the palm, the relation of thumb and fingers that enables gripping and grasping. If this kinetic proposition looks inward to the composition of an individual body (hence the term longitude), the dynamic proposition extends outward, laterally to the relations between that body and world. The dynamism of a body involves how it might affect/be affected and the capacities or thresholds of affection, the limits beyond which the body cannot pass without becoming something else. Deleuze loves the example of a tick, an insect with three affects: seeing light to climb to the top of branches, smelling mammals, and sensing heat so they know where to burrow. These affects include certain capacities, an 'optimal threshold and a pessimal threshold in the capacity for being affected: the gorged tick will die, and the tick capable of fasting for a very long time' (Deleuze, 1988:125).

These two defining aspects of bodies Spinoza labels a 'mode'. As Deleuze (1988:123–4) writes, 'Every reader of Spinoza knows that for him bodies and minds are not substances or subjects, but modes'. 3D computer animators call them models, not modes, yet the models are similarly composed of a longitude and latitude. Animators begin by defining the relations of movement and rest between the parts of the model. This process is called rigging, where the modeller establishes a range of motion and relationality between the various parts of the body. As Disney and Pixar animator John Lasseter explains, 'In effect, the modeler of a moving, living character is a digital-age marionette maker, attaching hundreds of interconnected "strings" that pull surfaces in concert to make them look alive' (Lasseter and Daly, 1995:43). No such process exists in hand-drawn or stop-motion animation, which create the appearance of these longitudinal relations without the existence of a rigged model. They create substances rather than modes: a drawing, a posed object. Thus analogue animators must draw or reposition the substance's movement, the in-between steps from pose to pose, whereas computer animators establish two poses and allow the computer to execute the in-betweens. In other words, drawn animation's characters do not exist outside each drawing, while computer animations' models pre-exist any image of it, earning them the moniker of digital object. As Pixar animator Rich Quade says:

> The models for the characters are created by somebody else. They're there. I never have to worry that Woody's head is suddenly looking a little too big, or that I didn't draw it square enough from this angle. That's a given. All I have to do is make it move. (quoted in Lasseter and Daly, 1995:60)

In the construction process, the modelling and animating screens frequently look like abstract spatial grids, yet the rendered models do not move in abstract space: they walk on simulated ground, drive simulated cars, grasp other digital objects. Thus, animators must also construct a latitude for the bodies, defining ways that the bodies affect and are affected by the 3D world. Like the digital models, the 3D world has a pre-existence that demands establishing foundational affective capacities and limits. 'It's not like drawn animation, where you have to paint a new background every time you want a different angle,' explains Pixar technical director Bill Reeves. 'Our sets get built once, to fixed dimensions. As you position and move your camera, you see the changing view you'd have walking through an actual physical space' (quoted in Lasseter and Daly, 1995:53). The physics of these actual spaces and models can be altered in a nearly infinite number of ways; yet, however the parameters are set, the animators engage in defining the latitudes of computer animated bodies, telling the software how one body affects and is affected by another.

It is at this latitudinal level that the implicit question of CG animation becomes explicit, and the animators' work to address the resultant problems. Because the models and 3D worlds are made from the same stuff, artists must define the parameters of their interaction. Without establishing these parameters, digital objects would blur and mix in decidedly unrealistic and unexpected ways. As Lasseter (1995:75) writes, 'The chief problem [...] is "intersection," where one object appears to cut right through the surface of another'. He quotes animator Kelly O'Connell, who explains, 'Modeled objects aren't solid, they're just information in the computer. There's nothing to tell the edges to bounce off each other. As soon as you start piling things at odd angles, it gets hard to keep them distinct' (quoted in Lasseter and Daly, 1995:75). For instance, the animators of *A Bug's Life* repeatedly ran up against the problem of making the bugs' feet appear to touch the ground, since too close would make them merge with the ground and too far would make them appear to float, a task that was particularly difficult when the ground was uneven and bumpy (Kurtti, 1998:67–70). Thus, Pixar employs multiple animators whose chief job is to hide the intersections, adding details to make the touching appear more realistic.

Computer animation's problems of intersection present a distinct issue from hand-drawn animation. With hand-drawn animation, artists ink clear celluloid layers for the foreground, middle ground, and background. These layers are then stacked and a photograph taken of the resultant combination. The layers of the image actually touch, which created a different problem – one of creating the realistic semblance of depth. If the camera moved closer to the foreground image, all the layers would change size in the same proportion, distorting the space. Whether in real life or live-action cinema, when your eye or the camera moves towards the foreground figures, those get bigger in proportion to the background. Because the layers of hand-drawn animation were actually touching, in contrast, all of the layers would enlarge at the same rate. This was the problem and implicit question of hand-drawn animation – how to make the layers appear separate when they were actually touching. In *Special Affects*, I label this the issue of *transferability* and detail techniques such as drawing the foreground lines bolder and the multiplane camera that evolved to address the question (Jenkins, 2014:87–99). The multiplane camera stacked the layers apart from, rather than directly on top of, one another, so that the camera could move closer to the foreground layer and the background would not resize at the same rate. The multiplane camera was a major innovation enabling artists to imitate the three-dimensional spaces of live-action cinema, moving animation from a gag-filled, two-dimensional play of line focused on flat characters to the semblance of life in round characters. Answering the implicit question in this way launched a new era of animation, beginning with the full-length features of 'golden age' Disney animation.

As the medium changes from celluloid to computer, the problem reverses. Hand-drawn animation tried to make the layers *not touch*, whereas computer animation tries to make digital objects touch. Indeed, hand-drawn, stop-motion, and computer animation alike deal with questions of touch in different ways. Drawn animators must both learn how to touch the celluloid with their pen and how to manage the touching of layers. Stop-motion animators must touch the figures, moving them from pose to pose to create apparent motion. Digital animators must rig the models and then instruct them in how to touch the world. The problem of touch, then, remains central to animation of all forms. Stop motion and hand-drawn animators work in the realm of the actual, puzzling over how to touch the substances and how the substances touch. Digital animators, in contrast, work in the realm of the virtual, addressing the problems of touch by defining the (latitudinal) parameters of the models: how the characters might touch and be touched by the world.

The striking resemblance of computer animation's construction of bodies to Deleuze's depiction of bodies-as-modes expands when recognizing these questions of touch. Touch is a prototypical example of affect understood as affecting and being affected, since touch, alone of all the senses, always entails both touching and being touched. Animation, the art of answering questions of touch, is quintessentially, then, an art of affect. Animation in general, and computer animation specifically, raises the question of how to relate the world and the characters, of how to make the figures and the ground affect and be affected – of how, in short, to make them touch and be touched.

On the Pixar feel: marvellous astonishment as special affect

According to Schaffer, Pixar's answer to these questions generates the unique Pixar feel and thereby explains the corporation's astounding commercial success. In Schaffer's terms, the Pixar feel is the feel of being plastic. Constructing characters as plastic beings addresses the limitations of characterization in computer animation, particularly the problems of the images looking too pristine and hence soulless, and the oft-discussed issue of the uncanny valley in which artificial human representations feel uncanny when they cross a threshold too close to the real thing. For Schaffer, the plasticized characters do not feel cold or soulless but instead are 'warm, nostalgic, and loyal' (Schaffer, 2004:89). As he writes:

Before *Toy Story*, digital images may have recalled the artificial, depthless textures of plastic in the bad sense. After *Toy Story*, digital images recall the intimate, animated, resonant plastic of childhood toys. Digitality is thus never cold or distancing in *Toy Story*, as parents raised on warm, soft, analogue features like *Bambi* might fear. (Schaffer, 2004:88)

Schaffer's (2004:74–5) great insight is to recognize how the implicit '*aesthetic questions*' – that is, 'the constraints and possibilities of CGI' – beckon Pixar's '*singular* and coherent response' and thereby underlie the Pixar feel. In particular, these constraints and possibilities relate to the prospects for photorealism; the Pixar feel is 'inseparable from a subtly differentiated attitude to the potential "realism" of digitally rendered imagery' (Schaffer, 2004:83). Schaffer criticizes other scholars who envision Pixar as a failed attempt to accomplish a predetermined teleology of computer animation towards photorealism. Instead, Pixar balances photorealism with the plastic feel of the characters, deliberately engineering 'a tension between the photo-realism of things and the unreality of the lives they are seen to lead' (Schaffer, 2004:83). Pixar constructs photorealistic worlds and inhabits them with synthetic, fantastical characters, which according to Schaffer look and feel plastic.

Developments since the time of Schaffer's publication question, however, whether Pixar's answer to these questions is so singular, whether a plastic feel is their consistent approach. The feel of plastic constitutes only one of many potential answers Pixar offers to computer animation's implicit question, which vary from movie to movie. In *The Incredibles*, for instance, the characters feel more like rubber than plastic. What remains consistent is the central question – how to relate the world and characters, how to make them touch. And although Pixar's answer to this question varies, all of the answers abide by a similar solution. Pixar consistently crafts photorealistic worlds and relates them to synthetic characters made of artificial materials such as plastic (*Toy Story*), rubber (*The Incredibles,* the human characters in *Wall-E*, *Toy Story*, and most Pixar movies), metal (*Wall-E*, *Cars*) or faux fur (*Monsters Inc.*). In this relation can be discerned two of the central forces or tendencies of computer animation, which form an economy in the energetic sense of a tension or exchange between two poles. The forces or poles are photorealism and caricature, the semblance of reality and the transmorphing plasmaticness common in animation. Computer animation enables both more photorealism and more caricature, more three-dimensional stability and more plasmatic transformation. Pixar relates world to character, seeking to balance these poles, with the characters embodying the force of caricature and plasmaticness and the world tending ever more towards the photorealistic.

So rather than the feel of plastic, Pixar's various solutions generate a special affect that is here labelled the *marvellous astonishment*. Before depicting this special affect, it is important to note that the label 'marvellous astonishment' is drawn from the historical record; people often used the terms marvel and astonishment to describe early animation and film. However, the label is less important than the depiction of the special affect, which stems from two predominant affective attractions found in earlier live-action film and animation, as shown in *Special Affects*. In *Special Affects*, I proceed from the premise that new media enable new affections and illustrate this premise through the examples of the cinema of attractions, classical Hollywood, early animation, and classical Disney. The cinema of attractions, a term coined by Tom Gunning, describes pre-classical films which were typically one-scene films that most frequently showed actual events happening such as trains leaving the station or someone riding a unicycle. Such 'actualities', as they were called, 'astonished' early filmgoers due to the realistic semblance of movement. Prior to the film camera, any perceived movement was accompanied by the presence of the moving thing. After, filmgoers were astonished that they saw movement but knew that the movement occurred elsewhere, that the moving thing was not present. Thus astonishment 'designates the spark from perceiving lifelike movement occurring in the here-and-now that took place in another time and space', the never-before-experienced split between the presence and the motion of the moving thing (Jenkins, 2014:30).

Today, commentators would likely be bored by actualities, as common as this split in perception has become, yet they remain astonished by the photorealism of digital animation. Mihaela Mihailova (2013:141) makes the comparison to the cinema of attractions, contending that one of the central pleasures of CGI is its capacity to 'generate a fully-fledged, detailed, and technologically advanced imaginary world [...] Admiration is a frequent spectatorial response to the latest achievements of digital animation. Computer-generated images flaunt their technological mastery and the audience derives pleasure from witnessing it'. Similarly, Dan North (2008:151) remarks, 'Just as, in the early cinema period, audiences may have been fascinated by rustling leaves, water and other simple, natural views, now there is a trend for celebrating the CG rendering of simple things; the dust on a shelf [...] or the fur on a creature'.

Movie reviewers also express astonishment and admiration at the realistic detail of Pixar's CGI. For instance, New York Times reviewer Manohla Dargis (2018) writes about the 'sheer loveliness' of the images in *The Incredibles 2*:

> It's still a fantasy 1962 or thereabouts as the boxy cars, clothing and midcentury modern flourishes suggest, but advances in computer animation make everything – from downy hair to brick buildings – look far sharper and more fine-grained. Here, you can almost count the

stubble on Bob's unshaven face and trace the swirls in the billowing, churning dust clouds that form after an explosion.

All that detail is so exquisitely rendered that it would be easy to get lost in the movie's particulars: to bask in the silvery glow of Elastigirl's uniforms, to ooh and aah over the striking design of a luxurious hideaway worthy of a Bond villain, to meditate on the David Hockney-esque patterns of the water in a motel pool seen at night.

Likewise, reviewer Ryan Cracknell (2008) expresses his astonishment with Pixar's realistic imagery:

(I)t's easy to marvel at the film's computerized beauty […] Like all Pixar films, *WALL-E* strives to push the technical boundaries of computer animation. This time out the focus is on the smallest of details: dirt, grime, dust storms, fire extinguisher foam floating in space. The line between live-action and animation is further blurred […] Foreground or background, the details are everywhere with vivid clarity.

Marvel, in contrast to astonishment, entails the appreciation of perceiving motion from an artificial form, a perception not available before the advent of animation devices. Marvel denotes admiration for the superb or extraordinary, and this term was chosen to signify how the appreciation for artifice rests behind this special affect, like how one might marvel over a magic trick. As I wrote in *Special Affects*, 'The marvellous indicates the spark felt by an audience who knows the images are constructed, but who marvels at their movements and transformations nevertheless'.[1] Marvel results from the split between a form known to be false and a movement sensed to be true and hence relates to the oft-discussed plasmaticness and metamorphosis of animation. One of the first commentators on Disney animation, famed director Sergei Eisenstien (1986:3), called Disney a 'marvellous lullaby' due to its plasmatic transformations that generating feelings of ecstasy. Einsenstein (1986:55) described the split in perception thus:

We know that they are … drawings and not living beings.
We know that they are … projections of drawings on a screen.
We know that they are … 'miracles' and tricks of technology,
    that such beings don't really exist.

But at the same time:

We *sense* them as alive.
We *sense* them as moving, as active
We *sense* them as existing and even thinking!

Besides Eisenstein, many commentators marvel over animation's capacity for plasmatic transformation, with some even contending that this capacity properly defines animation. For instance, Paul Wells (1998:69) depicts this marvellous metamorphosis as unique to animation, maybe even being its core and certainly one of the primary attractions of the animated fairy tale. Vivian Sobchak (2008) also credits the great appeal of animation to the morphing of the line, and Keith Broadfoot and Rex Butler contend that animation presents a 'time-image' due to this marvellous metamorphosis. As they write, 'The characters in cartoons are only this endless series of metamorphoses, the unchanging form of change, perhaps what might be called time' (Broadfoot and Butler, 1991:270–1). The marvellous affect is not simply about fantasy, or otherwise live-action film would 'satisfy in the same way', as Michael O'Pray (1997:201) notes.

> On the contrary, in animation especially, the satisfaction depends not simply on the ability to represent other impossible worlds, but rather to remind us of the skill and virtuosity involved [...] In this way it is true that animation is often at its best when we marvel not only at the subject matter [...] but at its means of achievement. (O'Pray, 1997:201)

Marvellous astonishment thus describes a special affect of computer animation, the combination of marvel over the plasmatic, transmorphing animation and astonishment over its photorealistic likeness. Like Eisenstein's split in reference to classical Disney, viewers know this is computer animation, yet they marvel over its technical magic tricks and are astonished by its lifelike scenes. In this way, marvellous astonishment is the special affect innervated by balancing the poles of photorealism and caricature, three-dimensional semblance and plasmatic animation. Lasseter (quoted in Schaffer, 2004:83) acknowledges just such a balancing act, in ways quite similar to Eisenstein's split:

> At Pixar, we like to think we use our tools to *make things look photo realistic, without trying to reproduce reality*. We like to take those tools and make something that the audience knows does not exist. Every frame they know this is a cartoon. So you get that wonderful visual entertainment of, 'I know this isn't real, but boy it sure looks real.' I think that's part of the fun of what we do.

In sum, Schaffer correctly isolates the economy between realism and caricature behind Pixar's solution to animation's implicit questions of touch, of how to relate the figures and the world. Yet rather than the feel of plastic, which constitutes just one of many of Pixar's answers, Pixar potentially innervates the affect of marvellous astonishment by crafting synthetic characters related to photorealistic worlds. Such marvellous astonishment results from this particular solution to the limitations and capacities of animation, its prospects for creating somewhat photorealistic images that nevertheless can look too pristine, soulless, or uncanny. By caricaturing characters composed of synthetic materials, Pixar avoids these possibly negative affections while enhancing both the astonishment over the realistic lifelikeness of the scenes and the marvel over the magical, transmorphing animations.

Unsurprisingly, this relation of world and character, this balancing of astonishing photorealism and plasmatic marvel, also ties back to the issue of touch. As Disney animator Thomas Schumacher (quoted in Lasseter and Daly, 1995:18) contends:

> The tactileness of this world, even though it has never existed – the sense that you can reach out and hold what you see on the screen – is very significant to the appeal of the film. If you tried to make it look like real life, you would fail, because it will never look like real life, but it can be touchable life.

The characters are synthetic but tactile, the worlds photorealistic but magical. This balanced solution to the implicit question of animation is responsible for the Pixar feel: that is, the special affect of marvellous astonishment. And it is marvellous astonishment that rests behind Pixar's commercial success. As Jennifer Barker (quoted in Neupert, 2016:54) writes about *Toy Story*, the 'nostalgic charm and kid appeal are inseparable from its tactile allure [...] The film entices us to run our fingertips over it, and its tactility invites a childish kind of tactile enjoyment in its viewers, both young and old'.

Impact images: when photorealistic worlds collide with synthetic characters

For all figures in this section, please see https://theimpactimage.blogs pot.com/

Touch relates not just to the problematic of animation and the feel of marvellous astonishment but also to the images in the films, particularly those moments when the synthetic characters come into contact with the photorealistic world. Although world and character are deliberately designed to appear to be made of different stuff, they are really both made from the same stuff – computer code – and, as we have seen, this presents intersection issues when the character 'touches' the world. Diving into scenes from *Incredibles 2* can thus help illustrate how marvellous astonishment derives from Pixar's particular solution to touch and how, in particular, Pixar crafts 'impact images' as part of that solution.

Incredibles 2 picks up where *The Incredibles* left off – a scene in which the villain Underminer uses a giant motorized drill to break into a bank from underground. The scene takes place in a large downtown, with multiple skyscrapers and other city buildings, as well as streets and parked cars in all directions. The only objects that look like cartoons are the characters – the Incredibles, human bystanders, the Underminer. Subtract these characters and the buildings, cars, streets, crumbling concrete, and spraying earth (as the giant drill pierces the surface) can hardly be distinguished from a live-action film. The objects are pristine in detail and texture; the 3D world is impressively photorealistic. I did not reproduce an image of this scene here because the transformation of the scene into a still shot reproduced in a book would not do the level of photorealistic detail justice. Suffice it to say that nearly every scene in the movie also features stunningly realistic and detailed settings, so the reader may watch any scene to confirm my claim. This stunning photorealism accounts for the astonishment part of Pixar's marvellous astonishment.

This leaves the characters, who, while still presented in great detail, appear made of rubber and exhibit the marvel of animation's plasmaticness. After the Underminer pierces the surface, Mr Incredible and Elastigirl spring into action, with Mr Incredible calling out for his wife to 'Trampoline me!' She immediately stretches flat and wide, grasping two parallel cars, while Mr Incredible leaps and trampolines off her elastic chest, propelling him onto the top of the giant drill. Elastigirl obviously embodies animation's plasmaticness, since her superpower is to bend and stretch into any shape, like elastic. Yet the other characters also exhibit the marvellous, morphing capacity of animation, mostly in ways that match with their superpowers. The son, Dash, has the power of speed, and when he runs his body stretches and blurs, his hair pulling out horizontally, as if the force of his speed bends his body. The daughter, Violet, has two powers: invisibility, so she is shown frequently transforming into invisible states and showing up elsewhere; and force fields, which look like glowing, pulsating pinkish-purple balls of electricity that bend and flex on contact with explosions and the like. These force fields appear out of nothing, like a sort of magic trick, adding to the marvel. We later discover that the infant son, Jack-Jack, has multiple powers, the most significant of which is being a polymorph who takes the various shapes of a demon flame baby, a full metal baby, a giant baby, and a hobgoblin baby, as well as being able to self clone into multiple, simultaneous instantiations. He also shoots lasers out of his eyes, has the power of telekinesis, can walk through walls and doors, can teleport, and can create interdimensional wormholes and travel through them. Although all of this plasmatic transformation is ascribed to their superpowers, the movie remains committed to the marvellous transmorphability of animation, pairing it with the astonishing photorealism to endow that feel of marvellous astonishment.

Mr Incredible's power – super strength – lends itself less to such transmorphing than the other characters, yet in the impact images he flexes, stretches, and changes shape nevertheless. After trampolining off Elastigirl onto the drill, he is hit by a flying rock and flies past us on the screen. As he lands, his body elongates and contorts well beyond what could be sustained by an actual body, into an extreme 'wheel pose' (for those familiar with yoga) as he bounces off the ground. He then attempts to stop the giant drill, leaning against the tank treads in another impact image. Here, his body squashes and stretches, bouncing like rubber, as each link in the tread impacts him. He then gets sucked under the tread and flattened like a pancake before coming out the other side. He throws a light pole into the treads, and this pole exhibits none of his rubbery flexibility, exploding in a photorealistic shower of seemingly hard concrete and metal.

These initial impact images are relatively simple compared to the animating done in many of the other impact images throughout the movie. In each, we not only see the transmorphing characteristics of the rubbery bodies but cinematic details – flashes of light, colour, sound, and other materials – that both help hide the intersection and add to the spectacular quality of the images. The scene where we first learn of Jack-Jack's powers features a battle with a pesky raccoon in their yard. The raccoon has realistic looking fur, but both characters demonstrate a rubbery composition as they crash and collide. At one point in their battle, the raccoon leaps off the patio table onto Jack-Jack's head (see Figure 1 and all figures at https://theimpactim age.blogspot.com/), which promptly bends like rubber or a water balloon. The raccoon pulls on Jack-Jack's head, which stretches and morphs again in a rubbery manner (see Figure 2). Throughout this scene, as the raccoon or the ground or the table or the trashcan collides with Jack-Jack, we discover some of his powers – his eyes shoot out lasers, he transforms into the demon flame baby, he multiplies into clones and dogpiles the raccoon, he pushes against the glass of the back door only for blue glowing lights to appear as the baby slips through matter. Each of these powers comes accompanied with flourishes of light and colour that signify the impact and also help to hide the intersection.

Such flourishes, as well as the extending and distending of rubbery bodies, remains consistent throughout the frequent impact images in the movie. When Violet fights in a hallway with the brainwashed superhero Voyd, they slam each other against the walls and the rails, with their rubbery bodies bending and flexing as the sounds of crashing ring out (see Figure 3). Violet uses a force field to slam Voyd against the ceiling, and Voyd's body bends while the colourful field radiates around her torso (Figure 4). When Violet saves the kids from a long fall and crash onto the deck of the main villain Screenslaver's yacht, even her purple-pink forcefield seems to become rubber, bouncing off the deck as its shape, as well as the kids' bodies, bend and flex like a glob of plasma. In Figure 5, one can see the dripping from the blubbery force field at the bottom, the result of the impact with the deck. Other flourishes include flashes of light and electricity, such as when the brainwashed superhero Brick hits Mr Incredible and a flash of light appears before Mr Incredible flies and slams into the control panel, with more sparks flying and his rubbery body bending and waving; or when Elastigirl hits He-Lectrix (who has the power to manipulate electricity) with a force field, and He-Lectrix's body lights up, showing his skeleton like in an X-ray.

Likewise, when Elastigirl chases a runaway train after being enlisted in her new role as an advocate for superheroes (who are currently illegal in the movie), her motorcycle lands on top of the train and her body extends like elastic as the back half of the motorcycle slides off the edge. At the moment of collision, yellow-gold sparks fly, again hiding the intersection and adding spectacular flair to the crashing impact image (Figure 6). When Elastigirl battles with a brainwashed person she believes to be Screenslaver, they slam each other against the floor and walls, with their bodies distending like rubber (Figure 7). Frequently, the collisions feature flying sparks of light and colour during the moment of impact, such as the scene when the brainwashed villain slams Elastigirl against a computer panel (Figure 8). The villain pokes Elastigirl's leg with a red, glowing electric prod, as her leg bends backwards and the red laser-like lights spread around her thigh (Figure 9). He also jabs the prod at Elastigirl as she reaches out her hand to stop it. This impact image, shown in close-up, features the same glowing red lights encircling her hand but is also instructive for computer animation's problem of touch. When frozen in a screenshot (Figure 10), one can readily see that the prod does not actually touch her hand, but the flourishes of glowing red light disguise the (lack of) intersection when seen at full speed.

It is also instructive to compare these impact images with other moments of collision or touch in the movie, especially those moments that do not involve characters crashing into the world but that involve static objects of that world. One such image is repeated throughout the movie, when the superheroes tear the brainwashing glasses off of other characters and fling them to the ground, usually followed by a smash of the glasses by their foot. These are pivotal moments that change the course of the action for the better, so they are frequently shown in close up and with a dramatic pause before the foot slams down. As the glasses clank on the ground, we see that they are made of the same stiff substance as the world. They look composed of hard plastic, not the rubbery material constituting the characters. The glasses do not bend and flex, and none of the dramatic flourishes of light and colour are included (see Figure 11). Indeed, the glasses have a plastic feel; they feel like hard plastic and collide with the similarly hard, material world around them. When they do, they bounce but do not distort and bend, and when the foot comes smashing down, they crumble into pieces rather than morphing into another shape. Such scenes maintain a high level of photorealism, reinforcing the perception that the world is made from a different substance than the characters. They are thus not what I am calling impact images, which are properly those moments when characters collide with the world, when the models encounter the 3D environment.

These impact images serve not only to hide the intersections but also to convey the idea that the photorealistic 3D worlds are made of a different substance than the rubbery, synthetic characters, hiding their sameness in compositional substance via lines of code. In the impact images, the harder surfaces of the world collide with the rubbery characters, with a flourish of light, colour, and sound, balancing both poles of the economy undergirding marvellous astonishment. The impact images feature the morphing, bending, flexing, and transformations of animation's plasmatic heritage, articulating to the marvellous side of this affective economy. The images also maintain the photorealism of the world, which remains less bendable and pliant than the characters, more like the hardness of the built environment, articulating to the force of astonishment. The aesthetic questions of CGI – how to relate characters and world, how to approach photorealism while maintaining the marvellous transmorphing of animation – beckon a solution, with Pixar's answer most evident in the impact images. This solution is responsible for the Pixar feel, that special affect of marvellous astonishment behind their commercial success. This solution also affects the narrative of *Incredibles 2*, as the rubbery characters express an ideology fit for control society.

Pixar's ideological expression and control society

Rubber constitutes not only the feel of the Incredibles but also becomes reflected in the movies' narrative content as the characteristics of rubber – namely flexibility and adaptability – show up as esteemed characteristics of the heroes. Just as Pixar's animation relates flexible, pliant, rubbery characters to harder, stiffer, less moveable worlds, the Incredibles express a similar relation. In short, the movies suggest that individuals should be flexible and adaptable. Elastigirl must put aside her desire to be a mother in order to pursue the greater good of making superheroes legal again. Likewise, Mr Incredible must abandon his desires to be a superhero in order to take care of the children. These characters even voice this ideological translation. At one point, Elastigirl proclaims, 'I'm not all dark and angsty. I'm flexible.' Her husband attributes his ability to handle the domestic labour to a similar flexibility: 'How do I do it? By rolling with the punches, baby. I'm Mr Incredible, not Mr So-So. I can handle it.'

These ideological translations suggest that the world is fixed and stable and thus individuals must be flexible enough to adapt to it. The rubbery, pliant computer models become translated into a model subjectivity, the neoliberal subject who accepts precarity, authoritarianism, and submission as inevitable and who adopts tactics of flexibility and adaptability simply to survive. Although the superheroes try to save the world, they do so to return it to 'stability', to eliminate the problems threatening domestic tranquillity for the Incredibles. Changing the world is too hard because the world itself is hard, stable, concrete, as the images reflect. Instead, subjects should expect to be hit by this world, to feel its collisions and impacts, and just roll with the punches and bounce back – like the very rubber behind Pixar's solution. Such a perspective *makes sense*. In other words, it is a translating of the affective encounter between animation and computer and of the social world of neoliberal capitalism.

In this way, the *Incredibles'* narrative content illustrates Massumi's point about ideology being an effect of affective encounters, in this case the effect of the encounter between computer and animation and the resultant questions it poses to animators. As Massumi explains:

> Power can no longer be construed as resting on an ideological ground that is predetermining [...] There is no ideology as determining in the first or last instance. Power structures are secondary effects of affective encounters, and ideologies are secondary expressions of power structures. Ideology is on the side of effects – twice over. It is not fundamentally on the side of causes. (Massumi, 2015:93)

Affect, in contrast, is on the side of causes, rather than being a secondary effect of ideology or the glue that holds it together. In other words, rather than ideology shaping affect, affect shapes ideology.

According to this view, *Incredibles 2* is not a representation of a prior, given, transparent ideology held by Pixar and imposed on viewers, but is an outcome of the affective problematic presented by computer animation. Confronted with the questions posed by computer animation, Pixar grapples for an answer, settling on the rubbery characters and stiff worlds characterizing marvellous astonishment. From there, Pixar seeks out ideological content fit for this affective experience, with the narrative reflecting these affective parameters. In other words, the feel of Pixar – in this case, of the feel of rubber – beckons an ideological representation befitting that feel. The emergence of computer animation, as event, constitutes certain intensities – the tensions between the poles of photorealism and plasmaticness – and certain potentialities – those aesthetic questions, limitations, and possibilities – that move from inhering in the event of the encounter (of animators and technology) to ideological expression in a particular narrative.

Just as Schaffer shows how *Toy Story's* narrative replicates a marketing strategy with 'perfect vertical integration' in which the characters 'embody and thematize [...] consuming desire', similarly so does the *Incredibles 2* narrative perfectly match the ideology of neoliberal control society (Schaffer, 2004:92). Neoliberalism demands a flexibility and adaptability like rubber from its subjects, and as Pixar discovers rubber as a potential answer to the aesthetic question of CG animation, they craft content which expresses such neoliberal ideology. In this way, the narrative helps mask the processes underwriting the feel of marvellous astonishment. We do not see, for instance, that it is animators who craft the rubbery flexibility of the characters and the stiff unchangeability of the world. These are, instead, presented as given. This presentation elides the practice of making animation, erasing the fact that the animators construct models of individual bodies and that it is those models that dictate how the body may affect and be affected. Individuals do not choose to be flexible in neoliberal capitalism or in Pixar movies; *they are made to be*. Nevertheless, Pixar carefully hides this reality with a spectacle of flashing lights and dramatic sounds. Same as it ever was.

Indeed, such an expression makes sense of control society, a society in which power increasingly operates by modelling subjects and controlling them by subjecting them to those models. Take social media. Much recent research illustrates how advertisers construct models of consumers by gathering big data about their preferences and practices. Those models then redound onto actual individuals, as the models guide the algorithms that determine what is and is not seen. The models help shape targeted advertising, even as the advertising tells us that we are all unique individuals. Deleuze (1995) calls this process dividualization, where the individual subject is broken down into component parts – likes, desires, activities – and then categorized into markets. Data on those markets then produce models of consumers, which in turn guide which information is presented and which is hidden. In short, similar practices to those of Pixar's have become predominant in control society. Pixar and other corporations create models and then use those models as a way to sort and attract potential consumers.

In sum, Pixar's movies are an ideological expression not of an evil cabal at Pixar but instead of the encounter of computer and animation. Pixar discovers rubber and other synthetic materials as a solution to the affective questions posed by CG animation, and this solution entails a controllable body and fixed world. No wonder, then, that their movies, in turn, translate that solution into content that likewise emphasizes bodily flexibility and resiliency (the ability to bounce back). Such an expression ends by promoting ideas of individual adaptability and flexibility even as models, operating behind the scenes, increasingly control options. A more perfect message for neoliberal capitalism in control society can hardly be imagined. Pixar not only sells marvellous astonishment but the desirability of rubbery, flexible, adaptable subjects and a rigid, given, inflexible world. Such a narrative hides the real lack of flexibility and adaptability under existing regimes of power based on modelling and control, just as the movie aesthetically hides the modelling of characters and world from the same sources and with the same substances. As Pixar makes sense of the aesthetic questions presented by computer animation, their answer *and* their narratives express a neoliberal ideology fit perfectly to control society.

Note

1 Jenkins (2014:90). In *Special Affects*, I define 'sparks' as sharp affects that sting or prick audiences, similar to Roland Barthes' *punctum* of the photograph.

References

Broadfoot, K. and Butler, R. (1991) 'The Illusion of Illusion', in A. Cholodenko (ed) *The Illusion of Life: Essays on Animation*, Sydney: Power Publications, pp 263–98.

Cracknell, R. (2008) 'WALL-E', Movie Views, 7 November [online], Available from: https://movieviews.ca/wall-e.

Dargis, M. (2018) 'Review: "Incredibles 2" Is a Fast Blast (With Red Flags)', *The New York* Times, 13 June [online], Available from: https://www.nyti mes.com/2018/06/13/movies/incredibles-2-review-disney-pixar.html

Deleuze, G. (1988) *Spinoza: Practical Philosophy*, translated by Robert Hurley, San Francisco: City Lights Books.

Deleuze, G. (1995) 'Postscript on Control Societies', in *Negotiations, 1972–1990*, translated by M. Joughin, New York: Columbia University Press, pp 177–82.

Eisenstein, S. (1986) *On Disney*, edited by Jay Leda, translated by Alan Upchurch, Calcutta: Seagull.

Jenkins, E.S. (2014) *Special Affects: Cinema, Animation, and The Translation of Consumer Culture*, Edinburgh: Edinburgh University Press.

Kurtti, J. (1998) *A Bug's Life: Art and Making of an Epic of Miniature Proportions*, Glendale, CA: Disney Editions.

Lasseter, J. and Daly, S. (1995) *Toy Story: The Art and Making of the Animated Film*, New York: Disney Editions.

Massumi, B. (2002) 'Introduction: Like a Thought', in: Massumi, B. (ed) *A Shock to Thought: Expression after Deleuze and Guattari*, London: Routledge, pp xiii–xxxix.

Massumi, B. (2015) *Politics of Affect*, Cambridge: Polity.

Mihailova, M. (2013) 'The Mastery Machine: Digital Animation and Fantasies of Control', Animation, 8(2): 131–148.

Neupert, R. (2016) *John Lasseter*, Urbana, IL: University of Illinois Press.

North, D. (2008) *Performing Illusions: Cinema, Special Effects and the Virtual Actor*, London: Wallflower Press.

O'Pray, M. (1997) 'Eisenstein and Stokes on Disney: Film Animation and Omnipotence', in Pilling, J. (ed) *A Reader in Animation Studies*, Bloomington, IN: Indiana University Press, pp 195–202.

Schaffer, W. (2004) 'The Importance of Being Plastic: The Feel of Pixar', *Animation*, 12(1): 72–95.

Sobchack, V. (2008) 'The Line and the Animorph or "Travel is More than Just A to B"', *Animation*, 3(3): 251–65.

Wells, P. (1998) *Understanding Animation*, London/New York: Routledge.

6

Player and Avatar in Motion: Affective Encounters

Daniela Bruns

Introduction

Complex code and advanced algorithms are traversing nearly every part of our mediatized everyday life: automotive workshops do not only replace spare parts but run software to detect programme errors; search engines are not only useful sources of knowledge but evaluate and exploit every query; today's virtual assistants are smart conversation partners with a personality instead of simple programmes with very limited dialogue options. Therefore, research on algorithmic systems has become essential for understanding the world we are living and acting in. But code as part of a smartphone that accompanies us every second, longing for gaze and touch, and causes anxieties when untraceable, evoke different affective responses than code implemented in objects that demand little or no interaction. Always implemented in a processing machine that we encounter, there is no such thing as pure code without matter. This also applies to video games, which are not only simple programmes but programmes running on platforms with specific controls, captivating our senses with their multifaceted output. Alexander Galloway (2006) describes video games as an action-based medium consisting of machine and operator actions, both equally important for the gaming experience: 'People move their hands, bodies, eyes, and mouths when they play video games. But machines also act. They act in response to player actions as well as independently of them' (p 4). The human encounter with game hardware and software takes place on eye level instead of being controlled or dominated by the operator input: 'Humans do not simply manipulate or control machines, data, and networks any more than machines, data, and networks simply manipulate or control us' (Paasonen et al, 2015:2).

This change of perspective has brought algorithms more and more into the focus of research. Nevertheless, the machinic act in form of processing algorithms should not be overstated in the experience with video games. In her book *Playing with Feelings*, Aubrey Anable (2018) criticizes the current fetishization of code in combination with the simultaneous neglection of the audiovisual output and haptic quality, that stimulates our senses, in game studies. Her critique is a reaction to the formalist approach of proceduralism which privileges strategically utilized code and computational architecture over its actual realization through hardware coming together with a sensitive and active subject. This transforms the player into a mere button-pushing entity, following the predefined interaction system of the game designer. The playing subject itself becomes an automatic script, a reflection of precisely these algorithms it is interacting with. In contrast, Anable sees the experience of playing a video game as shaped by complex entanglements between meaning, body, hardware, and code:

> Video games are affective systems. When we open a video game program on a phone, computer, or gaming console, we are opening up a 'form of relation' to the game's aesthetic and narrative properties, the computational operations of the software, the mechanical and material properties of the hardware on which we play the game, ideas of leisure and play, ideas of labor, our bodies, other players, and the whole host of fraught cultural meanings and implications that circulate around video games. (Anable, 2018:xii)

The way we perceive and feel a specific game is therefore neither programmed into a code nor completely dependent on the subjective experience with a game 'text' but arises from manifold encounters between human and machine. Seth Giddings (2005) pictures the process of starting to play a video game as plugging oneself into a cybernetic circuit, where computer as well as human components are working together to create the gaming experience (p 1). In his article 'As We Become Machines: Corporealized Pleasures in Video Games' Martti Lahti (2004) describes the gaming experience in a similar way:

> [The] delirium of virtual mobility, sensory feedback, and the incorporation of the player into a larger system thus tie the body into a cybernetic loop with the computer, where its affective thrills can spill over into the player's space. This desire is perhaps best exemplified by players' attempts to control the game world more fully with their own empathetic bodily movement. (Lahti, 2004:163)

Encountering a video game does not just mean setting virtual bodies or items in motion but also being set in motion. The playable avatar as a link between player actions and game world is particularly well suited for emotional and affective connections. Daniel Muriel and Garry Crawford (2018) state:

> Video games push players into the shoes of others, allowing them to experience the world from their perspective. However, players are not exactly experiencing what others feel or what it means to be in a specific situation, after all, video gaming is a mediated experience, not the experience itself; but it lets players at least connect with other realities in different ways. (Muriel and Crawford, 2018:86)

This contribution breaks down the cybernetic circuit of gaming as a physical as well as mental connection between controller, audiovisual stimuli, game world, avatar, and player's body. The first part examines the executing bodies of player and avatar, mediated through the game's controls. The second part illuminates the avatar as a carrier of meaning, situated in a specific game environment. The last part deals with gaming situations where the player's body is sensitive to the machinic activity of the game world that surrounds the avatar. The main goal of those remarks is to focus on the varying quality and intensity of human–machine interactions in gaming.

Executing bodies and controls

In the public realms of virtual entertainment and pleasure, namely, the video game arcades of the 70s and 80s, the physical body was a crucial part of the human–machine interaction: 'In arcades, players can sit astride a motorcycle or stand on a pair of skis, feeling bumps and vibration through these apparati, and using their whole bodies to control the game world by, for example, leaning into the curves as they round corners [...] represented on-screen' (Lahti, 2004:162). Not only the gameplay was characterized by intense bodily activity but also the social context of playing in arcades: mutual encouraging, switching bodies on the 'hot seat' of multiplayer games, collective celebration of high scores or seriously fought out competitions reflected the ongoing action of the virtual settings. The physical simulation of firing a toy weapon or riding a model of a motorcycle in arcades does not necessarily need a visual representation of the corporeal self on the video screen. The whole body of the player is part of the input device for the game and stands for itself. The movement of specific body parts directly affects what happens in the virtual world in a mimetic way while the audiovisual feedback of the machine closes this cybernetic circle between actual and virtual. A simulation technology that was too expansive for the usage in private households back then but has regained particular attention since the Wii motion-sensing controller was successfully introduced to the gaming market in 2006.[1]

Many of the games currently played, however, are mediated seemingly less body intensively: the control schemes are limited to a mouse, keyboard, joystick, or gaming controller, with user input visualized by a cursor or an animation on screen. The touchscreen of smartphones or tablets is input and output device at the same time, and therefore it seems to be controlled more immediately or instinctively. Nevertheless, the user has to learn when to tap, to swipe, to linger, to turn the screen, to use two or more fingers, and so on. In both cases, the bodily interaction with the specific hardware of the gaming system is generally not a natural or intuitive one but is governed by an arbitrary programming. Andreas Gregersen and Torben Grodal (2009) differentiate between primitive actions (P-actions) as the ones that are 'merely a movement of the body' – for example, pushing one button with a finger – and gaming actions that result out of a combination of several P-actions (p 70) like a low-hitting attack in the fighting game *Tekken 7* (2017). P-actions as well as gaming actions performed on screen are functionally mapped into the game system to make them meaningful actions in their respectively designed virtual environment. Even though the movement of a combination of P-actions and the movement of the representative in the game world are not straightforwardly identical, the feeling of authorship in game action can be very immediate, as Janet Murray (1997) states:

> The most compelling aspect of the fighting game [genre] is the tight visceral match between the game controller and the screen action. A palpable click on the mouse or joystick results in an explosion. It requires very little imaginative effort to enter such a world because the sense of agency is so direct. (Murray, 1997:146)

While Murray's description emphasizes the simplicity of the interaction with the input device – just clicking on a mouse or pressing a button – and focuses on the given agency as outcome initiated through the audiovisual feedback on screen, Graeme Kirkpatrick (2009) draws attention to a deeper understanding of its corporeal preconditions. As a transmitter of the player's finger movements, the gamepad controller operates best when it is not recognized:

> No one talks about pressing 'X', then 'O', then 'Δ', and no one feels that this is what they are doing [...] Good play is about feeling, and being able to feel what we are supposed to be feeling is, at least partly, a function of *not* looking at or thinking about our hands. (Kirkpatrick, 2009:130–1)

He criticizes that just because the controller tends to be not as present as the things happening on screen, it is often ignored by researchers as well as game designers. This is even more true for traditional gamepad controllers than for motion-sense controllers or 'mimetic controllers' as Keogh (2015) calls them. A motion controller, for example the Wii Remote, is used in an open space, where the player can perform relatively free motions with their whole body. When playing tennis on a Nintendo Wii console, the sensors keep track of its spatial position and transmit player movement into the game. In contrast, the gamepad controller lies relatively still in the hands of the player, which often leads to the misconception that the player's body and physical experience are of less importance. Kirkpatrick (2009) counters that while pushing the gamepad's buttons, the resistance of a physical object is noticeable: '[s]omething of the experience of throwing a javelin – its tension in the body, its discipline, its conscious manipulation of weight and energies – gets condensed into the hand' (p 134). This unconscious physical tension of holding a controller can also apply in more inactive moments: for example, when the player is waiting for a cutscene to end to dive back into the gameplay.

A fitting example is the bow shooting in *Shadow of the Tomb Raider* (2018) on the PlayStation 4, where the player has to keep pressing a shoulder button (L2) to equip the bow, pressing another (R2) to draw the bowstring, and letting the arrow go by releasing the latter one. Because both hands are needed for this action it mimics the use of an actual bow in miniature. If the bowstring is drawn too long, the DualShock controller gives a haptic feedback in form of vibrations. These vibrations feel like the shaking of an over-exerted muscle – and in combination with a wobbling crosshair – making it difficult to hold up the focus that is needed for aiming a target. Shortly after, the arrow will be released automatically, which transfers the tension of the pressing fingers also into a mental tension because arrows are a limited resource and missing targets regularly results in a higher need. If the player knows how, it is possible to drop the bow altogether and start from the beginning. While this example illustrates tension triggered by machinic action through realization of code, tension can also be influenced by operator action: Letting the controller go in a calm situation, for example, a long cutscene, releases the tension in hands and body and reduces the intensity of the connection to the input device. Another expression of this temporary disentanglement is flinging away the controller because of frustration or anger or disagreement with the events represented on screen.

Learning process

Johan Blomberg (2018) calls the position of the controller a paradoxical one: it becomes only fully functional by disappearing from the player's perception, but is all the more noticeable if it does not work as usual. He describes the neglect of the controller as the effect of a learning process that shapes the game experience to a great extent: 'Over time, there has been a gradual progression towards complete controller integration in the player's experience. Only the inexperienced player is painfully reminded of the controller's indispensable nature' (paragraph 4). As a gaming novice, the player has to constantly check the controller buttons to archive the required actions on screen. As habitualization progresses, the player gets used to the control scheme and focuses their attention on the game's audiovisual output. Blomberg compares this learning process to the process of learning a new language: rules of grammar, spelling, and pronunciation are extremely present at the beginning but are used automatically after mastering it. While the language student tries to reconstruct the appropriate linguistic expression so that the dialogue partner understands them, the player learns the language of the game so that interactivity can flow between them (paragraph 4). Following this comparison, different languages can be equated with the 'game language' of different gaming platforms and genres: controller and control schemes relate to conventions evolving over time and got inscribed into the gamer's habitus, developing a tacit knowledge (Merleau-Ponty, 2002/1945) or 'feel for the game' (Bourdieu, 1998), which is not only relevant for mastering a game – or games with similar controls – but also as embodied capital in the gaming community. This learning process is not possible to derive from code or algorithms but depends on the person who is playing. Therefore, not only the designed interface on screen with the left-sided position of the avatar and its face directed to the right triggers the urge to press the button for running to the right side of the screen in *Sonic Mania* (2017), but also our experience with other platform games – for example *Super Mario Land* (1989) – eventually makes the left to right movement in side-scroller video games feel natural for us.[2] Skilled players navigate through game worlds effortlessly without consciously thinking about finger movements or design affordances, while the physical connection of gaming novices to the actions on screen requires constant reflection and adjustment, resulting in 'thinking about' instead of 'just doing'. Zach Whalen (2004) uses the terms immersion and engagement to differentiate the human–machine interaction in video games qualitatively:

> [I]mmersion is the act of relying on learned behavioral scripts at a level of instinct – being 'in the moment' without having to be aware of what it takes to be in the moment – while engagement is the process of learning the script and requires an objective awareness of the object supplying the new schema. (Whalen, 2004:paragraph 3)

Moments of alienation

Some game designers play with conventions, challenging the player's internalized movement patterns and breaking their immersion in favour of a more distant and reflective relationship of player and game controls. Blomberg (2018) mentions an example that describes this kind of alienation perfectly: the Psycho Mantis boss fight in the action game *Metal Gear Solid* (1998). Because the player's opponent Psycho Mentis can predict every movement of the avatar, he seems to be undefeatable at first. To win this fight the player must come to the realization that changing the physical controller port on the console will disconnect Psycho Mentis's mental connection to the avatar and can therefore be beaten. On the one hand, this unconventional solution is mentally challenging because eventually, the player has to conquer the socially constructed separation of virtual (gaming) world and his/her material environment to master this fight. On the other hand, it momentarily breaks the close tie between controller and body by pulling the player out of the moment: they have to put the gamepad away, get up from the chair and focus on objects of the physical world.

A more recent example of alienation can be found in *Brothers: A Tale of Two Sons* (2013). On the adventure to find a magical medicine for their sick father, the two brothers Naiee and Naia must overcome many dangerous circumstances. While playing on a game console, the player moves the two avatars individually with the two thumbsticks on the controller. Inevitably, the elder brother dies near the end of the game, which leaves one of those thumbsticks unusable and renders one of the player's hands superfluous. Because most time of the game the player feels the tension of holding the controller and the pressure of the thumbsticks in both hands, the brother's loss is physically palpable by losing the usefulness of one of the own hands.

For Kirkpatrick (2009) those moments of alienation are of particular interest, because they bring the materiality of the controller and the player's own machinic-like actions – repeatedly pressing the right buttons in the right moment – back into consciousness (Kirkpatrick, 2009:136). Following the previous argumentation, this is especially true for players who are experienced enough to get immersed into the game action. However, contrary to the first impression, video games with gamepad controllers are not rendering the player's body motionless and physically inactive, while all the action is transferred to the screen. Although the movement seems to be limited to fingers and hands, the whole body is part of the cybernetic entanglement between human and machine. The experience of various sensations in different quality and intensity depends not only on the gaming programme and the physical controls of the game but also on player's body instincts that are formed through practice.

Embodied actions

The previous examples show clearly that the player's body occupies an extremely important role in playing video games. Connecting oneself into a cybernetic loop does not mean leaving the body behind and transferring the mind from the real to the virtual, in the form of a disembodied state in cyberspace. On the contrary, '[to] play a game is to *experience* the game: to see, touch, hear, smell, and taste the game; to move the body during play, to feel emotions about the unfolding outcome' (Salen and Zimmerman, 2004:314). Gregersen and Grodal (2009) illuminate the concept of embodiment for video gaming based on Maurice Merleau-Ponty's work. Their starting point is the realization that the experience of ourselves cannot be reduced to the actual, physical body. Instead they understand the body as a system of possible actions and differentiate between the *body image*, as the mental perception of one's own body, and the *body schema* as the sensory-motor ability to move. They state that the interaction with video game interfaces connects both to a 'body image in action – where one experiences both agency and ownership of virtual entities' (p 67). Two neurological approaches support their claim. The 'shared circuit' approach states that we physically react to the movements of other bodies. When observing a person who performs a dance or recoils in fear, we are likely to activate parts of our own motor system – which can be congruent or incongruent to the perceived movement of the other. Seeing movement on screen awakes the urge to move our own body. The other approach relates to the 'flexibility of the body schema to incorporate tools and other objects, including those virtually represented' (Gregersen and Grodal, 2009:68–9). Due to bimodal neurons that keep track of somatosensory and visual information, tools we are thoroughly familiar with get integrated into our body sensation. Britta Neitzel (2010) argues the same way when she writes that tools not only expand our abilities and possible actions but get incorporated into our own body through habituation and practice. This is the reason why the usage of a computer mouse as well as its interplay with the represented cursor on-screen works almost automatically, without our thinking consciously about it. This incorporation of an input device is also recognizable in immersive gameplay, when skilled players are 'in the moment', following their instincts.

Following Mike Featherstone (2010), this can be traced back to the 'body without image, the more incomplete and open body. Which is affected by other people's bodies in a variety of ways, which […] work beneath the level of consciousness and language' (p 199). He suggests that contemporary culture produces two ways of conceiving the body: 1) the body image as a static picture of our physical appearance that defines who we are by how we look; 2) the body without image, driven by an instinctive sensibility closely linked to one's proprioception. While the first is clearly based on a subject–object relation between self and body, the latter offers a more ambivalent and incoherent connection. Excitations are recognized by the visceral sensibility before being fully processed by the brain, making it possible to register intensities and tension physically. This unidentified bodily reaction, preceding a conscious, discursive and emotional localization, is called an affect (Featherstone, 2006:234–5).

When playing a video game at a skilled level, the players incorporate the controls as if they are part of their own body. Immersion becomes possible, putting the players in a state of immediate embodiment that leaves everything aside but the body in motion, the executive body, until moments of alienation interrupt this bond. Based on this bodily and instinctive driven experience, video games are well suited to offer affective encounters between human and machine. At the same time, they are not free of objectified bodies that are carriers of social signs, meaning, and power relations: bodies that can be emotionally engaging as part of narrative and game world. The sexualized images of female avatars, for example, were of particular interest for gender studies in the early discussions of video games. However, an essential point of criticism was also triggered by first examinations: the avatars were analysed as body images instead of bodies in motion, 'looked at' rather than 'played', undermining its most important purpose.

Meaningful bodies and avatars

The word 'avatar' originates from Hinduism, where it describes a 'manifestation of a god in bodily form on earth' (OED, 2023) or an 'incarnation, embodiment, or manifestation of a person or idea' (POED, 2013). Jessica Aldred (2014) defines it in the context of video games as 'the user's representative in interactive digital space, responding to their inputs via the game or computer interface, however simple or complicated those inputs may be' (p 356). While this definition reflects a broad understanding of the avatar, Benjamin Beil (2012) tries to narrow it down when he answers the question: what is the difference between the Sonic the Hedgehog (1991) figure and a block from the game Tetris (1984)? The tetromino is controllable by turning it around or moving it from right to left and back. Like a cursor, this block allows the player to interact with the game. Nevertheless, it is not an avatar in Beil's understanding, whose definition is based on the following comparison of avatar and tetromino: first, an avatar is part of a rather complex narration while the tetromino is embedded in an abstract setting of different shaped blocks that are falling from the sky; second, the bond between player and avatar lasts longer than the short takeover of one controllable building block of Tetris – after bringing it in position, the player gains control over the next one. Even though some games offer different playable avatars as well, in many cases their swapping is embedded in the game's storyline. Ultimately, the player spends more time with each of these different characters than with one tetromino, which results – and this is the last differentiation point of Beil (2012) – in a deeper bond to the playable avatar than to the whole cascade of building blocks in Tetris (pp 16–17).

In contrast to a mouse, crosshair cursor, or tetromino as a tool to interact with the computer system, the avatar is therefore an entity that also affords the possibility for emotional investment. This corresponds with the popular understanding of the avatar as both: the representation of a protagonist/figure/personality on one hand and a tool/prosthesis/shell that enables player actions on the other. In *Rules of Play* Salen and Zimmerman (2004) call this avatar experience the double-consciousness of play:

> A protagonist character is a persona through which a player exerts him or herself into an imaginary world; this relationship can be intense and emotionally 'immersive'. However, at the very same time, the character is a tool, a puppet, an object for the player to manipulate according to the rules of the game. (Salen and Zimmerman, 2004:453)

Britta Neitzel (2010) emphasizes the role of representation by stating that the avatar can only provide meaningful gameplay if it is embedded into a narrative and becomes therefore a combination of figure and tool. The situatedness of the avatar in the virtual world gives meaning to game actions and offers a body for identification to the player. It is hardly conceivable that someone playing Tetris feels emotionally connected to every individual brick and mourns their disappearance after fitting together a completed masonry.

Identification with and as the avatar

Jonathan Cohen (2001) defines identification with audiovisual media characters as 'a process that culminates in a cognitive and emotional state in which the audience member is aware not of him- or herself as an audience member, but rather imagines being one of the characters in the text' (p 252). The manifestation of identification is that we feel *with* the character instead of having feelings or attributions *about* the character. Video games as interactive media are not films or novels, but contemporary games offer a wide range of experiences, including those based on sophisticated stories and complex characters. Nevertheless, the bodily involvement in gaming also generates significant distinctions. Adrienne Shaw (2014) understands identification with video game avatars on a level of an affective embodiment rather than based on representation and cognitive processes. In her book *Gaming at the Edge,* she demonstrates that players from the margins of gaming culture enjoy games with a lack of diverse representation as much as the typical heterosexual, male, cis-gendered gamer, for whom many video games were originally designed. For her, identification is generally 'a process by which we come to feel an affective connection with a character on the basis of seeing that character as separate and yet a part of us in some way' (p 94). Ragnhild Tronstad (2008) provides a more differentiated approach: when characters offer their own personality and/or history as part of the game narrative, it is only possible to identify *with* them because then the player adapts their actions to their role in the game; whereas a truly 'avatarial' entity is one that can be played as a virtual extension of the player, just taking up an executing position, and letting the player identify themselves *as* their in-game character. Even though Tronstad's use of the true avatar is less common, his more nuanced perspective does make sense because of today's immense spectrum of different games on the market. Therefore, avatar design could be a good starting point to examine the connection between embodiment and identification further.

Different types of avatars

René Schallegger (2016) divides the avatar–player relation into three subcategories that are organized in a spectrum from *shell*, over *role*, to *personality*. Shells do not have a personality or will of their own; their only purpose is to transfer the actions and intentions of the player into the game world. Schallegger uses the term 'virtual prothesis' (p 25) to describe this type of avatar, which compliments the view of Gregersen and Grodal about the tool as an extension of our body. The avatar as empty vessel is a virtual representation of the player's actions and projections and therefore tends to establish a very close, 'quasi-physical' relationship between avatar and player. The shell as a body that the player borrows to perform their own actions reflects Tronstad's definition of the 'avatarial' the best.

The second type of playable characters are called 'role'. Here the avatar plays its own part in the diegesis of the game, but the player can individualize it on different levels. Classic role-playing games (RPGs) are a perfect example of this kind of avatar: in the fantasy world of *Dragon Age: Origins* (2009) and *Dragon Age: Inquisition* (2014) the player can choose between different races, classes, backgrounds, and attributes. Depending on the selected traits, the avatar will be treated differently in the game world and can even become a victim of discrimination by non-player characters (NPCs). Many games with RPG elements – *Mass Effect: Andromeda* (2017), *The Witcher 3* (2015) or *Horizon: Zero Dawn* (2017), for example – allow the player to choose from different dialogue options to form the character of the avatar to the player's own liking. Mostly, these decisions have no consequences for the game's outcome but they offer the possibility to identify with the avatar's expressions on the basis of homophily: 'players could identify with those characters and situations that reflect, somehow, one or more aspects of their lives, comprising their lifestyle, gender, sexuality, ethnicity, political perspectives, class, level of education, taste, personality, and so on' (Muriel and Crawford, 2018:131).

The last type, the avatar with its own 'personality', is the one that seems to be most distant from the player's interventions because it banishes them to the spectator seat. The construction of such an avatar, with its predefined character traits and a fixed narrative background, relies heavily on character designs from novels, movies, and television. Often, the development of its attitude, values, and traits is part of the game narration, and the player feels connected to it on an emotional or intellectual level. From Tronstad's perspective, this type of avatar offers most likely the possibility of identifying *with* it instead of *as* it, and is therefore not truly avatarial in his understanding.

While Schallegger's trisection can be productive for describing different manifestations of the player–avatar relation, the following example demonstrates its underlying complexity and fluidity. The playable personality in the action–adventure game *Hellblade: Senua's Sacrifice* (2017) is the Norseman girl Senua, who suffers from a psychosis with visual hallucinations and hearing voices. The player has no chance to individualize the character or contribute a personal touch by making dialogue decisions. Her preformulated past remains uncertain at the beginning of the game but is revealed as the plot unfolds. Because the player hardly learns anything about her personality and her motivations at the beginning of the game, the focus lies on an affective embodiment rather than an emotional empathetic connection at first. Therefore, when starting the game, identification *as* Senua, through controls and the executing body, is more likely than an identification *with* her figure as a sovereign personality. Nonetheless, the game situates the player as something outside the avatar from the start: one of the voices in Senua's head offers the player the opportunity to join the adventure, and Senua herself shows a moment of recognition when she breaks the fourth wall by looking straight into the 'camera', as if the player is just her hallucination, another voice in her head telling her what to do. While on a diegetic level, Senua refuses to be an empty vessel for the player, affectively marking them as something outside herself, on the level of performance Senua offers the player a physical connection by acting through her. Only after the player has learned more about Senua's personal history, where she comes from, and what her motivation is, the executing body – the player's actions mirrored on screen – is also framed meaningfully, offering a deeper connection to the avatar's persona. Which meanings the player actually activates for themselves during gameplay, and how the avatar is received and played as part of the game world ultimately depends on the player and gaming situation.

Embedded avatar

Based on Merleau-Ponty's understanding of the body as both subject and object, as the experience of the body and the objectified body, Rune Klevjer (2012) describes how the player's feeling of the latter is also channelled into the space on screen. While sitting safe and sound on the couch, their own body becomes an object of minor importance, and the virtual avatar becomes the new object-body for the player. The feeling of ownership is directed to the displayed avatar instead of lingering on their own body. Due to the extension of the subject-body, Klevjer argues, this happens independently from fictional configuration on a phenomenological plane. So while offering a specific role the player can engage with, still important for the overall experience in many games, it is not necessary for the feeling of being immersed in the fictional world as someone else. His considerations are therefore compatible with Shaw's (2014) findings that an appealing representation is not the main requirement when identifying with a video game avatar. However, while the players slip into a virtual body and recognize this body as their own image, the virtual body is not a blank sheet either. Rune Klevjer (2012) argues further that playable avatars differ from tools and instruments because they allow the players not only to act in but also from within the virtual world. So they expand and relocate the player's body at the same time:

> When we play, because the avatar extends the body rather than pure agency or subjectivity, screen space becomes a world that we are subjected to, a place we inhabit and where we struggle for survival. We learn to intuitively judge, like we do in the real world, the opportunities and dangers of the environment. (Klevjer, 2012:13)

James Paul Gee (2008) describes video game characters as projective beings, stating that players are inhabiting not only the body but also the mind of the avatar, while simultaneously projecting their own intentions, goals, and desires into it. When talking about the avatar's mind, Gee means the player's concept of what it could be like in the present circumstances of the game:

> As a player, you must – on the basis of what you learn about the game's story and the game's virtual world – attribute certain mental states (beliefs, values, goals, feelings, attitudes, and so forth) to the virtual character. You must take these to be the character's mental states: you must take them as a basis for explaining the character's actions in the world. (Gee, 2008:258)

Through the avatar and the fictional world it is embedded in, specific affordances and disaffordances occur for the players, providing them with goals and possible actions. Within this framework, the players are able to develop their own goals, intentions, and expectations, bringing them to life via the avatar's actions. However, Gee's description of player–avatar interaction stays on a very harmonious level, picturing an ideal state, without mentioning situations where this balance is questioned or even threatened, whether intentionally or unintentionally by the player.

The contradiction of one's acting as someone else, the vagueness of being oneself but also being the other, is reflected in language: players often use the first-person pronoun 'I' when describing the actions their avatars perform in video games, but also referring to them in the third-person (see Cogburn and Silcox, 2009:1–2). In this regard, the mission 'By the Book' of the open-world action-adventure *Grand Theft Auto V* (*GTA V*, 2013) turns out to be an interesting assignment: in the role of Trevor Philips, who is characterized by antisocial, aggressive, and psychotic behaviour, the player must torture the technician Ferdinand Kerimov to obtain information about a terrorist for the secret service. This task differs from other assignments because the player's agency is minimized to choosing a torture instrument and activating it by simply clicking buttons. This is reflected in its common designation as a 'torture scene', although it is not a cutscene but has interactive elements. Furthermore, the man the player must torture is represented as a victim with a name, a family, and a personal past that he is willingly talking about to the avatar/player. While the whole game is based on criminal activities, killing people, stealing cars, and committing heists, the connection between player and avatar is disturbed in this sequence, both on the level of embodiment – due to changed control schemes – and identification with the avatar who tortures an innocent victim. Forum and blog entries of the gaming community reveal different practices to deal with this mission like quitting the game, searching for a possibility to skip the mission, or holding the psychotic character Trevor accountable for the performed actions. Accordingly, some of the players interpreted the required actions as something that fits the character Trevor, opening a possibility to distance themselves from their actions, whereas others cannot stand what they must do, debonding completely through quitting or skipping the scene.

The previous considerations suggest that the player–avatar relation is not something fixed but oscillates between moments of affiliation and alienation, depending not only on controls and avatar design but also on player skills and emotional engagement. However, in addition to identification through actions, the identification through representation can be relevant for the player's feeling of connectedness towards the avatar as well as the world it is embedded in. In many contemporary video games both levels are intertwined during gameplay, so that the differentiation between identification based on player's emotional engagement with the avatar's role (*with*) as well as player's actions in gameplay (*as*) must not be acknowledged as two end points of a continuum but as two possible factors that can support or contradict each other. This can lead to diverse intensities and qualities of the felt connection between player and avatar.

The previous examinations were mainly based on active players who use the interactive medium of video games to participate in game events with controller and avatar. The last section gives an insight into what happens when player activity comes to a halt.

Sensitive bodies and machines

Early jump-and-run, fighting and shooting games – in arcades and at home – have taught us to move our avatar or crosshair on-screen persistently. The consequences of not being in motion means a lost life, lost points, or a lost game. The machine demands input from its operator to activate its algorithms and produce output. This is reflected in Alexander Galloway's (2006) statement when he writes about the unique nature of video games: 'What used to be primarily the domain of eyes and looking is now more likely that of muscles and doing, thumbs, to be sure, and what used to be the act of reading is now the act of doing, or just "the act"' (p 4). With that, he draws a line between the mass media of film, literature, and television and the action-based video game where looking and reading were replaced by the 'instigation of material change through action' (p 4).

The game's coding and bodily interaction are focused in this approach, emphasizing the interplay of operator and machinic action. Galloway (2006) coined the term 'ambience act', which 'is the inverse of pressing Pause. While the machine pauses in a pause act and the operator is free to take a break, it is the operator who is paused in an ambience act, leaving the machine to hover in a state of pure process' (p 10). During an ambience act, the machine takes over and runs the programmed algorithms without getting input from the player via control device. In these situations, micromovements of the avatar often have a demanding character like the break animation of *Sonic the Hedgehog* (1991): by impatiently tapping his foot the player's body should be activated by the movement of the avatar. The lingering possibility of the player's return to action, is the reason why Galloway sees the ambience act as charged with expectation. Additionally, micromovements also communicate an organic feeling of avatar and game world because complete motionlessness would seem very mechanic. Both aspects are combined in the interactive storytelling game *Detroit: Become Human* (2018). It revolves around the narration of three playable androids developing human emotions. At a key moment, while controlling the housemaid android Kara, the player can decide whether to break the android's programmed code to protect a girl from domestic violence or to follow the orders of the abuser to not move.

When not interacting with the controller at all, the avatar remains completely stiff like a lifeless being. The decision to break the programme code transforms the static machinic body posture into a dynamic one, desperately waiting for player input. The player's decision to act is pressed ahead by the system's feedback in form of the avatar's micromovements, simultaneously symbolizing character development: the ethical decision of the player to act and protect the girl is what transforms the android into a human-like being. If the player decides against this transformation by not acting, the avatar will die shortly after. In this case, as in many others, interaction with the game is rewarded with progressing in the game.

Then again, Aubrey Anable (2018) illustrates that visualization – activating looking rather than doing – has always been an important aspect of video game history by referring to the story of video games' origin. The two early video games *Tennis for Two* (1958) and *Spacewar!* (1961) 'were used in demonstrations for laypeople visiting the labs because the games made visible – in some sense externalized and made available to the senses – the otherwise invisible and incomprehensible process of the mistrusted machines' (p 24). Later, the gaming industry of the early 2000s, especially the producers of video game consoles, strove for high performance, and its visualization in the form of hyper- and photorealistic graphics became the holy grail.[3] Besides innovations in game interfaces, this has been a relevant issue because those computer-related aspects are perceptible – literally sensible – for the public, whereas enhancements concerning game engines, the processing of code, and technical aspects are mainly relevant to people with the necessary expertise.

Technological progress in computer performance, as well as memory capacity and the integration of (audio)visual media characteristics into video games (see King and Krzywinska, 2006), like cutscenes, photorealistic graphics, and composed music, resulted in new practices of playing and new affective encounters. More and more contemporary video games feature gaming situations where the player is not urged to act but invited to pause the action without stopping the processing of the system. Machinic interludes, independent from player input, also convey the impression that the fictional world does not rely on the player's actions, that it is a vital simulation on its own. Instead of encouraging instant player action, the following examples celebrate the independent machinic act: the video game *Brothers: A Tale of Two Sons* (2013) allows the player's avatars to sit on benches, lingering in different locations with a beautiful view; in *Life is Strange* (2015) the player can let the avatar play guitar and just listen to harmonic tunes for a while; in *Rise of the Tomb Raider* (2015) the player can attain a 'Quiet Time Achievement' for sitting on a chair and enjoying the photorealistic view of a mountain range; Andy Kelly in the *Guardian* (2015) even gives travel recommendations for the fictional state San Andreas of *GTA V* (2013) with a screenshot gallery, 'Ten places every *Grand Theft Auto V* player should visit'.

In these moments, where the player becomes a 'tourist, an observer, a witness' instead of an executive body, they 'can forget about the mission and just start [...] observing the in-game universe' (Muriel and Crawford, 2018:40). But even though the operator pauses their input while the machine keeps acting, as Galloway states, the player's body does not become irrelevant. The avatar, its quests, character traits, and representation, as well as the controller, do not feel important while admiring the visual and auditory richness of the virtual world, but in the next moment the player can go back into their executive body to fight off an enemy or take a decision relevant to the avatar's fate. Therefore, admiring video game environments is always charged with the promise to act in this environment, which demonstrates an important distinction between viewing a picture and absorbing the scenery in video games. The player's body, accustomed to the immersive feeling of embodiment and identification, remains sensitive for potential actions, maintaining bodily tension even in situations of motionlessness.

Notes

[1] The 1993-introduced *Sega Activator* was a commercial failure; for motion-sensing controllers, see Isbister, 2017, pp 73–108, and Gregersen and Grodal, 2009, pp 73–7.

[2] Additionally, the left-to-right movement is also culturally learned as Spalek and Hammad (2005) show in their study about reading directions. This is presumably also the reason why western designers have chosen this level design in the first place.

[3] Nicely illustrated in Günzel (2014): *Push > Start, The Art of Video Games.*

References

Aldred, J. (2014) 'Characters', in M.J.P. Wolf and B. Perron (eds) *The Routledge Companion to Video Game Studies*, New York: Routledge, pp 355–63.

Anable, A. (2018) *Playing with Feelings: Video Games and Affect*, Minneapolis: University of Minnesota Press.

Beil, B. (2012) *Avatarbilder: Zur Bildlichkeit des zeitgenössischen Computerspiels*, Bielefeld: Transcript.

Blomberg, J. (2018) 'The Semiotics of the Game Controller', *Game Studies*, 18(2), Available from: http://gamestudies.org/1802/articles/blomberg

Bourdieu, P. (1998) *Practical Reason: On the Theory of Action*, Stanford: Stanford University Press.

Cogburn, J. and M. Silcox (2009) *Philosophy through Video Games*, London/ New York: Routledge.

Cohen, J. (2001) 'Defining Identification: A Theoretical Look at the Identification of Audiences with Media Characters', *Mass Communication & Society*, 4(3): 245–64.

Featherstone, M. (2006) 'Body Image/Body without Image', *Theory, Culture & Society*, 23(2–3): 233–6.

Featherstone, M. (2010) 'Body, Image and Affect in Consumer Culture', *Body & Society*, 16(1): 193–221.

Galloway, A.R. (2006) *Gaming: Essays on Algorithmic Culture*, Minneapolis: University of Minnesota Press.

Gee, J.P. (2008) 'Video Games and Embodiment', *Games and Culture*, 3(3–4): 253–63.

Giddings, S. (2005) 'Playing With Non-Humans: Digital Games as Techno-Cultural Form', *Proceedings of the 2005 DiGRA International Conference: Changing Views – Worlds in Play*, Available from: http://www.digra.org/wp-content/uploads/digital-library/06278.24323.pdf

Gregersen, A. and T. Grodal (2009) 'Embodiment and Interface', in M.J.P. Wolf and B. Perron (eds) *The Video Game Theory Reader 2*, New York: Routledge, pp 65–84.

Günzel, S. (2014) *Push Start: The Art of Video Games*, Hamburg: earBOOKS.

Isbister, K. (2017) *How Games Move Us: Emotion by Design*, Cambridge, MA: MIT Press.

Keogh, B. (2015) *A Play of Bodies: A Phenomenology of Videogame Experience* (PhD thesis), Melbourne: RMIT University.

Kelly, A. (2015) 'Ten places every Grand Theft Auto V player should visit', photo gallery, *The Guardian*, 16 April [online], Available from: https://www.theguardian.com/technology/gallery/2015/apr/16/gallery-ten-places-every-grand-theft-auto-v-player-should-visit

King, G. and T. Krzywinska (2006) 'Film Studies and Digital Games', in J. Rutter and J. Bryce (eds) *Understanding Digital Games*, London: Sage, pp 112–28.

Klevjer, R. (2012) 'Enter the Avatar: The Phenomenology of Prosthetic Telepresence in Computer Games', in J.R. Sageng, H. Fossheim and T.M. Larson (eds) *The Philosophy of Computer Games*, Dordrecht: Springer, pp 17–38.

Kirkpatrick, G. (2009) 'Controller, Hand, Screen: Aesthethic Form in the Computer Game', *Games and Culture*, 4(2): 127–43.

Lahti, M. (2004) 'As We Become Machines: Corporealized Pleasures in Video Games', in M.J.P. Wolf and B. Perron (eds) *The Video Game Theory Reader*, New York: Routledge, pp 157–70.

Merleau-Ponty, M. (2002/1945) *Phenomenology of Perception*, translated by Colin Smith, London and New York: Routledge.

Muriel, D. and G. Crawford (2018) *Video Games as Culture: Considering the Role and Importance of Video Games in Contemporary Society*, London/New York: Routledge.

Murray, J.H. (1997) *Hamlet on the Holodeck: The Future of Narrative in Cyberspace*, New York: Free Press.

Neitzel, B. (2010) 'Wer bin ich? Thesen zur Avatar-Spieler Bindung', in B. Neitzel, M. Bopp and R.F. Nohr (eds) *»See? I'm real…«: Multidisziplinäre Zugänge zum Computerspiel am Beispiel von ›Silent Hill‹*, Münster: LIT, pp 193–212.

Oxford English Dictionary. (2023) s.v. 'avatar, n., sense 1.a', https://www.oed.com/dictionary/avatar_n?tab=meaning_and_use#32513733.

Paasonen, S., K. Hillis and M. Petit (eds) (2015) *Networked Affect*, Cambridge, MA: MIT Press.

Pocket Oxford English Dictionary. (2013) s.v. 'avatar, n., sense 1.a.i'.

Salen, K. and E. Zimmerman (2004) *Rules of Play: Game Design Fundamentals*, Cambridge, MA/London: MIT Press.

Schallegger, R. (2016) 'WTH Are Games? Towards a Triad of Triads', in J. Helbig and R. Schallegger (eds) *Digitale Spiele*, Cologne: Herbert von Halem, pp 14–49.

Shaw, A. (2014) *Gaming at the Edge: Sexuality and Gender at the Margins of Gamer Culture*, Minneapolis: University of Minnesota Press.

Spalek, T.M. and S. Hammad (2005) 'The Left-to-Right Bias in Inhibition of Return Is Due to the Direction of Reading', *Psychological Science*, 16(1): 15–18.

Tronstad, R. (2008) 'Character Identification in World of Warcraft: The Relationship between Capacity and Appearance', in H.G. Corneilussen and J.W. Rettberg (eds) *Digital Culture, Play, and Identity: A World of Warcraft Reader*, Cambridge, MA: MIT Press, pp 249–64.

Whalen, Z. (2004) 'Play Along – An Approach to Videogame Music', *Game Studies* 4(1), Available from: http://gamestudies.org/0401/whalen/

Ludography
505 Games (2013) *Brothers: A Tale of Two Sons*.
Bandai Namco (2017) *Tekken 7*.
Brookhaven National Laboratory (1958) *Tennis for Two*.
CD Project (2015) *The Witcher 3*.
Electronic Arts (2009) *Dragon Age: Origins*.
Electronic Arts (2014) *Dragon Age: Inquisition*.
Electronic Arts (2017) *Mass Effect: Andromeda*.
Konami (1998) *Metal Gear Solid*.
MIT (1961) *Spacewar!*.
Ninja Theory (2017) *Hellblade: Senua's Sacrifice*.
Nintendo (1989) *Super Mario Land*.
Nintendo (1984) *Tetris*.
Rockstar Games (2013) *Grand Theft Auto V (GTA V)*.
Sega (1991) *Sonic the Hedgehog*.
Sega (2017) *Sonic Mania*.

Sony Interactive Entertainment (2017) *Horizon Zero Dawn*.
Sony Interactive Entertainment (2018) *Detroit: Become Human*.
Square Enix (2015) *Life is Strange*.
Square Enix (2015) *Rise of the Tomb Raider*.
Square Enix (2018) *Shadow of the Tomb Raider*.

PART III

Data Visualization: Space and Time

Animation, Data, and the Plasticity of the Real: From the Military Survey of Scotland to Synthetic Training Environments

Pasi Väliaho

To ANIMATE, in a military sense, is to encourage the troops by the power of language. That art, that power, which can on singular and critical occasions so animate the spirit of man, as to cause it to give an elasticity, a strength, a velocity, to the corporeal matter of the being, which unanimated it would be incapable of doing; such art, such power, must be ever necessary to a leader of soldiers. (Smith, 1779:n.p. [entry 'to animate'])

So Captain George Smith, who was appointed Inspector of the Royal Military Academy at Woolwich in 1772, described the use of the verb 'to animate' in his *An Universal Military Dictionary* (1779). In late-eighteenth-century military jargon, 'animation' responded to the needs of galvanizing soldiers to overcome their fears when facing a battle, or of maintaining troops in ordered formations in the fog of war. Somewhat paradoxically, animation meant enlivening, indeed, giving life to individuals in the face of their potential death. Smith was undoubtedly aware of the word's etymological roots in Latin *animare*, which Samuel Johnson's (1755) English dictionary described as 'to quicken; to make alive; to give life to', as well as 'to give powers to; to heighten the powers or effect of any thing', and 'to encourage; to incite'. But etymology aside, noteworthy here is how a couple of hundred years before theorists like John Langshaw Austin or Gilles Deleuze, Captain

Smith recognized how linguistic utterances could shape souls and transform states of affairs. By the sheer power of discourse, Smith contended, bodies could be rendered as elastic, strong, and speedy; by the power of discourse, they could be made to perform tasks they were not able to or did not want to do. By means of what Smith called 'animation', individuals could be programmed to become operative units of the war machine.

Fast-forward about 240 years: commanders' enlivening elocutions have been replaced by more mundane logistical operations of images and sounds. We are familiar with how contemporary war machines abound with digital visuals of all sorts, especially computer-generated animations circulating on various video games and virtual reality platforms. Their programming functions have expanded from elevated cries as incitements to battle, to encompassing the whole cycle of warrior production from recruitment to post-combat therapy. The extent to which the US military, among others, today harnesses video games for training and operative purposes – ranging from drilling individual motor and reaction skills (such as shoot or no-shoot situations) to the coordination of teamwork – is common knowledge (see Lenoir and Caldwell, 2018). At the other end of the spectrum, affordable virtual reality technology applications have been developed for the treatment of the psychological traumas (what is nowadays called "post-traumatic stress disorder") arising among soldiers on duty.

What connects such present-day operations with the late-eighteenth-century commander's enunciations is one key function defining both types of animations: to render bodies and minds as plastic and prone to shaping and enhancement. This is above all a governmental function. Its goal is the 'right disposition of things arranged so as to lead to a suitable end', to use the words borrowed by Michel Foucault (2009:26) from the French Renaissance writer Guillaume de la Perrière to explain his concept of government as the administration of lived realities. I have previously discussed the governmental powers of animation with regard to the human mind as a surface on which military programming is variously executed, the genealogy of which extends back to seventeenth-century experiments with optical media, animated images, and mental influence (Väliaho, 2017). In what follows, let me take a slightly different direction, and explore animation's potential in the preparation for war, and in transforming the surface of the earth into a 'fully actionable space' for military operations.

Consider the US Army's recent investment in 'synthetic training environments' (see Judson, 2019) that combine three-dimensional virtual topographic maps with training simulation platforms and software (Figure 7.1). The virtual maps are part of the army's ambitious programme called 'One World Terrain', to 'provide detailed 3D maps of anywhere the US military might need to train, deploy, or fight' (Freedberg, Jr, 2019). Its development outsourced to private companies, One World Terrain is

Figure 7.1: US Army's 'mixed reality' environment

Source: USC Institute for Creative Technologies.

meant to procure a single database of three-dimensional topographic maps sufficiently detailed for training simulations and mission planning. 'The idea', we are told, 'is to be able to click on any place on a virtual globe and go there, sometimes with door-knob fidelity. Soldiers can then train virtually in an exact environment in which they can expect to operate in reality' (Judson, 2018). Compiled from the sensor readings of drones during intelligence and surveillance missions around the globe, among other data, One World Terrain is meant to allow combat training in an augmented, or 'mixed', reality environment, which resembles a multiplayer gaming platform where live gamers mingle with algorithmic 'intelligent entities' (representing enemies as well as civilians).

The smallest and furthest corner of the earth, if not ideally the whole planet at once, can thus be animated as a virtual battleground, mixing the real with anticipated and hypothetical events and outcomes, and expanding the state of war potentially anywhere at any time. These animations are primarily purposed for spatiotemporal and cognitive management: to play out a spectrum of possible and/or probable events and thereby ideally weed out contingencies, thwarting the spontaneity of the real. And they adhere to a particular concept of the plasticity of the real – a concept according to which the course of events and their consequences can be subjected to influence and manipulation.

The genealogy of such animations is two-fold at least, extending to the later eighteenth century and even earlier. While war games have historically been used to simulate and therefore manage randomness and contingency, topographic visualizations, on the other hand, have aided in generating virtual workspaces where actual data has been employed in simulating hypothetical scenarios (see Engberg-Pedersen, 2015:103–83). The following historical excursion will start from the latter, tracking the US Army's synthetic training environments functionally back to an eighteenth-century military cartographic practice, and then further back to seventeenth-century camera obscuras, the key 'mixed reality' devices of early modernity that contributed to animating the world as a repository of data. Overall, the following paragraphs investigate the historical development of the perceptual and cognitive assemblages which today's military applications partly derive from.

The survey

In 1747, 16-year-old Paul Sandby, who later became one of England's most celebrated landscape artists, joined a small group of young men in mapping the Highlands of Scotland. In the aftermath of the Jacobite risings, the English army's Board of Ordnance had initiated a comprehensive survey of Scotland, assigning its engineers to 'make Draughts and Estimates of what Works would be needfull to be done effectually to secure' this part of the kingdom (Anderson, 2009:76). The military survey was to facilitate the planning of operations in the location, while also supporting the governmental programme of annexing peasant holdings and common lands into large private estates (Bonehill, Daniels and Alfrey 2009:14). During the summer, surveyors travelled across the country with their measuring and drawing instruments. During the winter, in the Board of Ordnance's Drawing Room in Edinburgh Castle, the records and sketches of data from the field were compiled into maps (Anderson and Fleet, 2018:118–19).

Sandby was working in an already well-established environment of various types of apparatuses and techniques designed for producing mixed realities where symbolic worlds were projected and mapped onto the actual one. Perspectival and cartographic grids were perhaps the most dominant ones. The latter facilitated mapping out the earth onto a two-dimensional surface with a geometrical grid of meridians and parallels from a viewpoint that combined human, earthly agency with a panoptic overlook. The cartographic grid, as Christian Jacob (2006:2) reminds us, projected 'an order of reason onto the world and [forced] it to conform to a graphic rationale, […] a conceptual geometry'. Designed for the expansion of empires, the grid set up an intellectual frame that fostered visual harmonizing, systematization, and uniformization, indeed, 'optical coherence' (as Jacob puts it) against disorder, chance, and the unforeseen. On the other hand, the perspectival grid, introduced by Alberti in *De pictura* in the 1430s, constituted a plane intersecting the visual pyramid and aided in determining the positions, proportions, and scale of objects depicted by projecting and mapping them on a two-dimensional surface, and, furthermore, in securing and immobilizing the position of the viewer into a fixed point at the apex of the visual pyramid. The perspectival grid, notably, contributed to the programme of rearranging space according to geometrical rules. In this sense, perspectival projections coincided functionally with cartographic ones (Cubitt, 2014:214; Edgerton, 1975:106–23). Both perspective and cartographic projections made spatial relations measurable. Both, essentially, reduced things and beings into purportedly objective epistemological content, which allowed the world's subsequent translation into repositories of information, or what we today call 'databases'.

Such was also one of the military survey's key objectives. Diverse visual information on grids and rules was compiled into a gigantic twelve-by-eight-metre map by means of which this part of the country, 'so very inaccessible by nature, should be thoroughly explored and laid open', as William Roy (1785:386), the Scottish military engineer in charge of the survey, put it. Yet the views drawn by Sandby did not simply adhere to the rules of conventional cartographic and/or perspective projection. For Sandby – what is important to the topic of this essay – cartographic visualization joined a different kind of purpose to geometrical ordering: the perceptual and cognitive translation of the real into an actionable and animated environment.

Take, for example, Sandby's 'Plan of the Castle of Dunbarton' from around 1747 (Figure 7.2). A bird's-eye view of the rock where the castle of Dumbarton is located (near Glasgow), which juxtaposes a schematic plan of buildings, walls, and cannon stands with the location's topography, is accompanied by two smaller pictures. Emphasizing a serene rural landscape, the latter unfold single perspectival views, or 'prospects', onto the castle from the front and back sides as seen across the River Clyde. The aerial view presented in the main illustration, however, is much less conventional in style. It strangely emerges from what appears as a perspectival view onto the surrounding landscape in the upper part of the picture, and combines a ground plan of the fortification with an oblique projection purposed to portray the rock in relief. Oblique views had become commonplace in military illustrations of fortifications and other architectural elevations by the early seventeenth century (Scolari, 2012:6–9, 287–300). Sandby's approach, however, was not to rely on the abstracted straight lines of the 'soldier's perspective', but to visualize the castle's location as a dense network of topographical features with differing contours, from steep flanks to relatively flat terrains (see Kaplan, 2018:57, 64). Skilled brushwork careful about detail sought to provide information about the rock's dramatic heights by means of shading, in a sense, to animate the rock's topographic features with hachures. John Bonehill and Stephen Daniels (2017:230) point out Sandby's 'virtuoso style of terrain drawing' where aligned brushstrokes were used to indicate the direction of slopes, and graduation of tones steepness and height. Here, Sandby's goal, it appears, was to render topographical features in a perceptually 'direct' and embodied, or actionable, manner – a point I will return to.

Figure 7.2: Paul Sandby, *Plan of the Castle of Dunbarton*, c.1747

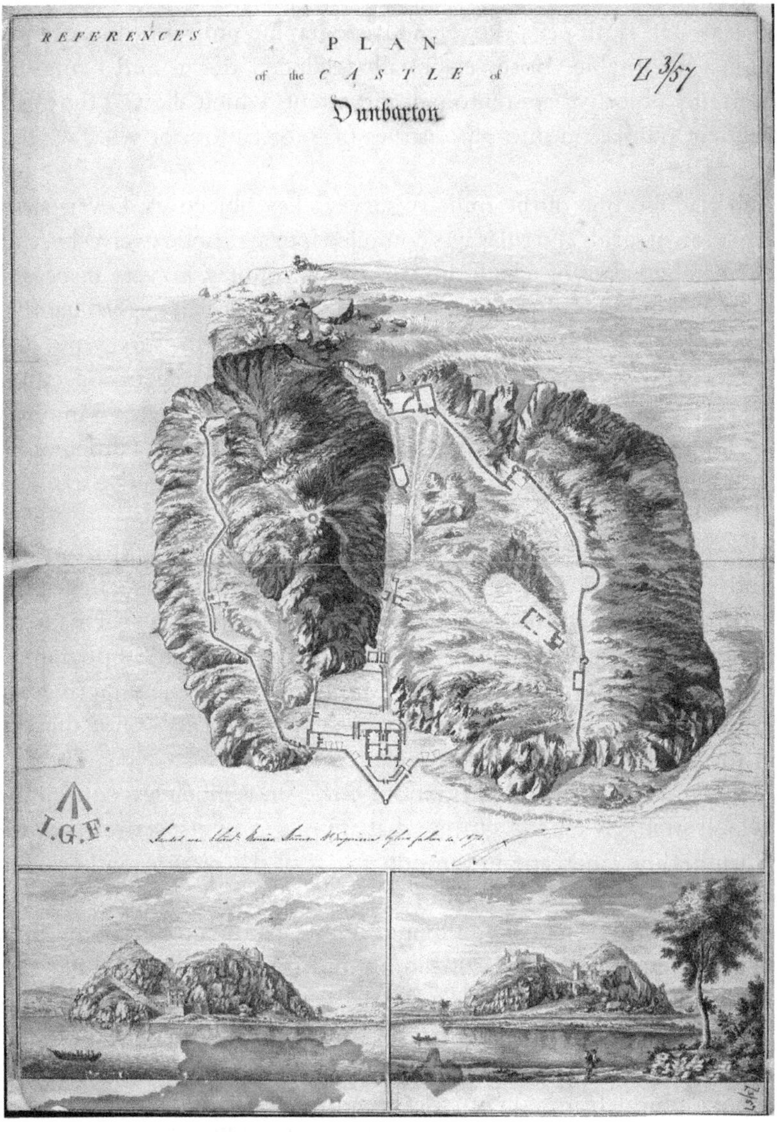

Source: British Library MS.1649 Z.03/57. © National Library of Scotland.

Taken together, the Dumbarton Castle sheet puts forward an intricate cognitive composition, which approaches its subject from multiple perspectives combining first-person vistas with a diagram of the fortification, as well as a bird's-eye view of the location's topographic features. The military survey's sheets were drawn for tactical and operational purposes; they were to aid in strategic mastery in occupying and governing, in addition to the planning of potential battles. David Watson, who was appointed Deputy Quartermaster-General in Scotland in 1747, explained the survey's goals: 'As the Encampments, Marches, and every possible movement proper for an Army to make in the field, entirely depend on a just and thorough knowledge of the Country, the greatest care & Exactness should be observed in Examining minutely the Face of that Country' (quoted in Anderson and Fleet, 2018:119). With its visual intelligence of topographic features (the 'face') of terrains, the military survey strove to turn landscapes and locations into what one might call, borrowing from today's video games jargon, 'fully rendered actionable spaces' (Galloway, 2006:63). The visualization of movement was pivotal to the military survey's pursuits. Views such as Sandby's onto the Dumbarton Castle implicated a range of implicit vectors and trajectories – possible lines of attack and defence manoeuvres, 'prospects and refuges, vantage points and lines of fire' (Bonehill, Daniels and Alfrey, 2009:17). Of course, such movements were only potential, located in the beholder's imagination as the capacity to reckon and, indeed, mentally animate virtual actions based on the information presented on the data sheet.

Caren Kaplan associates the survey's visual products with ideas about the commander's scopic and intuitive powers in vogue during the period, crystallized in the concept of '*coup d'oeil*' that meant the 'almost mystical belief in the innate capacity of gifted individuals to take in details of a landscape in an instant and to transform this information into actionable data' (Kaplan, 2018:55). In his *An Universal Military Dictionary*, Captain George Smith discussed the commander's genius in terms of the 'quick eye', which enabled the commander 'to judge of an advantageous post, of a manoeuvre to be made, and of a good disposition for the troops, whether with respect to that of enemy, or to the situation or nature of the country' (Smith, 1779:iv). Topographic visualizations were precisely meant to assist the 'quick eye'; that is to say, the commander's intuitive understanding of strategy and situational awareness. But insofar as they were to turn things and beings into actionable data, to thwart the world of unknowns and contingencies for optimizing operationality, their task was also, to this end, to formalize or 'proceduralize' perception. Turning the visual field into vectors of potential movement, they were to exclude any additional element of interpretation and/or imagination. In this sense, we could label a visualization such as Sandby's of Dumbarton Castle as a 'data-animation', referring to images that render the world as actionable informational content, and contribute to the development of a systemic mode of cognition that appropriates this data as a functional element in a governmental procedure.

Tracing shadows

Using the concept of 'data' to describe the military survey's concerns and outcomes is not entirely anachronistic. While the concept may today be most ordinarily associated with mathematical information specific to electronic computing, 'data', as David Rosenberg shows, was in fact introduced into English language already in the seventeenth century, mainly in the context of theology. The concept was naturalized over the course of the eighteenth century when its connotations also shifted to referring to 'facts in evidence determined by experiment, experience, or collection' (Rosenberg, 2013:33). It might not be an entire coincidence that, at the same moment in time, practices and techniques of gleaning and aggregating pictorial information based on observation expanded and evolved as part of the European colonial project (within the pursuits of the Royal Society of London in England, for example), while the epistemic nature of visual images evolved into making sense of real-world objects and processes by correlating sensory information with conceptual schemata and frames – the most notable example here being the pictorial catalogue accompanying Denis Diderot and Jean le Rond d'Alembert's *Encyclopédie* project from the latter half of the eighteenth century (see Bender and Marrinan, 2010). While these developments, to be sure, predated the rise of the great statistical and bureaucratic machineries of the nineteenth century – machineries where also technologies of visualization, mainly photography, played an intrinsic role (see Sekula, 1986) – their impetus was in the mapping and diagramming of the world into an ideally systematic and standardized repertory of actionable facts.

The notion of trace was important to such an enterprise of recording and collecting visual 'facts in evidence', and particularly palpable in Sandby's black hachures seeking to minutely delineate the shadows of slopes, dips, and elevations on the Dumbarton rock. This concept also takes the military survey's topographic data collection practices back to their pictorial roots and archaic traditions of picture-making revolving around the concepts of shadow and animation. Consider Pliny's legend about the origins of painting, for example. 'All agree', Pliny expounded in book 35 of *Natural History*, 'that [the art of painting] began with tracing an outline round a man's shadow [*umbra hominis lineis circumducta*]' (Pliny, 1961:271). Further on, he elaborated on the story of the potter Putades and his daughter who was in love with a young man. Just before her lover was bound abroad – we are not told where or for what reason he was leaving – the daughter 'drew in outline on the wall the shadow of his face thrown by a lamp'. Putades then pressed clay on his daughter's drawing and 'made a relief, which he hardened by exposure to fire with the rest of his pottery' (Pliny, 1961:373). Notably, the young man's 'clay likeness' (*similitudo ex argilla*) was afterwards preserved in the Shrine of Nymphs – suggesting that the young man had not returned from his journey, and that his sculpted semblance had instead become a cult object (Stoichita, 1997:18–19).

Noteworthy in Pliny's story is how it associates both drawing and clay modelling with a single origin: shadow projection. First, the young woman 'captured' (*circumscripsit*) the image of her lover as a shadow cast on a wall, creating an externalization of his being. Second, the woman's father gave this outline volume and substance; the drawn shadow acquired a body. From sketching to pottery, the young woman's lover gradually fused with his shadow, which offered a spectral substitute for the absent original. What resulted from the collaboration between Putades and his daughter, as Victor Stoichita (1997:18) notes, was 'the symbolic creation of a "living" double, a surrogate figure'. Animation was critical for this surrogate to become alive – animation in the archaic sense of attributing an inorganic being with the qualities of living through emotional, mnemonic, or other kinds of attachment. Pliny's story is indeed about love, longing, and loss, corroborating Hans Belting's insight that every type of image perception is to be considered basically an act of animation whereby beholders enliven pictures as part of their embodied and mental reality; 'whereby we give life to images that we want to believe in as living' (Belting, 2011:130). And, as Gerhard Wolf points out, Pliny's story 'should be read within an anthropology of the shadow in the classical world (and in other ancient societies), where the insubstantial eidola of the dead were called "shadows"' (Wolf, 1999:61). The Greeks' *Hades* was populated by shadows, which were immaterial images of the dead who had lost their bodies. Pictorial creations, on the other hand, as Pliny's legend tells us, re-embodied the dead, which became alive – animated – through affective investment.

This anthropology of image, shadow, and animation entangled in the mystery of absence and death seems distant to the kinds of concerns Sandby was tackling as part of the military survey. Sandby's shadings animated an enterprise the objective of which was to conquer, colonize, circumscribe, and defend. More generally, they participated in the modern visual concept of shadow that links with the reproduction of the actual and the 'objective' scrutiny of the visible. The proper rendering of shading and cast shadows was critical to perspectival imaging and the adjacent idea of verisimilitude (the gaze as a measure of truth) – what Roger de Piles (1708:34) in his authoritative handbook of perspective painting considered the picture's credible appearance of truth (*vraisemblance*). De Piles (1708:381–3) emphasized the importance of shadows to the expression of the unity and harmony of objects (Figure 7.3). Leonardo da Vinci already pointed out how shadow was 'the medium through which the body reveals its form' (quoted in Belting, 2011:17). Optically accurate visualization of shadow also carried out more technical functions, above all in skiagraphy, a subgenre of linear perspective focused on the two-dimensional representation of calculated

Figure 7.3: Illustration from Roger de Piles, *Cours de peinture par principes* (1708)

projected shadows. Treatises dealing with skiagraphy, such as Edme-Sébastian Jeaurat's *Traité de perspective à l'usage des artistes* (1750), proliferated in France in the eighteenth century as they responded to the demands of the developing technical culture of mining, engineering, architecture, and military science (Baxandall, 1995:84–8). Precise methods of shadow projection were needed for registering spatial relations and planning distributions of light and shade: indeed, the government of the 'right disposition of things' in a visually functional sense.

This brief glance suggests how the tracing of shadows, in the modern sense, was indispensable to what Svetlana Alpers (1983:135) calls the 'art of describing', an art that wanted to arrive at epistemic certainty about appearances through attentive observation as well as by blurring 'distinctions between measuring, recording, and picturing'. Shadows were mobilized in an epistemic campaign over the real through observation and reckoning. A key optical technology promoting this campaign during the seventeenth and eighteenth centuries was, as Alpers points out, the camera obscura – a machine generating animated projected pictures that, for seventeenth- and eighteenth-century observers, displayed 'the momentary, unfixed aspect of nature's passing show' (Alpers, 1983:13). The camera obscura set up a specific realm of machinic perception and cognition, which, to quote Martin Kemp's vivid description at length:

> produces condensed enhancement of tone and colour, providing subtle intensification without harshness or glare. Nuances of light and shade which seem too diffuse or slight to register in the original scene are somehow clarified, and tonal effects gain a new degree of coherence. The shapes of forms, miniaturized in such a way that they seem to be condensed to their very essence, acquire a crystalline clarity. Striking juxtapositions of scale at different planes, which we remain largely unconscious in the actual scene, become compellingly apparent. (Kemp, 1990:193)

In early modern Europe, the camera obscura virtualized one's incipient concept of the real into a mechanical perception – a trajectory of development that also has been integral to the contemporary concept and practice of augmented reality. For instance, Constantijn Huygens, father of the famous Dutch scientist Christiaan Huygens, exclaimed after witnessing a catoptric camera obscura shown to him during his trip to London, in 1622, by the engineer and experimenter Cornelis Drebbel: 'All painting is dead in comparison, for here is life itself, or something more elevated, if one could find the words for it' (Huygens, 1911:94; my translation). Huygens gave expression to a common sentiment about how directly and accurately, beyond the confines of verbal description and even human vision, the device was able to depict, indeed, trace the movements, colours, and shapes of the natural world. The camera obscura's projections equalled naturalness and 'life itself', surpassing techniques of picture-making relying on the human hand in their perceptual objectivity and truthfulness. As such, the apparatus' screen spurred the development of a mode of knowing that wanted to rid itself of the knowing subject while keeping firmly grounded in the observation of 'facts in evidence'.

The camera obscura's screen contributed to the kind of proceduralization, even automation, of perception and cognition discussed earlier in relation to Sandby's topographic work. From early on, the optical medium found one of its key early applications in the field of surveying. Constantijn Huygens' son Contantijn Jr. utilized the camera obscura in producing topographical drawings while serving with Willem III on his campaign against the French in 1672 (Figure 7.4), probably in the vanguard of operationalizing vision for military purposes by means of optical media. Here, Contantijn Jr. reiterated a topographic sensibility palpable already in Johannes Kepler's use of the camera obscura for the world's reproduction in pictures, as reported by the British ambassador Sir Henry Wotton in a letter to Francis Bacon from December 1620. Wotton visited Kepler at his home in Linz and was fascinated by a landscape drawing he saw in Kepler's study. To Wotton's query about how he had made it, Kepler replied: '*Non tanquam pictor, sed tanquam Mathematicus*' ('not as a painter but as a mathematician'). 'He hath a little black Tent', Wotton explained the secret behind the drawing:

Figure 7.4: Constantijn Huygens, Jr., *View of the Ijssel*, 1672

Source: © The Samuel Courtauld Trust, The Courtauld Gallery, London.

which he can suddenly set up where he will in a Field, and it is convertible (like a Wind-Mill) to Quarters at Pleasure, capable of not much more than one Man, as I conceive, and perhaps at no great ease; exactly close and dark, save at one hole, about an Inch and a half in the *Diameter*, to which he applies a long perspective Trunk, with a Convex glass fitted to the said hole, and the concave taken out at the other end, which extendeth to about the middle of this erected Tent, through which the visible Radiations of all the Objects without, are intromitted, falling upon a Paper, which is accommodated to receive them, and so he traceth them with his Pen in their natural Appearance, turning his little Tent round by Degrees, till he hath designed the whole Aspect of the Field. (Wotton, 1685:300)

The drawings Kepler drafted, crouching in his portable camera obscura, concretized his notion of *pictura* that referred to the traces of objects projected onto a screen – a key conceptual innovation whereby Kepler challenged the optical theories of his times (see, for example, Smith, 2015:322–72). Kepler's gesture was to rid optical theory of ontological speculation on the emanation of likenesses in favour of a geometrical account, which was based on the premise that light was the only agent of optical phenomena. For Kepler, images were products of light, including images on the retina. 'Since hitherto an Image [*imago*] has been a Being of the reason, now let the figures of objects that really exist on paper or upon another surface be called pictures [*picturae*]', Kepler (2000:210) wrote, making an important distinction between *pictura*, a projected image that 'really exists', and *imago*, an image existing in the mind; between optics and psychology. The *imago*, Kepler (2000:77) claimed, was 'practically nothing in itself, and should rather be called imagination'. The retinal picture, like the camera obscura's projected image, on the other hand, was a causal effect of light, and had in principle nothing to do with how the world was interpreted by the subject. The camera obscura's animations implemented a model of what one could call (not without a certain contradiction, however) 'subjectless' perception purified of mental, interpretive content. As Alpers (1983:36) argues, Kepler's concept of *pictura* 'deanthropomorphized vision', severing connections between seeing and imagining. Not surprisingly, this machine-based model of perception resonated closely with the concerns of topographic visualization. Kepler's tent camera obscura, Wotton wrote to Bacon, could find 'good use made of it for Chorography'; that is to say, 'the art of describing or mapping a region or district', as the dictionary definition goes. Kepler's *picturae* could be considered an early version of the concept of visual 'data' – something objective and autonomous produced, or 'gleaned' mechanically as it were.

Later in his career, when working in commercial landscape art, Sandby turned the camera obscura's subjectless animated visions into an aesthetic axiom. 'All [his] endeavors', Sandby's son remarked, 'were to give to his drawings a similar appearance to that seen in a camera–obscura, and when looked at with this impression, their beauty becomes very conspicuous; the truth in the reflected lights, the clearness in the shadows, the aerial tint and keeping in the distances, and skies' (Sandby, 1811:440). This quasi-mechanical principle of visual clarity and truth devoid of subjective impression could already be located in young Sandby's military topographical drawings. Both the survey's charts and the camera obscura's screen were purposed to trace the world as a surface of data, outlining things and beings as 'facts in evidence'. Both, in this respect, presented a mere distant echo of Putades' daughter's nocturnal drawing session. Where the daughter's sketch of her lover's profile ended up being eternalized as a clay likeness and animated as the person's virtual double through memory and affect, the survey's charts and the camera obscura's projections were ideally cleaned of any supplementary mental content. The latter operationalized pictorial tracing not as an entry point for bonding with spirits but as a means of survey and scrutiny to disclose potential spaces of action with an optimal 'clearness in the shadows'.

Plasticity

Let us return to the 'synthetic training environments' purposed by the US Army to turn topographic maps into virtual battlefields. Here images have, to be sure, become visual after-effects of computer algorithms; but beyond the digital per se, their perceptual and cognitive arrangements reiterate old(er) histories. At least, the US Army's 'mixed realities' find an immediate and significant genealogy in modern visualization practices purposed for the Western powers' military-financial expansion over the globe. Consider how, even in formal terms, Sandby's topographic sheets are echoed in the army's new augmented reality systems: the sheets' first-person vistas onto (real or fictive) locations doubled by '3D' topographic renderings have now grown into virtual maps and other kinds of data screens superimposed onto one's perceptual field – an arrangement that basically emulates popular first-person shooter interfaces. The eighteenth-century military survey's data animations feeding into the government of the globe thus become remediated in the augmented reality technology's ludic frame. The US Army's 'One World Terrain' seeks to make temporally or spatially distant locations present as enactive content akin to Sandby's topographic charts that multiplied viewpoints and animated details in view of operability.

Both instances are (or were) epistemically predicated on making the world available for action, by adapting the observer cognitively as an agent in the represented surroundings. Around the same time as the military survey of

Scotland, models of perception and experience emerged in English thought that sought to reconfigure the mind's relation to its environment, insisting that seeing was not to be simply associated with (geometric) representation but understood as embedded in the world, close to objects and surfaces, changing constantly in a moving viewpoint (see Kramnick, 2018:57–97). This eighteenth-century 'aesthetics of perceptual presence' within which the senses were above all purposed to make the world available, as Jonathan Kramnick points out, in many ways anticipated present-day accounts in philosophy and cognitive science of perception 'as a kind of skilled attunement to what the world affords' (Kramnick, 2018:60, 62). For instance, Alva Noë's (2004) 'enactive' concept associates perception with the body's skill to move about and probe the environment. Experience, in this account, is a complex dynamic between the perceiver and the world where the latter gradually makes itself present and available for action. Such a concept, one should note, comes across as particularly apt for making sense of perception in augmented or 'mixed' reality environments where images are no longer to be considered more or less static representations of an external or internal reality but in themselves as hybrid worlds to explore. These environments are animated as sites of action – as surfaces that enable the execution of a movement or an operation – and perceptually speaking their difference from our actual physical surroundings is merely a matter of degree (see Noë, 2004:224–5).

Yet these environments, crucially, differ from the actual one in their fundamental lack of facticity. The US Army's synthetic training grounds, say, present the realization of a possibility. They are based on a conviction according to which, through repeated rehearsal, actual outcomes can be determined before they are materialized. They embody a particular perception of the *plasticity* of the real, which leans on the powers of data animation to shape reality into a desired design. The concept of plasticity often focuses our attention to the individual's capacity to adapt and reshape under external influence (as in 'neural plasticity', for instance), but I am employing it to account for animated projections of a new kind of form or quality, not just on the subject, but onto processes and relations.

In the context of data practices, the history of the concept of plasticity goes back to the latter half of the seventeenth century at the latest, and the work of Sir William Petty in particular, who famously promoted his ideas about economic government based on what Petty called 'political arithmetic'. Petty's ideal was a governmental rationality that worked in terms of quantitative data – 'Number, Weight, or Measure' (Petty, 1899:244) – based on gradually amassed numerical records about production, consumption, trade, longevity, and so forth. In Petty's reasoning, 'facts in evidence' needed to be gleaned for the proper understanding of tendencies and probabilities, which were to serve the basis of an economically sound rule. But the key purpose of this projection of the world as data charts and maps, for Petty, was also to actively intervene into and refashion demographic and social processes. Data observation was to become part of what Petty (1899:157) called 'political alchemy', that is to say, the work of 'transmuting one People into the other' (for example, transforming the poor Irish population into a successful English colony). Here Petty was using an old alchemical concept – transmutation – of turning base metals into precious ones, a concept suggesting the plasticity of things and beings to readily change not only their form but also their substance.

Petty's political alchemy might appear as far removed from the visuality of digital and other kinds of animations, even if it shares a colonial history with Sandby's topographic charts and the US Army's 'One World Terrain'. Yet the concept discloses a crucial point about how data, including visual 'facts', should be understood as a form of animation – and animation today considered part of the larger histories of Western political, economic, and military practices of rendering the real as supple and plastic for desired transformations, or, to use eighteenth-century jargon, perpetual 'improvements'.

References

Alpers, S. (1983) *The Art of Describing: Dutch Art in the Seventeenth Century*, Chicago: The University of Chicago Press.

Anderson, C.J. (2009) *Constructing the Military Landscape: The Board of Ordnance Maps and Plans of Scotland, 1689–1815*, PhD dissertation, University of Edinburgh.

Anderson, C. and Fleet, C. (2018) *Scotland: Defending the Nation, Mapping the Military Landscape*, Edinburgh: Birlinn for the National Library of Scotland.

Baxandall, M. (1995) *Shadows and Enlightenment*, New Haven: Yale University Press.

Belting, H. (2011) *An Anthropology of Images: Picture, Medium, Body*, translated by T. Dunlap, Princeton: Princeton University Press.

Bender, J. and Marrinan, M. (2010) *The Culture of Diagram*, Stanford: Stanford University Press.

Bonehill, J. and Daniels, S. (2017) 'Designs on the Landscape: Paul and Thomas Sandby in North Britain', *Oxford Art Journal*, 40(2): 223–48.

Bonehill, J., Daniels, S. and Alfrey, N. (2009) 'Paul Sandby: Picturing Britain', in J. Bonehill and S. Daniels (eds) *Paul Sandby: Picturing Britain*, London: Royal Academy of Arts, pp 12–27.

Cubitt, S. (2014) *The Practice of Light: A Genealogy of Visual Technologies from Prints to Pixels*, Cambridge, MA: MIT Press.

Edgerton, S.Y., Jr. (1975) *The Renaissance Rediscovery of Linear Perspective*, New York: Harper & Row.

Engberg-Pedersen, A. (2015) *Empire of Chance: The Napoleonic Wars and the Disorder of Things*, Cambridge, MA: Harvard University Press.

Foucault, M. (2009) *Security, Territory, Population: Lectures at the Collège de France, 1977–78*, edited by M. Senellart, translated by G. Burchell, London: Palgrave Macmillan.

Freedberg, S.J., Jr. (2019) 'Special Ops Using Army's Prototype 3D Maps on Missions: Gervais', Breaking Defense, 13 October [online], Available from: https://breakingdefense.com/2019/10/ste-army-3d-mapping-software-so-good-special-ops-uses-it-for-missions/ [Accessed 15 January 2020].

Galloway, A.R. (2006) *Gaming: Essays on Algorithmic Culture*, Minneapolis: University of Minnesota Press.

Huygens, C. (1911) *Briefwisseling, volume 1: 1608–1634*, edited by J.A. Worp, The Hague: Martinus Nijhoff.

Jacob, C. (2006) *The Sovereign Map: Theoretical Approaches in Cartography throughout History*, edited by E.H. Dahl, translated by T. Conley, Chicago: The University of Chicago Press.

Johnson, S. (1755) *A Dictionary of the English Language*, 2 volumes. London.

Judson, J. (2018) 'Army creating virtual world for multidomain battle training', Defense News, 26 March [online], Available from: https://www.defensenews.com/digital-show-dailies/global-force-symposium/2018/03/26/army-creating-virtual-world-for-multidomain-battle-training/ [Accessed 15 January 2020].

Judson, J. (2019) 'US Army's jumping to the next level in virtual training', Defense News, 17 May [online], Available from: https://www.defensenews.com/land/2019/05/17/us-armys-jumping-to-next-level-in-virtual-training-world/ [Accessed 15 January 2020].

Kaplan, C. (2018) *Aerial Aftermaths: Wartime from Above*, Durham, NC: Duke University Press.

Kemp, M. (1990) *The Science of Art: Optical Themes in Western Art from Brunelleschi to Seurat*, New Haven, CT: Yale University Press.

Kepler, J. (2000) *Optics: Paralipomena to Witelo & Optical Part of Astronomy*, translated by W.H. Donahue, Santa Fe: Green Lion Press.

Kramnick, J. (2018) *Paper Minds: Literature and the Ecology of Consciousness*, Chicago: The University of Chicago Press.

Lenoir, T. and Caldwell, L. (2018) *The Military-Entertainment Complex*, Cambridge, MA: Harvard University Press.

Noë, A. (2004) *Action in Perception*, Cambridge, MA: MIT Press.

Petty, W. (1899) *The Economic Writings of Sir William Petty, volume 1*, edited by C.H. Hull, Cambridge: Cambridge University Press.

de Piles, R. (1708) *Cours de peinture par principes*, Paris: Jacques Estienne.

Pliny (1961) *Natural History, volume IX: Books 33–35*, translated by H. Rackham, Cambridge, MA: Harvard University Press.

Rosenberg, D. (2013) 'Data before the Fact', in Lisa Gitelman (ed) *'Raw Data' Is an Oxymoron*, Cambridge, MA: MIT Press, pp 15–40.

Roy, W. (1785) 'An Account of the Measurement of a Base on Hounslow-Heath', *Philosophical Transactions of the Royal Society*, 75: 385–480.

Sandby, T.P. (1811) 'Memoir of the Late Paul Sandby, Esq', *The Monthly Magazine* (June 1): 437–41.

Scolari, M. (2012) *Oblique Drawing: A History of Anti-Perspective*, translated by J.C. Palandri, Cambridge, MA: MIT Press.

Sekula, A. (1986) 'The Body and the Archive', *October*, 39: 3–64.

Smith, G. (1779) *An Universal Military Dictionary: A Copious Explanation of the Technical Terms etc. Used in the Equipment, Machinery, Movements, and Military Operations of an Army*, London.

Smith, A.M. (2015) *From Sight to Light: The Passage from Ancient to Modern Optics*, Chicago: The University of Chicago Press.

Stoichita, V.I. (1997) *A Short History of the Shadow*, translated by A.-M. Glasheen, London: Reaktion Books.

Väliaho, P. (2017) 'Animation and the Powers of Plasticity', *Animation*, 12(3): 259–71.

Wolf, G. (1999) 'The Origins of Painting', *Res: Anthropology and Aesthetics*, 36: 60–78.

Wotton, H. (1685) *Reliquiae Wottonianae, or, a Collection of Lives, Letters, Poems*, London.

8

Chronoclasm: Real–Time Data Animation

Sean Cubitt

It is only a slight exaggeration to say that Fordism crashed into its own projection of infinite progress; and that in 2007 financialization smashed into the foreclosure of the present by debt. Chronoclasms are crises of time that occur when practices and concepts of time come into contradiction. There is undoubtedly an ontological time of the quantum foam subtending perceptible reality. Likewise there is equally undoubtedly a geometric administration of time that we inherit from Newton and Kant. The clash between the sovereign authority of the clock that is the material heartbeat of every computer and every network and the bubbling billions of subatomic interactions enables another time to emerge, the time we call history. Into this third, historical form of time emerge ideas about the ontology of time and practices for managing it that are themselves historically mutable. Close attention to techniques of animation, the art of giving movement to inanimate pictures, can give us a privileged entry to the analysis of chronoclasm as crisis and as the underpinning structure of time under capital.

Noise and abstraction

The sun is light–giving, life–giving, but also blinding and dangerous. NASA's Solar Dynamics Observatory (SDO) carries several instruments designed to cope with its visible and invisible spectra. Among them, the Atmospheric Imaging Assembly (AIA) measures solar light in ten wavelengths. NASA and Lockheed Martin, the constructor, upload daily movies from the data. It is slightly pushing the terminology to call these real–time animations, but they are clearly animations because they produce apparent motion from stop–motion capture, the earliest animation technique in cinema (Crafton, 1982/1993,

1990), and approximate to real time, especially if we consider each daily movie a component of a much larger animation of the sun's activity accumulated in NASA's databases. Indeed, the delay only makes apparent that terrestrial sunlight is always eight minutes old, and the telemetry from the SDO likewise. Animation is always an intervening process.

The AIA animations condense hours of individual images caught 12 seconds apart in the 120 angstrom waveband. When a flare arrives (shortly after the 3:30 mark on the video from 9 September 2017 – do look away if you're susceptible to flashing images), the electromagnetic pulse creates interference patterns and causes the sensors to shut down between frames.[1] The MPEG codec used to compress and decompress the images for transmission struggles to fill the gaps. Such noise is an intrinsic element of observation. It arises from external events like this solar flare in 2017, and from internal conditions of the equipment of capture and transmission, constantly generating and trying to codify noise. Data animations are necessarily also noise-reduction and noise-management systems. By analogy with Mary Douglas's definition of dirt (Douglas, 1966:2), noise is data in the wrong place. It is such anomalous data that, since Galileo's discovery of the moons of Jupiter, has driven both cosmological enquiry and its pursuit of ever more sophisticated instruments.

Noise has equally been a characteristic of animation since the pioneering animations of Blackton and Cohl. The miraculous year of 1914–15, that saw the introduction of a series of devices like pin registration for controlling noise in production systems, also introduced new possibilities for noisy systems, notably in the first moves towards rotoscoping and multiplane rostrum cameras.[2] The anarchic spirit of cartoons was always in dialogue with controlled industrial production at houses like Disney. This dialogue continues in the automation of foreground-background parallax, outline thickness, character gait models and in-betweening (discussed below) and in recent motion capture devices like the Xsens MVN, a Lycra suit fitted with seventeen motion-capture sensors, capable of animating avatars in real-time games engines to develop animated performances.

The archaeology of the Xsens mappable bodysuit takes us back to Etienne-Jules Marey's motion capture suit (Dagognet, 1992; Mamber, 2006), initially propounded as a scientific instrument in pursuit of more-than-human observation of human motion, but rapidly assimilated into the quasi-science of Frank and Lillian Gilbreth's time and motion studies, where factory work became the subject of disciplinary techniques guiding workers away from distraction and irrelevant gestures (Rabinbach, 1990; Crary, 1999; Canales, 2009) – in short, from noise. If only Foucault had thought of using Marey's instrument as the metaphorical technology of *Discipline and Punish*...

Motion capture, mo-cap for short, follows the 1914 inventions in its devotion to the Gilbreths' credo of efficiency and economy. Wrapping an animated shell around a wireframe capture of a performer gives films like the forthcoming *Avatar* sequels rapidly realized effects, swiftly quality-controlled through the production chain, and easily assimilated into the workflow, especially of animation industry software leaders like Adobe and Autodesk. A related process – a photographic shell applied to a digitally generated entity, known as a sprite – gives digital effects the apparent grit and scars of authenticity that they have sought since Adobe provided its very first plug-in, a lens flare, to make entirely artificial shots look as if they had been made with the aid of a camera by replicating the most egregious noise that cameras produce. Animating from mo-cap works in the opposite direction, abstracting from the idiosyncrasies of performance a simplified, rarefied and, crucially, replicable essence. Abstraction, the process of abstracting, is as integral to real-time data animation as is the noise it aims at excluding.

The intertwining of these operations is clearer when we take the original metaphor of noise literally. Alexander G. Kosovichev's solar sonifications developed from one of NASA's earlier helioseismographic projects, this time derived from 40 days of observations from the Michelson Doppler Imager processed by Kosovichev, who started 'with doppler velocity data, averaged over the solar disk, so that only modes of low angular degree [...] remained' (Stanford Solar Center, 1997). Subsequent processing removed spacecraft motion effects, instrument tuning, and some spurious points. Then Kosovichev filtered the data at about 3 mHz to select clean sound waves. Finally, he interpolated over the missing data and sped it up a factor 42,000 to bring it into the range of human hearing. The slow-developing harmonies of these recordings required averaging the original data, removal of system-generated interference, selection, interpolation, and scaling, premised on judgements of what constituted 'spurious' data: again, something we might describe as data in the wrong place, or perhaps (in the case of echoes, for example) in the wrong time. To the degree that this was an aesthetic exercise, these operations are as formal as Bach's reversals and inversions in the composition of a fugue; but to the extent that it had and still has some observational kudos, the exclusion of internal instrument noise and external supergranulation are processes that are as intensely disciplinary as matching playback to the capabilities of a human ear. Supergranules are solar convection cells over 30,000 kilometres. Even allowing for the immense size of the sun, ignoring features of this scale seems remiss *unless* the choice is indeed about the pleasure of listening, a pleasure which for hundreds of years has been inseparable from a care for both formal and mathematical logic. This case pitches formal elegance against careful observation: a scientific and sociological division, certainly, but also a significant aesthetic one – structural harmony versus care for the details of solar events and the instruments that record them.

Recognition and simulation

These abstracting processes are integral to data visualization, especially in real time. The NECS NeoFace system trialled by the Metropolitan Police in London since 2017 measures distances between eyes, nose, mouth, and jaw, a minimum of seven points. This is still crude compared to professional systems used in the movie and TV industries; but it provides sufficient accuracy to at least rule out faces gathered on watch-list databases. Ironically, changing expressions and motion – the very features that animate a face – are treated as noise in a system that emphasizes the stability of recognition factors over time (Kember, 2014; Kember also notes the inscription of gender and racist stereotypes in the software). Everyone who has passed through airport security with a biometric passport knows that successful navigation of the gates demands a static and expressionless visage. Live facial recognition in crowd situations operates without these controls over the living, but must abstract the data points that correspond to its algorithms from their living mobility, and do so on the fly. Relations between points matter more than the points themselves, and relations between faces in the crowd more than individual faces, while both are elevated above concern for features like eye movement, hair colour, or the smile that means so much to human observers. Unlike a smile, there is no reciprocity in live facial recognition.

An intriguing, perhaps ominous, development appeared in May 2019 in the form of animations of the Mona Lisa produced by Samsung's AI Center in Moscow and the Skolkovo Institute of Science and Technology (Daley, 2019). Using a generative adversarial network (GAN) architecture, researchers wrapped the painting's features around a 3D model derived from a library of head scans. Other scientists and engineers work on CCTV-captured gait recognition, captured without the need for 'geek suits' of the kind used to date in motion capture in the movie industry. Combining multiple angle scans and gait analysis offers the prospect of animating a photorealistic doppelganger, as in the BBC's 2019 conspiracy thriller *The Capture*. Credible deepfakes, like credible fake photographs, require not only skill but speed in transmission: *The Capture*'s real-time re-animations are only marginally ahead of the speed of the networked AIs operating in a GAN architecture. The paranoid vision of real-time animations generated from the traits of living people is in many respects only a technical acceleration of a long-established practice of projecting fantasies on screen. Since Freud, we associate such projections with desire and its perversions or vicissitudes; but before Freud the term most widely used, especially among the Romantics, was 'imagination'. Whenever I imagine a friend, how we will reconnect after an absence, even after bereavement, I am exercising a talent for picturing things that have not yet occurred. Because the word has slipped out of use, it is harder for us to recognise that the uncanny of the GANs animations is that they mimic imagination, not reality. Imagination is the subjunctive mood in action. It belongs to our constant faith in the emergence of a future other than the present, a future we do not plan or cause, and which contains multiple possibilities, some of them mutually contradictory in the manner of all fantasies, of a world, events and encounters which escape the iron hand of the present. This is the kind of possible, rather than probable, futurity, a radical and utopian chronoclasm that GANs give an unexpected solidity to, hovering between the 'may happen' of imagination and the 'will happen' of planning, an unexpected marriage between administration and imagination. That such indefinite, subjunctive accounts of the future exist here and now in our present reopens the question of where and when the present exists in animation – what is live, what is real-time, what is computed on the fly, and whether the viewer exists in the same time as the playback.

Live video broadcast can be dated, with the usual provisos, to 11 November 1937. By the 1950s, the use of charts in live broadcasts was already common. Any animation was performed live in studio or as expensive filmed inserts, which also risked being anachronistic by the time of transmission. Like early children's television cartoons such as *Captain Pugwash*, and for similar economic reasons, data animations were performed live to camera using stick- or wire-manipulated cardboard cut-outs. Live-in-studio, live-to-camera and live-to-air, these techniques form another genealogy of live data visualization during the pre-internet era.

Time management

Geometric diagrams are at least as old as Euclid; cartography even older. True data visualization arrives, again with provisos, in Playfair's *Statistical Breviary*. Playfair drew on Joseph Priestley's *Chart of History* and *New Chart of History* of 1765 and 1769, which for the first time laid out a graph with a time axis along the lower edge. These chronological diagrams informed William Playfair, author of the *Commercial and Political Atlas, & Statistical Breviary* of 1786 and 1801 (Rosenberg and Grafton, 2011). With a modicum of training, Playfair's reader learned to read the horizontal t-axis, a precursor to animation video editing timelines, to observe change across the chart. The *Breviary* graphs, like timelines in software interfaces, followed both the temporal dimension of writing and the old form of the scroll. The presentation of time as spatial dimension had been used before to express algebraic functions, including change over time, but Playfair was the first to use them to express empirical data. Playfair's time-series graphs, like time-lapse solargrams, negotiate the space between contingent external events and the chart of their expiring durations, but with the additionally convincing feature of having no gaps between frames. Animated data visualizations similarly venture into the hinterland between elegance and empiricism.

175

The consequences for the perception, manipulation, and management of time, in predictive sciences like meteorology but also for trend projection and the exploitation of futurity in commodity and derivatives markets, are significant. These are dominant media, in the sense of media that the dominant use when they dominate. At the cultural and aesthetic levels, they either reflect or set into action new phenomenologies of time, a tension between cartography and liveliness that we have already observed in facial recognition software. Animating a timeline adds to segmentation and interpolation the abstraction, as we just observed in facial recognition, not just of data points but of relations between them.

The MPEG codec governing the vast majority of video transmission was developed on the industrial model of animation, which separated the more expensive and creative work of key animators from the more mechanical labour of artists responsible for the frames between keyframes. It segments its data stream at keyframes marked by edits between shots or major changes in colour values within them. Checking for statistically stable areas of successive frames, it erases redundant – and thus noisy – elements, like the blades of grass on a football pitch, and where necessary inserts algorithmically deduced elements back into the frame on playback to ensure smooth transitions for the duration of the shot. Keyframes are sent in greater detail, and areas of the image where the greatest change occurs between keyframes are the objects of the greatest attention from the algorithm, which typically follows the interest marked by camerawork, such as focus on faces. Data fields like the solar disc do not typically present themselves in the same way. The prickling of data points across the face of the sun in the AIA animations, which human eyes find hard to pick out precisely because they appear as noisy irrelevancies, are liable to be compromised by the codec's hunt for key frames, zones of maximum change, and its tendency to interpret relative or probabilistic instability as irrelevance. Likewise, they may be overly enhanced at the decompression phase. It is not just the local instrument in orbit round the sun but the whole telemetric and network distribution that becomes the source of instrument noise. The distinction between this and actual electromagnetic interference from events like the 2017 solar flare is extremely difficult to descry.

Crucial to regulating this practice is the stability of key elements like screen aspect ratio, number of lines scanned, and the clock regulating the progression of scans, fields, frames, and sequences, as important as 1914's rotoscope and reprinted backgrounds or the efficiency gains of motion capture. One of the most fascinating things about the seismograph, another genealogical root of data visualization, is that though we perceive the pen as moving, in fact it is being held stable, while the rest of the apparatus moves, including the drum holding the writing surface. Very early Chinese designs used relative motion of a pendulum and its writing surface; early twentieth-century seismographs used spring-loading and inertia; more recent designs use electromagnets to hold the pen in place, but rather than read the data from the drawing, they take it from the amount of power drawn down by the magnets holding it in suspension, collecting information about energy use in numerical form and producing graphs from this second-tier evidence.

This design offers additional affordances when compared to inertial springs, picking up the direction of forces as well as their magnitude, delivering three-dimensional information. The data output looks familiar, except that the unit measurements on the vertical axis are given in microvolts, a form that makes it much easier to transmit live data to distant observers. The characteristic chrono-aesthetic of animation expands into real time not only through acceleration and magnification but extension into a third dimension. A timesheet from a single seismograph forms a single frame in a much larger animation produced in vast networks of seismometry operated by agencies like the US Geological Service. Live pages from US Geo's earthquakes service require skilled reading, though in some vivid instances can indicate cause for immediate concern even to untrained eyes, and undoubtedly services are already mobilized even while the website updates. Which is to say that these are performative images.

Future proofing

Everyone checks the weather before making plans for the day. Earth. nullschool.net, authored by Cameron Beccario, pulls down data from seven live research sources including the Goddard Earth Observing System and the Real Time Global Sea Surface Temperature network, updating anywhere between 30 minutes and five days, depending on the source, and delivering animations on open-source software, with displays of wind speed and direction, particulate matter, wave and current information, and aurora observations among others. In one sense the result is just art. You wouldn't rely on it if you were rowing the Pacific in an open boat, because the problem with live weather reports is that it is already too late to do anything about them; and the scale is either too small for spatial or temporal comparison and planning, or too large to give local cover.

Nullschool is precisely as inaccurate as it is open-source. Real-time accuracy over larger and smaller scales costs money. The money to overcome the scale problem is available in finance markets. Nanex, a financial software corporation, offers, according to its sales page, 'a high-performance real-time streaming data feed that delivers the whole market to your desktop computer. NxCore easily handles today's option and equity markets which can exceed millions of quote and trade updates each second and billions of updates each trading day' (Nanex, nd). In this instance the granularity and acceleration of animation principles is evident from observing that the time units across the *t*-axis are in milliseconds, far swifter than any of the other systems discussed so far, and delivering, for a price, a seat at the high table where algo-trading – computer-based high-frequency bidding and selling – depends on millisecond advantages. The E-mini flash crash of 6 May 2010 is a neatly documented example. It appears to have been triggered by a single order for fifty thousand contracts coinciding with an otherwise slow day's trading due to the then current Euro crisis. A series of feedback loops in other electronic trading operations led to rapid, wild fluctuations in the specialist market, before crashing into the main futures market (Kirilenko et al, 2017). In that market, the stakes might be described as bets on the future value of commodities, but if market predictions of the price of beans collapse, so does investment in bean production. The automated trading that sparked and drove the E-mini crash had present effects on future production.

Algo-trading is no more human than the weather, but it is not as alien as solar flares. Like the weather, chaotic algo-trading is an outcome of human actions mediated through technologies, waste energy in one case, digital trading in the other, the latter specifically driven by the demand for profit above all other goods. Weather forecasting and economics deal for practical purposes with closed systems in equilibrium. Both treat external features as externalities in order to operate usefully. But the noise-generating capacity of both externalities and supposedly homeostatic systems are not inconsequential. In the ping-pong of over- and under-bidding as the Nanex flash-crash animation progresses, there is evidence that traders, market regulators, and technical managers are intervening in what might otherwise appear to be in some extended sense a wholly natural emergence of mathematical chaos. The animations are not representations but, linked to the immediately past processes they map and to the automated instruction sets that will trigger the immediately subsequent behaviour of trading computers, they are not simply animations but animators of the market they both depict and instruct.

No one has ever dared leave an economic market to evolve autonomously from human interests, despite the blandishments of the most devout believers in the invisible hand. The E-mini market, on which the sun never rose but which extracts so much of its energy from yesterday's, today's, and tomorrow's sunlight, has a hybrid human and inhuman life. It is in this sense exemplary of the corporate cyborg, a network of computers with human biochips inserted, part as environmental sensors, part as random number generators. It is also exemplary of a particular affordance of animation since its emergence from stop-frame techniques around 1900 that initiated the abstraction of motion into steps along a time axis, an affordance we might call 'chronoclasm'. A chronoclasm happens when several temporal regimes collide, in this instance the millisecond timescales of algo-trading and the annual or longer scales of the futures being traded, alongside the 30 Hertz frequency of the screen display and the slightly slower nervous and muscular response time of the user seated in front of it. Condensations and expansions of the t-axis, fugal variations, and technical performance of exclusions and interpolations are all elements of the dialectic of elegant form and observational accuracy that comes into chronoclasm in real-time data animations.

The iconoclasm (Mondzain, 2005:176ff) was a deliberate destruction of icons to allow direct experience of God. The chronoclasm may be a deliberate destruction of time as 'a moving image of eternity' (Plato, 2004:np) through which mortal beings experience the infinite, or an accident deriving from the internal inconsistency of timescales and practices of time. The impossibility of either stable systems or true autonomy – Gödel's theorem that systems are always either incomplete or incoherent (Nagel and Newman, 1959) – and consequent impossibility of self-equilibration, in the world observed or the observational system – suggests that truth, contra our most ancient faiths, can never be kept apart from time. This in turn implies that the modes of truth are not in the present indicative but in variations of what would, could, or should occur: the present subjunctive. The whole challenge of accelerating animation to the 'now' of real time is to arrive at the present; but truth is not necessarily in the now: truth may be already past by the time we realize, as when we are already engulfed by the storm when the weather report comes in, or realizable only in the more or less imminent future, like a meteorological prediction, in the same way that the truth of an artistic drawing of a building is the building as it used to be, but the truth of an architectural drawing is the building as it will come to be. The problem of real-time animation is not that it is too fast but that it is not fast enough to visualize the speed of truth in the subjunctive. The truth that data visualizations seek suffers three times over: from arriving too late, from deferral, and from the proliferation of presents.

Truth and time

I have argued that most potent examples of real-time animation are data visualizations. This hypothesis rests on the question of data. Facial recognition and gait-capture rely on the idea of data as the given, so that their screen visualizations count as evidence, as grounds for action, and as truths. It is surely an irony that truth has become an object of concern, and not only to social and media theorists, precisely in the era of 'post-truth'. We find ourselves in the ignominious position of defending the truth of journalism, current affairs, and documentary, and the truthfulness of broadcasters and newspapers, that we social and media theorists have collectively spent most of a century pillorying for their ideological or discursive subservience to wealth and power, leftists united in defence of the indefensible.

There can be little doubt that the dominant truth practice of the 21st century is data. Etymologically, data translates directly as 'givens', not just 'what is the case' (Wittgenstein, 1961:1), but what gives (or fails to give) itself (Heidegger, 1962:150ff). Yet data is rarely if ever given: it is, we say, captured, collected, harvested from the natural world and from human activities alike. In Lisa Gitelman's (2013) now well-used phrase, there is no such thing as raw data. The things 'given' are already shaped as things, and like some demented tyrant bathing in forced adulation, we accept what we wrench from the world and other people as if it were tribute freely given. And, like a tyrant, and more still like a colonist, we take from whatever might indeed be offered, but ignore the potlatch and refuse to exchange, preferring accumulation and, in a perverse reversal of Derrida's (1992) commentary on giving, treat the giver as though they did not exist. Data are as much the loot of empire as the Benin bronzes in the British Museum. In exchange for looted data, the internet offers beads, or pictures of Grumpy Cat, the constant tickle of entertainments, 'attractions', as Gunning (1990) would say, riffing on Eisenstein and Brecht but, as isolated fragments of pleasure, bereft of their political aesthetics. Exchange of data, were it not merely economic and thus intrinsically exploitative, might otherwise be angelic in the sense that angels are messengers between incommensurable worlds. The difficulty of truth in our time is that it is not the fruit or nature of exchange between humans and their world, but, where it is claimed at all, a commodity-based extraction of a single abstracted quality of the world – its numbers. Data, it is a truism today, is the oil of the 21st century; and like the fossil petroleum heritage, is given no intrinsic value of its own, valuable only when processed and consumed. Not only because of reluctance to claim permanence and universality in the sciences and arts, but because the only claims to truth come from governments and corporations, often with the least right to the word, who want its performative and instrumental power, truth has become a difficult, diminished, and diminishing concept over the last two decades.

Data-driven scientific models, in physical and social sciences, extract as truth what is not given, enclosing information as once they enclosed land, and later enclosed the skills Marx (1973:690–711) describes as dead labour. Those colonizing subsumptions of natural and human resources are completed in the subsumption of knowledge under capital. The new conditions of biopolitical and commodified truths are in the liberal sense democratic: they abandon hierarchies in favour of the flat ontology of commodity exchange and of relational databases. Under these conditions, Truth is only the accumulation of truths: the singular 'Truth' a collective noun for its discrete and interchangeable components, as the Market is the sum of commodity exchanges. Even as a lightning sketch, this depiction of truth reveals a specific quality of its approximation to presence: in place of actuality, the aggregation of data entities in perpetually unstable movement is an emulation of quantum effervescence, an unstill, unfinished, and unfinishable embroidery over the void of a present it cannot reach and therefore denies. This preliminary description of truth as it is practised in the currently dominant culture emphasizes its internally contradictory temporalities.

Truth as data aggregation rests on two mutually exclusive propositions. One: Truth is a something-out-there which is true whether or not we can see and understand it (being, gravitational waves, the arche-fossil [Meillasoux, 2008]). In a more recent, eco-critical variant, there is a non-human truth, which deep ecology notes has physical and spiritual effects on us, regardless of our knowledge. However, there is also the possibility that truth is not 'given' but withheld; that what is captured in data harvesting is not truth but appearance, specifically the aspects of a situation that fit the measurement criteria of the instruments recording them and the information storage and processing protocols designed to convert them into tradable values. Earthquakes are not microvolts, but can be made to *appear* as microvoltage read-outs. Animation gives privileged access to this mode of truth. Any animated picture is a series of still frames in succession. The space between frames, Bellour's (2002) *entre-images*, is a negative space without which cinematic movement is not possible. To the extent that the truth of animation is movement, it is indistinguishable from the blank between images, the site of those moments of picnolepsia, momentary gaps in perception, that Virilio analysed in *Lost Dimension* (1991; see Cubitt, 2011). The truth of movement is the non-existence of its interstices. The truth of the given is what is not given at all.

The second proposition underpinning truth as aggregate knowledge reverses the first: Truth is produced by knowing it. A thing becomes true when we can state it, implying that truth is a quality of statements. In this case, truth is produced by the method through which we approach it, the discourse that gives us rules for making well-formed statements that can be tested by the methods of that discourse (experiment, proof, probability, and so on). If so, then it is possible that truth is not exclusively discursive but produced by actions, among which verbal actions are only one type; and vice versa, only some discursive statements are performative actions, and truth depends not on descriptions but acts. In this case, discursive truths only become true when they act in the world. We (including non-human agents like futures trading software) make things true by enacting them. This explains how discourse operates as an agreement among a group to accept such-and-such a class of statement-actions as true: by an exclusive definition of the group capable of determining truth. Ascribing movement to animations is, then, not a matter of the *phi* effect in individual brains but a collective agreement to succumb to the non-existence of its truth. Here, truth as a property of animation is revealed not as existing in a discrete moment in time but as a process that emerges, a duration.

Discursive media formations cannot claim to produce situations or conjunctures by stating them. That great line from *Citizen Kane*, 'You provide the prose poems. I'll provide the war' only *seems* to ring true, then or today. Providing a war demands the mobilization of personnel and materials, not just rhetoric, though rhetoric plays its part. Truths are not constructed. Nor are they given. But they are mediated – by news agencies and scientific institutions but also by non-human systems: for example, weather events mediating anthropogenic and extra-planetary heat. Truths mediate between humans and situations, and vice versa, mediating humans to situations, but non-human occurrences are also mediated to and by non-human agents, such as scientific instruments or photosensitive plant cells. The mediation hypothesis acknowledges the formative (if not generative) power of media in mediations such as policy documents, measuring instruments, or landscape art, without thereby denying that there is a situation to be mediated, while preserving the corollary that mediation, as action, is not free from the situation, and to that extent not only translates it for another elsewhere and in another time, but acts in the situation by mediating it. A second implication of the mediation hypothesis, therefore, is that truth is a temporal phenomenon. Just as so-called real-time transmission actually occupies the time necessary to gather, format, encode, send, check, and open, supposedly 'raw' data must be encoded in countable form, organized for storage as information – that is, in relation to other data, typically including historical data sets – and packaged for interoperable relationships with other data, for example in GANs; while data capture itself must deal with signal delay, echo, and temporality (for example, of waveforms) as well as data cleaning prior to its second-order management in storage and processing, including transmission processes, which, in a return loop, determine the design and in many systems the objects and orientation of the capture mechanisms. These truth-claiming activities not only take time: they define it; for example, in the definition of real-time according to processing cycles. Truth takes time.

Temporalities, temporealities, and temporamentalities

To the extent that the non-existent gap between images is absent from the succession of discrete frames, even if it determines its apparent flow, the gap between images occupies a different temporal register to succession. The durational aggregation of images belongs to the linear temporality of apparent motion. The gaps belong to another truth, and another temporality. As picnolepsia, the time of absence is absence from time, a being without time that might therefore be described as ontological. Where the aggregate of apparent motion emerges as a result of collective action – whether of agreement between spectators that they are watching a *moving* image, or as the product of the cyborg operation of codecs – it is political. This political emergence might then be called a temporamentality – a government of time. The neologism needs to be distinguished from temporality, a term rooted in the distinction between the eternal, spiritual activities of the medieval Church and the 'lords temporal' engaged in mundane, time-bound rule, collection of tithes, and guardianship of land. Deriving from the mode of existing in time proper to mortals, the term now refers to the different modes of existing in time, like the circular time of the seasons or the ephemerality of consumerism. Wolfgang Ernst (2016) offers another neologism, tempor(e)alities, to refer to ontological times produced by technical means, such as the millisecond transport times so critical to financial networks and computer-to-computer algo-trading. Temporamentalities, with their memory of Foucault's (2000) 'governmentalities' and the *Annales* school concept of *mentalités*, are rather constructions of temporalities and temporealities (to simplify Ernst's styling) that have achieved the status of real abstractions, capable of changing how time is organized. The concept of Progress is such a temporamentality, a description of history that has become a political slogan, policy, and educational principle and ground of whole disciplines such as electrical and electronic engineering. A familiar question concerns whether temporal technologies like clocks and calendars determine temporamentalities, the tendency of Borst's (1993) and Mumford's (1934:12) analyses; or, in common with all technologies, are symptomatic of a broader collective *mentalité*; or, in a third analysis, designed entirely as servants of a dominant mode of production; or again if chrono-technologies and temporamentalities are relatively autonomous, interacting at a distance and according to their discrete internal logics. Or, as a final item in a potentially longer list, are temporamentalities and chrono-technologies in a relation of contradiction and negation? The relation between times and their measures is significant firstly because it forces the question 'When is truth?' and secondly because it clarifies the stakes in animation, which as the fundamental technology for the reproduction of movement is the chrono-technology par excellence of our era.

It is clear that movement existed before cinema. Cinematic representation of movement – animation – obeys the law that any representation stands in for a represented that is absent, implying that movement is absent from animations. However, the optical illusion depends on a human to be deceived: dogs, for example, with their swifter eyesight, see only stills where we slip into illusion at a rate of 25 frames per second. Of course, there must be movement for the illusion to occur, but like a magic trick, the decisive action has to be invisible. The shutter closes to hide the moment when the filmstrip ticks forward to the next frame (otherwise we would see a blur between frames), and in scanned images the fading of light from the pixels is obscured by their rescanning with a new frame, and the gaps between pixels and scanlines are just small enough to fool us. As a form of mediation, then, cinematic representation of movement is time-based, time-consuming, takes time, but unlike the time of the true movement it represents, this temporeality is subject to the temporamentality of a chronometer, the clockwork of a projector or the Herzian timing governing network protocols, computer processing, and scanning codecs.

A little less than a thousand years ago, St Anselm, considering the mystery of God's eternity, noted

> Whether, therefore, we are talking about what we may say (that truth does come to a beginning or an end), or about what we may intelligibly think (that truth does not come to a beginning or an end), truth is not circumscribed by beginning and ending. (*Monologion* paragraph 19. Anselm, 1998:32)

We might come to a similar conclusion in considering the mystery of the universal constant that underpins contemporary physics. Movement in this universal context is absolute and belongs to eternity, not clocks. In animation, therefore, we confront the clash of two modes of time in which a social temporamentality overcomes and absents eternity. From the standpoint of the temporamental apparatus, eternity is the timeless nothing between frames; but Anselm teaches us that the nothing is in fact something, in this instance the principle that allows the illusion to flourish. At the same time, the illusion also depends on Virilio's picnolepsia noted above, the neuropsychology of human optics shaped by what Virilio understands as our recurrent losses of consciousness in the interstices between images. It is not only real movement that is absent but the perceiving consciousness. The question 'When is truth?' thus also raises the question of who or what is present or absent in the mediation of truth, where truth is a quality of what is absented in the process of representation.

Transmitting video images today involves another temporamentality in the form of vector prediction. The near-universal MPEG codec, the compression-decompression algorithms, is defined by the Motion Picture Expert Group, a subgroup of the International Electrotechnical Commission and the International Standards Organization's Joint Technical Committee, published by the International Telecommunications Union, a UN body with, like its partners, powerful corporate members (Cubitt, 2014, MacLean, 2003). One technique for ensuring efficient transfer of the in-between frames is to send, not a pixel-by-pixel account of every frame, but a mathematical description of the likely trajectory of significant elements of the image from one keyframe to the next, a description known as a vector. These vectors are probabilistic: they do not recount the actual record of movement but a simulation based on the probable travel of, say, a cluster of red pixels representing a cricket ball across a field. Video animation is, then, not only picnoleptic but proleptic, representing real-time acts (in the case of live sports broadcasting) through representations of the likely future of those acts, or, from another perspective, showing the future as if it were already completed. In one sense this is, as prolepsis was at origin, a purely rhetorical effect; on the other, to the extent that discourse, including visual discourse, remediates what it represents, it is a performative action, perhaps most of all when coupled with the future-oriented simulations of Earth-observation networks, war gaming, and financial software.

Asking who is present during the picnoleptic blanks of real-time animated transmissions draws the answer: the codec is present, operating in real time, calculating with extreme rapidity the content of the next cluster of frames. This codec is, however, far from autonomous technology. It is an apparatus in Flusser's (2000) sense that embraces technical installations (the TCP/IP packet-switching protocol and with it the entire panoply of internet governance; construction standards in the electronics industry; the supply chains for metals, plastics, glass, and the fabrication of chips; the ongoing colonialism and endocolonialism of resource extraction; the energy supply engineered in consort with the electronics industry; the environmental impacts of energy use, resource extraction, and device fabrication; the ancient sunlight trapped in fossil fuels and the ancient energies stored in minerals; the distant echoes of the Big Bang...). As Dipesh Chakrabarty (2009) argues, we can no longer disentangle human history from natural history. Cosmic forces are at play in our screens. But they are occluded by the demands of corporate standardization, and a temporamentality that mirrors a temporeality that has risen to dominance with financialization in the period since the 1973 oil crisis: the colonization of the future.

Debt

We know that corporations are inhuman because they pursue profit not only at the expense of human lives but of their own survival. Unlike organisms, a corporation cannot foresee its own demise. Mining the Athabasca tar sands for oil makes bitumen too expensive for road building: oil extraction makes oil consumption increasingly difficult. But a corporation has no sense that it is destroying itself because the profit it seeks exists only in the present but self-destruction is always future. There is no future profit: profit can only be realized *now*. Thus the collapsing economies brought about by the combination of overproduction and wage reduction had to be resolved not by raising wages (or paying the taxes corporations also avoid, whose absence also sends road building into decline) but by offering credit. And what is credit? It is spending today money to be earned in the future. The debt crisis is a symptom of a chronoclasm brought about by the near-completion of capital's global expansion (assimilation of the Asian workforce, maximum exploitation of global resources, real subsumption of consumption) in space, demanding a new expansion in time: the colonization of the future. Debt is the mechanism capital uses to move both risk and crisis from capital to the poor, and from the present to the future. Its task is to ensure that each of us takes on the duty to pay capital today what we will earn tomorrow, so that it can accumulate profits that, however, it must remove from circulation if it is not to find itself in the position of having to repay itself for its own loans. Governments in the wealthy nations have agreed that they will pay the penalty, and subsidize the financial system with more debts, so as to avert a strike by capital, which, however, is inevitable as a consequence of its having already accumulated the profits that otherwise would accrue to it in future. No organism would act so suicidally. We can only hope that when it dies, capital will not take all of us with it.

This brief analysis helps understand why vector prediction becomes a characteristic technique of animation in the 21st century. The future, for a creature endowed with imagination, is subjunctive: it may or would or could become many things, and as futurity it can contain, fantastically, many mutually contradictory possibilities simultaneously. The future is the unplanned, the potential, the otherwise. For finance capital, however, it is reduced to a single function: a goldmine to be excavated in this instant, and foreclosed as soon as exhausted, leaving a decimated landscape of poisoned workers and toxic tailings ponds. This is the structural rationale for vector prediction, which estimates and realizes future economics in the now, before they actualize themselves. To the extent that the present is *not* the instant in which alone profit can be extracted, but the gateway between what has already been realized and the possibilities of what might emerge, this foreclosure of the future also forecloses the present. For capital, there is only the succession of still moments, presents in which the (pseudo-)given is taken, each present equivalent to the one before and the one after.

The mediation hypothesis proposes another understanding of this logic, a 'logic' because it depends on the axiom $A = A$. The foundation of commodity exchange and of logic, the principle of self-identity seems solid, but once written it becomes clear that the A to the right comes after the A to the left. This delay, marked by the equals sign, expresses a difference as well as a deferral, like the invisible darkness between animated frames. We can express it as $A \neq A$, where the 'unequals' sign is marked by the oblique stroke of noise entering from another direction, another dimension: systemic or external. It says, there is a relation between these As, a temporal and differential relation other than identity. The relation under erasure infects the simple A itself: we can no longer assume that any A obeys the axiom of self-identity. Mediation thus takes up a different axiom: A is non-identical. The noise of the $\neq$ transition between frames unsettles the frames around it to the point that they no longer cohere internally or in their relation of succession. The engine of contemporary capital demands a present where it can make profit, but that present falls apart under the pressure of its own instruments, those data tools that it requires to convert the future into the present and the present into real time. The scanned frame, unlike the film frames of the last century, is perpetually incomplete, fading before it can be refreshed: any message is intrinsically not-present, incomplete, and noisy. Ephemerality enters the still image, and the endless present of profit dissolves. Where technologies are relatively autonomous, they do not necessarily follow *after* some lodestar. Their structural innovations, developed according to their own internal needs and structures, may also *foreshadow* the future state of other relatively autonomous spheres. It is legitimate to simulate the future on the basis of our climate models and seismographs, politically astute to make plans around contingencies. But it is neither legitimate nor astute to expropriate the future or to reinflect it as an Aristotelean *telos*: our future is no longer a goal which things tend toward, but a boundary of all potentiality. Placed in the service of data visualization, financialization, and risk management, and governed by codecs that remove as much noise as possible from transmission in order to maximize efficiency, and most recently engaged in a two-way traffic that harvests data from viewing and interaction, animation has been drawn into the self-enclosed feedback loop described in the most powerful description we have of contemporary capital, and its dominant ideology, the mathematical theory of communication (Shannon and Weaver, 1949). The task of animation research is to liberate it, in all the explosive potential of its subjunctive non-identity, not to realize the future, but to reopen the not-yet-future of the present. Chronoclasm is not to be avoided but embraced as the means to increase the friction between temporealities and temporamentalities at the level of dominant ideology of communication and the foreclosure of the future in debt.

One way to understand this is by understanding that animation, especially data visualization in real time, depends on the enforced labour of attention for industrial data mining. This affective labour (Hardt and Negri, 2004:108) is by no means 'immaterial'. On the contrary, it thrives on producing the illusion of immateriality, which derives from the principle Marx (1976:165) observed in the 1860s: that social relations appear to workers in the fantastic guise of a relation between things. Only now the ecological relation appears to us in the fantastic guise of commodities too, and we ourselves not only separated from the world we posit as our object but from each other in the isolated cells of our prosumption (Andrejevic, 2003). The restriction of 'affect' to mere synonym of 'emotion' is inadequate for the embodied nexus of material and energetic flows that constitute the sensory and emotional life of affective labourers. The perverse ideology of this mode of employment is that because it is unpaid it is free, and because it increases the enervation of the workers it is enjoyable. Animated data visualization not only describes the world as data but recruits the affective attention of unpaid spectators to provide yet more data from which more animations can be made in a process whose only end will be the moment when all interactions are predictable and therefore redundant, and machines can respond to themselves while humans, supernumerary to a truly enclosed and noiseless system, can be left to die out. Affect is not a philosophical liberation: its recent ascendance derives from the accuracy of the account it gives of the new mode of exploitation under capital. Its one strength, which it draws from the same conjuncture, is that at its most useful it acknowledges that there is no discontinuity between the inner and material lives of humans, or between either and the continuum of worldly flux. But where affect theory celebrates this condition, its celebrations are premature (Clough, 2010). It celebrates an ontological temporeality that has yet to escape its subsumption under the temporeality of communicative capital on the Shannon–Weaver model. Continuity between human and non-human only exists under the conditions of contemporary animation, the historical reality of the moving image, a post-cinematic mode of production and consumption, to paraphrase Beller (2006).

Beller, however, was focused on the cinematic succession of frames. Electronic imaging uses interlacing, and now progressive scanning, to refresh each pixel as it fades away, erasing even more intensively the gap between images where non-being bubbled in the picnoleptic unconsciousness. That was a gateway into the affective relation with the non-being of the world, and the loss that underpinned the human desire to reconstitute movement from its fragmentation. The work of electronic, scanned images takes on part of that older cinematic mode of attention and its value-forming action that made it so valuable in an older industry. Today, affective relations must emerge in more oblique, transversal relations, critically in the form of interruptions of the signal at the more microscopic level of the pixel itself. Our value-forming labour of attention is focused on producing wholeness from the pixelated surface, as much as it is on leaping unconsciously across the gap between fully formed frames. The radically incomplete nature of electronic images, masked by their constant fading and refreshing, is harder to grasp so long as the apparatus performs perfectly and the viewer is sufficiently disciplined to observe the screen from a proper distance. As labour, affect still exploits the human/non-human relation. The purpose of critical action in and around animation is to expose and emphasize that exploitation in order to liberate both animation and its labourers on either side of the screen. Critical animations and animation studies will unpick the pretended wholeness of data visualizations to discover the constant tension, friction, and noise of the chronoclasm emerging between the temporamentality of the viewing situation and the temporeality of an affective universe, short-circuiting the division of the dataverse from natural worlds. Only so will humans retain their capability to produce values other than economic from their work in, of, and as reality.

Notes

[1] See https://svs.gsfc.nasa.gov/cgi-bin/details.cgi?aid=4491&button=recent

[2] John Randolph Bray – whom Donald Crafton (1982/1993:137–68) calls 'the Henry Ford of animation' – in 1914 took out a patent for an animation process in which 'the pictures are made in any suitable manner on separate sheets of material having such a degree of translucency as will permit the tone or shade-producing layer to be seen through the sheet with the desired degree of distinctness' (patent granted 9 November 1915; cited in Maltin, 1987:9), so that motion plates could be superimposed on a single background plate. On 19 December 1914, Earl Hurd pushed the same technique further in another patent application: 'I believe I am the first to employ a transparent sheet or a plurality of transparent sheets in conjunction with a background which is photographed therethrough upon the negative film' (cited in Maltin, 1987:9). This was the first process to stipulate the use of clear celluloid and to employ multiple transparent sheets. In 1915 Bray produced another patent, this time for stationary foreground sheets laid over the action elements, so characters would seem to pass behind them. In the same year the Fleischer brothers patented their rotoscope, a device for tracing from film footage (Walden, 2008). The final breakthrough in that *annus mirabilis* was the invention by Raoul Barré of the peg system, in which each drawing is perforated mechanically, allowing them to be perfectly aligned ('registered') with one another on a peg board.

References

Andrejevic, M. (2003) *Reality TV: The Work of Being Watched*, Lanham, MD: Rowman & Littlefield.

Anselm of Canterbury. (1998) *The Major Works, including Monologion, Proslogion and Why God Became Man*, edited by Brian Davies and G.R. Evans, Oxford: Oxford University Press.

Beller, J. (2006) *The Cinematic Mode of Production: Attention Economy and the Society of the Spectacle*, Lebanon, NH: Dartmouth College Press/University Press of New England.

Bellour, R. (2002) *L'Entre-images*, Paris: La Différence.

Borst, A. (1993) *The Ordering of Time: From the Ancient Computus to the Modern Computer*, translated by Andrew Winnard, Cambridge: Polity Press.

Canales, J. (2009) *A Tenth of a Second: A History*, Chicago: University of Chicago Press.

Chakrabarty, D. (2009) 'The Climate of History: Four Theses', *Critical Inquiry*, 35(2): 197–222.

Clough, P.T. (2010) 'The Affective Turn: Political Economy, Biomedia, and Bodies', in M. Gregg and G.J. Seigworth (eds) *The Affect Theory Reader*, Durham, NC: Duke University Press, pp 206–25.

Crafton, D. (1982/1993) *Before Mickey: The Animated Film 1898–1928* (revised edition), Cambridge, MA: MIT Press.

Crafton, D. (1990) *Emile Cohl, Caricature, and Film*, Princeton: Princeton University Press.

Crary, J. (1999) *Suspensions of Perception: Attention, Spectacle, and Modern Culture*, Cambridge, MA: MIT Press.

Cubitt, S. (2011). 'Vector Politics and the Aesthetics of Disappearance', in J. Armitage (ed) *Virilio Now: Current Perspectives in Virilio Studies*, Cambridge: Polity, pp 68–91.

Cubitt, S. (2014) 'Regional Standardization: MPEG and Intercultural Transmission', in L. Hjorth, N. King and M. Kataoka (eds) *Art in the Asia-Pacific: Intimate Publics*, London: Routledge, pp 134–45.

Dagognet, F. (1992) *Étienne-Jules Marey: A Passion for the Trace*, translated by R. Galeta with J. Herman, New York: Zone Books.

Daley, J. (2019) '"Mona Lisa" Comes to Life in Computer-Generated "Living Portrait"', Smithsonian Magazine, 28 May [online], Available from: https://www.smithsonianmag.com/smart-news/mona-lisa-comes-life-compu ter-generated-living-portrait-180972296/#uxdPYzDRVcUARGhO.99 [Accessed 10 October 2019].

Derrida, J. (1992) *Given Time: 1. Counterfeit Money*, translated by P. Kamuf, Chicago: University of Chicago Press.

Douglas, M. (1966) *Purity and Danger: An Analysis of Concepts of Pollution and Taboo*, London: Routledge.

Ernst, W. (2016) *Chronopoetics: The Temporal Being and Operativity of Technological Media*, translated by A. Enns, New York: Rowman & Littlefield.

Flusser, V. (2000) *Towards a Philosophy of Photography*, translated by A. Mathews, London: Reaktion Books.

Foucault, M. (2000) 'Governmentality', in *Power (Essential Works of Foucault 1954–1984, volume 3)*, edited by J.D. Faubion, translated by R. Hurley, London: Penguin. 201–22.

Gitelman, L. (ed) (2013) *'Raw Data' Is an Oxymoron*, Cambridge, MA: MIT Press.

Gunning, T. (1990) 'The Cinema of Attractions: Early Cinema, Its Spectator and the Avant-Garde', in T. Elsaesser (ed) *Early Cinema: Space, Frame, Narrative*. London: BFI Publishing, pp 56–62.

Heidegger, M. (1962) *Being and Time*, translated by J. Macquarrie and E. Robinson, Oxford: Blackwell.

Hardt, M. and Negri A. (2004) *Multitude: War and Democracy in the Age of Empire*, New York: The Penguin Press.

Kember, S. (2014) 'Face Recognition and the Emergence of Smart Photography', *Journal of Visual Culture*, 13(2): 182–99.

Kirilenko, A., Kyle A.S., Samadi, M. and Tuzun, T. (2017) 'The Flash Crash: High-Frequency Trading in an Electronic Market', *Journal of Finance*, 72(3): 967–98.

MacLean, D. (2003) 'The Quest for Inclusive Governance of Global ICTs: Lessons from the ITU in the Limits of National Sovereignty', *Information Technologies and International Development*, 1(1): 1–18.

Maltin, L. (1987) *Of Mice and Magic: A History of American Animated Cartoons* (revised edition), New York: Plume .

Mamber, S. (2006). 'Marey, the Analytic, and the Digital', in J. Fullerton and J. Olsson (eds) *Allegories of Communication: Intermedial Concerns from Cinema to the Digital*, London: John Libbey, pp 83–91.

Marx, K. (1973) *Grundrisse*, translated by M. Nicolaus, London: Penguin/ New Left Review.

Marx, K. (1976) *Capital: A Critique of Political Economy, Volume 1*, translated by B. Fowkes, London: Penguin/New Left Review.

Meillassoux, Q. (2008) *After Finitude: An Essay on the Necessity of Contingency*, translated by R. Brassier, London: Continuum.

Mondzain, M-J. (2005) *Image, Icon, Economy: The Byzantine Origins of the Contemporary*, translated by R. Franses, Stanford: Stanford University Press.

Mumford, L. (1934) *Technics and Civilization*, London: Routledge and Kegan Paul.

Nagel, E. and Newman, J.R. (1959) *Gödel's Proof*, London: Routledge and Kegan Paul.

Nanex. (nd) 'Welcome to Nanex', Nanex.net, [online], Available from: http://www.nanex.net/

Plato (2004) *Timaeus*, translated by B. Jowett, Internet Classics Archive, [online], Available from: http://classics.mit.edu/Plato/timaeus.html

Rabinbach, A. (1990) *The Human Motor: Energy, Fatigue and the Origins of Modernity*, New York and Berkeley: Basic Books and University of California Press.

Rosenberg, D. and Grafton A. (2011) *Cartographies of Time: A History of the Timeline*, New York: Princeton Architectural Press.

Shannon, C.E. and Weaver, W. (1949) *The Mathematical Theory of Communication*, Urbana, IL: University of Illinois Press.

Stanford Solar Center. (1997) 'Solar Sounds', Solar Oscillations Investigation, 2 March [online], Available from: http://soi.stanford.edu/results/sounds. html [Accessed 10 October 2019].

Virilio, P. (1991) *Lost Dimension*, translated by D. Moshenberg. New York: Semiotext(e).

Walden, K.L. (2008) 'Double Take: Rotoscoping and the Processing of Performance', *Refractory*, 14, Available from: https://refractoryjournal. net/double-take-rotoscoping-and-the-processing-of-performance-kim-louise-walden/ /

Wittgenstein, L. (1961) *Tractatus Logico-Philosophicus*, translated by D.F. Pears and B.F. McGuinness. London: Routledge and Kegan Paul.

PART IV

Image Formation and Embodiment

9

Deepfake Face–Swap Animations and Affect

Mette-Marie Zacher Sørensen

'Deepfakes' is the popular word term for *faked* videos (synthetic audiovisual media productions) produced by using *deep* learning techniques (artificial neural networks). According to Deeptrace, an Amsterdam-based company that provides tools to detect deepfakes, in 2019 there were 14,608 deepfake videos online, which drew more than 134 million views (Ajder et al, 2019:7). There is no doubt that the phenomenon generates fear and resistance. In November 2018 the *Guardian* published an article with the headline, 'You thought fake news was bad? Deep fakes are where truth is going to die' (Schwartz, 2018). The American government is working to 'combat the spread of misinformation through restrictions on deep-fake video alteration technology' (Clarke, 2019). The recent, rapidly accelerating developments in the field of artificial neural networks have made it possible for ordinary users to easily play with face-swaps. The Zao app, which is currently available only in China, enables its users to digitally swap faces with movie actors. The seamless integration and growing accessibility of face-swap technologies generate fear about their abuse: for example, in connection with fake news, advertisements, or hate crime strategies. The fear is that epistemic claims ('He said this', 'She did that') in a medium that is historically associated with authenticity may affect people differently from other media (writing, audio, still images). Deepfakes are not used primarily for fake news, but to create non-consensual pornography. According to Deeptech, 96 per cent of the deepfake videos online have sexual content (Ajder et al, 2019:7). American researcher Danielle Citron, an internet hate crimes expert, states, 'Deepfake technology is being weaponized against women by inserting their faces into porn. It is terrifying, embarrassing, demeaning, and silencing. Deepfake sex videos say to individuals that their bodies are not their own and can make it difficult to stay online, get or keep a job, and feel safe' (Ajder et al, 2019:6).

Just as it is illegal to write falsehoods about people, the United States Congress states that each and every person should be protected from being falsely visually presented (Clarke, 2019). Scientists, lawmakers, and journalists seem to concur in their criticism of deepfakes, but as Danielle Citron stated during a hearing, 'A ban on deep fake technology would not be desirable. Digital manipulation is not inherently problematic. There are pro-social uses of the technology. Deep fakes exact significant harm in certain contexts but not in all' (Citron, 2019:7).

In this chapter I present some theoretical concepts for analysing specific contexts of face-swapped deepfakes, where contexts are understood as medial and affective environments. I analyse two different generic face-swapped deepfakes – 'the public speech' and 'the porn scene' – through a theoretical perspective of what I term, 'the medial and attention ecologies of digitized bodies'. My aim is to contribute to the discussion around the fear and resistance regarding deepfakes by asking the theoretical question:

What is it like to be depicted in a deepfake face-swapped animation, and what terms are associated with denying them ('I never said that', 'I never did this')?

Traditional image theory has seldom addressed the actual affect of depicted bodies (Berger, 1972), but along with the proliferation of selfies on social networks (where the sender is the subject) (Tiidenberg and Gómez-Cruz, 2015), deepfakes bring to our attention, in a darker way, the way in which bodies in a moving image not only affect, but are also affected. I explore the question of the depicted body by applying affect theory (Spinoza and Deleuze) and media theory (Bernard Stiegler and Mark B.N. Hansen).

I am particularly interested in questioning the affect of the face-swap in an animated setting, where my take on the concepts of *affect* and *animation* may be explained by Spinoza's sense of the word 'affectio': 'to move'. I will outline why a face-swapped animation is different from a face-swapped still image, owing to the temporality of the animation, and in my analysis of generic face-swaps I will draw on Spinoza's insight that to affect is to move and be moved. I use Mark B.N. Hansen's distinction between life and artificial time to analyse the difference between 'the public speech' and 'the porn scene' in terms of phenomenological experience and denial. Also in connection with denial, by drawing on Yves Citton's concept of ecologies of attention, among other things, I argue that what we give our attention to is a question of affect. First, I question the concerns about the face in deepfake face-swap animations, by discussing the affective character of the face and its medial conditions.

The swapped face, media technologies, and affect

In 2010, German media artists Andreas Schmelas and Stefan Stubbe developed the *Artificial Smile* camera, which is used to investigate the possibilities of real-time auto-retouching of faces in digital photography. The subject's mouth is immediately replaced with someone else's smiling mouth – carefully selected and scaled so the photograph still looks as natural as possible.

Ten years ago, at the exhibition of *Artificial Smile*, videos with auto-retouched smiling faces were shown, and the audience could choose to have their portraits photographed (Figure 9.1). The audience laughs while watching the interaction take place. It is funny because it is artificial; it is like the two-dimensional sculptures in amusement parks, where one's head is transposed to the body of a famous superhero or a Disney character. It is funny because it is uncanny, but also because it is so unconvincingly executed, because the technology was still in the early stages of its development. So we laugh at the technology used. It is an indulgent laugh and indicates that we are in a confident state of control. The construction and the fakery are obvious.

Today, the *Artificial Smile* art project is already 'old media history' owing to improvements in the use of machine learning in photo-editing processes. In 2017 FaceApp was released. This app generates naturalistic-looking transformations of faces in photographs by using neural networks. The app can alter a face to make it smile, look younger, look older, or a different

Figure 9.1: Andreas Schmelas and Stefan Stubbe, *Artificial Smile* (2010)

Source: Courtesy of the artists.

gender. The difference between the 2010 art project, *Artificial Smile*, and the 2017 commercial FaceApp is that the retouching of the facial features has become naturalistic. The use of artificial neural networks and the amount of data involved makes the changes to the photographs much more accurate (machine learning also made users aware of the algorithmic bias that may occur in the data sets, because, for example, the 'Beauty filter' made people's skin lighter and their noses narrower). FaceApp is an example of how advanced image-editing tools that were previously available only to professionals, and that had certain limitations, have now become widely distributed, and thus also contribute to the dissemination of an editable digitized body. This also applies to face-swaps, which were previously reserved for expensive film productions, but which are now on the way to becoming widespread throughout society.

In the 2014 article 'Proxy Politics', German artist and critic Hito Steyerl remarks that on the internet, your face is becoming disconnected from your butt (Steyerl, 2014:6). We lose track of, and control over our faces and the uses to which they may be put: 'Face prints are taken. An image becomes less of a representation than a proxy, a mercenary of appearance, a floating texture–surface–commodity. Persons are montaged, dubbed, assembled, incorporated' (Steyerl, 2014:8). Deepfakes are the object of my study and with this concept I refer to 'synthetic video with digitized bodies'. By this I mean animations in which photography and/or moving images of an indexical character – that is, faces, bodies or body parts, voices (though in this chapter my interest concerns the visible body), and so on – are used in animations with a new purpose (unedited, unanimated photos or video can be distributed without consent and lead to violence; however, my object of interest is deepfakes). Deepfakes may depict a variety of things other than digitized bodies, although very often that seems to be the case; in particular, deepfakes seem to present faces in new settings. In the following sections, I use the term 'face-swaps' for the following reasons. In some versions of faked videos, a face is swapped onto the body of another. However, other animations may only transpose the mouth, or an entire body is animated. I keep the notion of the face-swap in deepfakes, following Gilles Deleuze and Felix Guattari's conceptualization of the face in their seminal text on the face, 'Year Zero: Faciality', in *A Thousand Plateaus* from 1987. Here, the face is distinguished from the head and body. The body is singular, whereas the face must be understood in terms of facialization. In this chapter, the face reflects an over-coding of the body and is a symbol of the process of subjectification: 'Dismantling the face is the same as breaking through the wall of the signifier and getting out of the black hole of subjectivity' (Deleuze and Guattari, 1987:208). In this context, 'subjectivity' is understood as negative, related to normative categories. The concept of facialization is related to the process that constitutes the face/subjectivity, and the aim should be to dismantle the face in favour of the body/singularity. The reason for keeping the notion of face-swaps, even on occasions where it is not literally a face that is swapped, is that deepfakes are face/body assemblages. Again, in this context, by 'deepfakes' I mean deepfakes with digitized bodies, and these bodies will never be singularized bodies. I am interested in the affect of deepfake face animations, and am particularly interested in the temporality of the face when the digitized body is a moving image (an animation). In the following sections, I will define the concepts of the identity and expression axes of the face, and through a theoretical discussion of the temporality of these two axes, analyse the affective encounter with a separation of these two axes, which, I claim, occurs in a deepfaked face-swap animation.

In 2008 Japanese media artist Daito Manabe developed the *Face Visualizer* technology for performances in which electrodes send electrical stimuli to the skin of the face, which causes the face to move, for example, to the rhythm of an electronic beat, or as an echo of another performer's rhythmic facial gestures (Figure 9.2).

Daito Manabe's performance clearly demonstrates a separation between identity and facial expression, or to put it more clearly: in the performance appears a more than usual distinction between the two questions, 'Who are you?' and 'How are you?' In 'Year Zero: Faciality', Deleuze and Guattari describe how the two axes significance and subjectification intersect in the face. These two axes are comparable to Jenny Edkins' description in her book, *Face Politics*, which describes how much of the scientific work

Figure 9.2: Daito Manabe, *Face Visualizer*, performance, 2008

Source: Courtesy of the artist.

on 'face processing' is based on the premises that the face (1) identifies someone, either as an individual or as a member of a group, population, or race; and at the same time (2) expresses an emotional state (Edkins 2015:55). For analytical reasons we will benefit from a distinction between an identity axis and an expression axis. Respectively, they correspond to the questions, 'Who are you?' (identity axis) and 'How are you/What are you doing?' (expression axis). One way to analyse the *Face Visualizer* is to note that there is an interesting relation between the two axes. One of the crucial aspects of the deepfakes is that they separate the two axes in a more extreme manner. By way of questioning the consequences of the separation of identity and facial expression, next I will outline a theoretical analysis of the affect of the two axes based on their different temporalities, among other things. The identity axis is complicated by the definition I outlined regarding the difference between faciality and the singularized body in Deleuze and Guattari's 'Year Zero: Faciality'. Or, as Deleuze writes in his book on Spinoza's philosophy:

> The important thing is to understand life, each living individually, not as a form or a development of form, but as a complex relation between differential velocities, between deceleration and acceleration of particles [...] It is by speed and slowness that one slips in among things, that one connects with something else. One never commences; one never has a tabula rasa; one slips in, enters in the middle; one takes up or lay down rhythms. (Deleuze, 1988:123)

As we see in the passage above, Deleuze and Guattari base the concept of the singularized body on Spinoza's thinking, and note the problem of identity and form, how one always 'slips in', 'enters in the middle'. This relates to temporality and affect, which are of interest to me in what I address next: bodies have the capacity to affect and be affected. They are always in the middle. I will further outline some of the uncertainties related to the 'expression axis'.

In his 1924 book on formalist film theory, *Visible Man*, Hungarian film-maker Béla Balázs carries out an analysis of the human face as a medium, which still seems relevant when it comes to understanding the relationship between expressions and temporality. The human face and its expressions are untranslatable into language. Balázs describes how the face is, metaphorically speaking, more polyphonic than language:

> There is a film in which Asta Nielsen is looking out of the window and sees something coming. A mortal fear, a petrified horror appears on her face. But she gradually realizes that she is mistaken and that the man who is approaching, far from spelling disaster, is the answer

to her prayers. The expression of horror on her face is gradually modulated through the entire scale of feeling from hesitant doubt, anxious hope and cautious joy, right through to exultant happiness. (Balázs, 2010:34)

A face can display the most varied emotions simultaneously, or rather, in a continuous modulation, and hence we experience emotions over time. Literary scholar Elisabeth Freeman (2019) describes how, of the various representational media, only the durational ones – the ones that unfold over time, rather than being apprehensible all at once – can capture the process of transmitting and otherwise transferring energies from one body to another. Here, 'energy' is to be understood as affect, and the point is that affect and temporality have a specific relationship with each other.

Although different from the moving image, the still portrait has a certain relationship to *identity* – the captured moment of a person, but according to some scholars the goal of capturing *emotions* in still images is a historical fallacy that still compromises many assumptions regarding physical expressions, emotions, and affects. This point is made by Jenny Edkins, who has investigated how the sciences examined facial expressions related to emotions, and the development of disputed theories of basic, universal emotions, which until recently was conducted through the use of still images. Edkins argues:

The examination of face processing tends, it seems, to carry out its experimental work with still images. Often these images are obtained by asking actors to pose facial expressions, and to produce these by moving muscles thought to correspond to certain so-called basic emotions.[...] There is an assumption here that is seldom unpacked: the assumption that emotion resides in the face, not in the body or the interaction, and that an expression can be abstracted from time and conveyed in a still image. (Edkins, 2015:56)

Some of our assumptions regarding the face seem to stem from techno-historical circumstances. In *Cinema 1* Deleuze writes, 'The face is this organ-carrying plate of nerves which has sacrificed most of its global mobility and which gathers or expresses in a free way all kinds of tiny local movements which the rest of the body usually keeps hidden' (Deleuze, 2005:90). This description of the facial close-up is a more positive notion of the face than the concept of facialization in *Thousand Plateaus*. The close-up belongs to film, and may be part of the reason that the face has gained such prominence. But deepfakes are not close-ups. The faces swapped into deepfakes do not have what Deleuze terms *face value*: the experience of a filmic close-up that causes the viewer to 'ask' the face, 'What is bothering you?'

Balázs emphasizes that film is the medium of the face and of emotions. The historical invention of the filmic close-up may have given rise to the assumption that the face is an expresser of emotions. I do not argue that the face expresses nothing, but to some extent the role of the face as the medium of emotions is an effect of media history. This argument relates to how American neuroscientist and psychologist Lisa Feldman Barrett has convincingly argued how we cannot detect specific emotions or emotional qualities from facial expressions. Barrett counters the assumption that our feelings are revealed by facial movements: 'Despite its immense influence in our culture and society, there is abundant scientific evidence that this view cannot possibly be true. Even after a century of effort, scientific research has not revealed a consistent, physical fingerprint for even a single emotion' (Barrett, 2017:14–15).

In an article about the neural mechanisms of face perception, researchers Behrmann et al write, 'Face perception is probably the most developed visual perceptual skill in humans, most likely as a result of its unique evolutionary and social significance' (Behrmann et al, 2016:247), but this view does not consider the techno-historical impact of what we see and how we see the face. American cultural theorist Kelly Gates opposes this perception of the face, arguing that sight and vision should not be understood as essential qualities or strictly physiological processes with universal, transhistorical meanings or functions. There is no such thing as natural or 'true' vision. Instead, referencing Donna Haraway, Gates argues that vision is always a question of the power to see and the struggle over how to see (Gates, 2011:11). Or, as Warwick Mules states about the face, '[T]he term face-to-face has become a signifier of pure communication – either an ideal to which all communication should aspire, or more critically, a false promise that obscures the entangled context of mediation as the real condition of any communicative event' (Mules, 2010:1–2).

In W.J.T. Mitchell and Mark B.N. Hansen's influential anthology, *Critical Terms for Media Studies* (2010), they define how they address the concept of *media* as a bridge between aesthetic, technological, and sociological traditions:

[W]hat the emergence of the collective singular *media* betokens is the operation of a deep, techno-anthropological universal that has structured the history of humanity from its very origin (the tool-using and inventing primate) [...] 'media' in our view, also names a technical form or formal technics, indeed a general mediality that is constitutive of the human as a 'biotechnical' form of life. (Mitchell and Hansen, 2010:ix; emphasis in original)

Such a broad concept of technology and media makes it impossible to assume that the human face was once untouched and 'now' is becoming contaminated by technique. In this perspective, the expression of the face (for instance, its ability to speak) would also be considered a historically emergent technique. It is relevant to reflect on the human face as a medium that, like all other media, is undergoing historical change owing to technological developments. Perhaps we should become accustomed to considering the face as an 'interface' that we had during one historical period and that is changing. In 2014, American 'small talk' consultant Debra Fine published the self-help book *Beyond Texting: The Fine Art of Face-to-Face Communication for Teenagers*. The book is based on the premise that today's teenagers are better at communicating in writing than in face-to-face communicative situations. They need to be taught the 'exotic' and 'new' 'live' way of communicating. Among other things, the book includes a diagram describing what may be achieved with a smile. The book argues that this physical way of communicating will provide the recipient with a positive experience. Although it uses superficial self-help language, the book presents an important media-theoretical position, because hierarchies of what is new and old, natural and mediated, dissolve.

Attention and affect

In May 2018 the Belgian political party, Socialistische Partij Anders, posted a deepfake of Donald Trump saying: 'As you know, I had the balls to withdraw from the Paris climate agreement [...] and so should you' (Schwartz, 2018). It provoked many comments, many expressing outrage that the American president would dare weigh in on Belgium's climate policy (Schwartz, 2018). In a political climate where lies from an elected democratic leader are accepted, other categories than facts and truth have already taken over, and by this I mean concepts such as attention and affect. It is not only a question of what is true and false but a question of what is being paid attention. Next, I argue that attention and affect are interrelated and note that deepfakes are already a part of an ecology of attention and affect. Images have the ability to move us. Belting wrote that from the perspective of anthropology, images have power because an image animates and is animated by the subject and, hence, becomes a part of the subject. Belting argues that we tend to think that we are in control, but in fact images colonize our bodies (Belting, 2014:10). I would rather argue, again, with Spinoza, that we are always in the middle, meaning that (moving) images do not 'attack' passive subjects with affect; we are always in some sort of state, including when it comes to attention and experience. As Bergson wrote of perception, '[P]erception is not the object *plus* something, but the object *minus* something, minus everything that does not interest us' (Deleuze, 1991:25; emphasis in original). This resonates with new research in the field of neuroscience and emotions:

In a traditional way of looking at the brain, perception was supposed to feed information into the brain, which in turn led to thoughts about the information, which then led to emotional assessment of the information and finally action [...] the situation is just the reverse: Our emotions gear us up for action, and then we search and scan the environment for relevant perceptual clues, which becomes conscious to the extent that they resonate with image schemas that was already in process of being developed in response to frontal-limbic emotional responses. (Ellis, 2005:169–70; emphasis in original)

The brain receives formidable volumes of information. Information about the surroundings flows to the brain through the eyes, ears, nose, mouth, and skin. The traditional five senses are not the brain's only input channels. Information about the state of the body and organs also flows continuously to the brain. This information about the body is called interoception (Tsakiris and De Preester, 2019). Sensing the body's signals is something you determine – you cannot possibly experience everything all the time. Meditation is a way to establish space to feel the body, or at least to be aware of one's own attention. N. Katherine Hayles describes how meditation is a way to give our system room for information on unconscious processes:

[M]editive practices have the effect of diminishing investment in the narratives of consciousness, partially or wholly clearing the global workspace, and therefore making room for feedforward information coming from nonconscious processes, particularly about body processes, emotional responses, and present awareness, thus centering the subject and putting her more closely in touch with what is actually happening from moment to moment within her body as it is embedded within the environment. (Hayles, 2017:61)

Meditation is not a practice of deciding to do nothing, but of deciding to give way to parts of the pieces of information that are otherwise filtered out. One cannot help missing something, and this is a condition of not only contemporary media culture but an ontological condition of perception and experience. Attention is a selective process that apparently attaches to the subject's agency. Our everyday language tells us that attention and experience are subjective. You cannot say to another person, 'You just experienced this': the individual subject must be the one to determine what they have experienced, and what we choose to give our attention to seems subjective. However, in the 2014 book, *The Ecology of Attention*, French cultural theorist Yves Citton argues that we should de-individualize the concept of attention, because collective processes determine what we consider exciting and relevant, and thus to what we pay attention. What is offered as a potential experience is not up to the individual. He calls this general principle *the formal principle of enthrallment*, and it reads as follows: '[H]uman attention tends to fall on objects whose forms it recognizes, under the spellbinding influence of the direction taken by the attention of others' (Citton, 2017:33). Collective attention, and not a logical or equitable distribution, helps determine whether the climate crisis or football finals receive a certain amount of attention. In his book *Psychopolitics: Neoliberalism and New Technologies of Power*, German philosopher Byung-Chul Han quotes artist Jenny Holzer's historical truism of the 1980s: 'Protect me from what I want' (Han, 2017:20). Today the request may be read as reflecting ambivalence about agency related to free will and potential manipulation at precognitive levels of impulses, desires, and fake news. As American aesthetic theorist Sianne Ngai has argued via science theorists Isabelle Stengers and Mikhail Epstein, even recognizing scientific theories is a matter of what we find interesting. What we choose to focus attention on, even at epistemological levels, requires the collective affective recognition that something is in the right place between desire and reason. Relativity theory and quantum physics have aroused interest because they contradict the common sense (Ngai, 2015:116), whereas a theory that affirms the obvious does not arouse attention. The interesting thing lies at the junction of something we already care about and something we do not know.

Every sort of attention – from perceptual sorting to accepted scientific disciplines – is a matter of affect (to be emotionally geared up for action and to be *interested* are affective categories.) Hence, attention is also related to power. To state that a video is fake demands attention-power. The distribution of attention is different in 'the public speech' and 'the porn scene'. When it comes to the way in which attention and affect are distributed, it is interesting to consider how a deepfake of Trump abuses his face by separating its identity and expression axes. The face-swapped face in the deepfake of Trump is a faciality face, and it is a face in which the identity axis is promoted and separated from the expression axis, to make the epistemic claim: 'Trump (identity axis) said this (expression axis)'. The problem is that a person should be able to control both axes. I argue that this case is not that different from using his name in a fake text or his signature in a forged letter (both these acts are illegal). The expression axis is not very effective in the Trump video, and hence the deepfake is a violation owing to the epistemic or semantic claim ('He said this') rather than because of the manipulation of the expression axis of his face. This relates to my earlier argument regarding the fact that the moving face affects us, but as a medium the face is not as expressive as the historic film close-up would have us to believe.

Affect and attention are related to power. As I just analysed in relation to the face-swapped deepfake of Trump, it demands power to be given attention while stating that this is fake: 'Someone has stolen my face'. The effect of this act is different in a situation where something false has been said while borrowing your face (the public speech) than when something has been done with a body with your face attached to it (the pornographic scene). Even though the person portrayed says, 'I never did this' (or I never gave consent to the distribution of this), she and others have already been affected by it. This is due to the medial, and therefore affective, character of moving images, in the case of the pornographic scene, where it is more difficult to separate the identity axis and the expression axis at an affective level. The face/body assemblage is stronger in an animation of less semantic character ('She did this' instead of 'He said that'). The pornographic scene *moves* the body, the subject, the person involved. To move is to exist and is hence related to identity. The consequences of the temporality of the animated pornographic scene will be discussed next.

Temporality, animation, and affect

Face-swaps with pornographic content are being used in interactive video games and virtual reality (VR) simulations: VaM is software for creating VR games and simulations with adult content, which is being exploited by some users to create non-consensual pornography by swapping faces onto the bodies of an animated character. Journalist Samantha Cole, from Vice Magazine, has been the keenest follower of this development in the field of deepfake pornography, and here she describes her encounter with VaM:

> The neutral, realistic face of a celebrity maintains eye contact, following the user and blinking as they move around her: the user looks to the right and pulls up VaM's control interface, which displays a long menu of sex positions the 3D model can be put into: doing a backward bend, squatting and touching herself, several versions of kneeling. The user picks a position from the menu that puts the model on her back holding her legs over her head, and looks back to the 3D model to find her in that position. (Cole and Maiberg, 2019)

As described in the statement, the animated character is bending, touching, kneeling, and so on. These action verbs denote movements made by the face/body assemblage (the digitized body). The temporality of movement and its relation to life and the artificial time of the film medium will be discussed next.

Roland Barthes famously outlined the concept of photography's *ça a été* ('it was'), and he analyses Alexander Gardner's portrait of Lewis Payne sitting on his bed, waiting to be hanged. Barthes points out how in this picture we simultaneously read, 'He is dead and he will die' (Barthes, 2000:95).

This will happen and this happened. Bernard Stiegler has analysed how the film's indexicality differs from that of photography, owing to the temporal dimension. In the 1987 Federico Fellini film, *Intervista*, the director visits Anita Ekberg, and with her watches the famous scene in *La Dolce Vita* where she bathes in the Trevi Fountain. Thus, she sees herself but also not herself, because she is in a role. Stiegler does not read this as Barthes's experience of her 'dying and will be dying' but Ekberg's own 'I, who will die', which is deadly. Stiegler explains how the film, in terms of its temporality, offers the potential for ghostly sensations. As he describes it:

> In cinema, as an after-effect, this sequence of fictional instants comes to us as a succession of moments from real life, from a progression that remains with us as a continuum of presents forming someone's past and future, informing us about the person; it is the (ghostly) past of the actress herself playing her past and present, while playing with them, the character's present in the actress's past, and the actress's present in the character's past. (Stiegler, 2009:22)

In his argument concerning the relations between time, technique, and memory, Stiegler uses and discusses Husserl's theory of inner time consciousness, with which he differentiates between primary and secondary retention (memory) and protention (expectation). Stiegler believes that this analysis of our time experience overlooks what he calls tertiary retention (memory). In principle, tertiary retention comprises all our common exteriorities outside the body. For example, a photograph represents a temporality that is not directly experienced by the subject because they were not necessarily there when the photographed event took place, but now the photograph represents a kind of shared memory. By extension, one may ask whether fake videos should be considered tertiary retention. They refer to the state of the production, not the state of an actual event.

Mark B.N. Hansen (2009) is interested in exploring how contemporary media is changing our experience of time. He is inspired by Bernard Stiegler, and he argues that that we have no experience of time at all without techniques/exteriorizations. In continuation and criticism of Husserl's theory of inner time consciousness, Stiegler argues that consciousness may seize the sense of the flux of time only through an experience of a temporal object – a 'surrogate'. Stiegler considers film (including television and so on) our exemplary contemporary temporal object, because its time dimension is reminiscent of passage of time in life as it is lived. Hansen counters this with examples of new media's aesthetic dealings with time. He argues that video artists such as Bill Viola and Douglas Gordon, by using extreme slow motion, provide a sharpened experience of time simply by not being in line with the 'world' pace, as film and television typically are. Hansen believes that we are experiencing a shift in what he calls 'the artefactualization of time', from cinematic media objects to much more detailed digital inscriptions that cannot be reduced to shaped objects. To exemplify this shift, he describes Wolfgang Staehle's *Empire 24/7*, which transmits live images from the Empire State Building to galleries and websites 24 hours a day, and Pierre Huyghe's 1994 *Chantier Barbès-Rochechouart, Paris* work, which is a video billboard right beside the subject it transmits (some workers on a construction site). As I see it, both *Empire 24/7* and *Chantier Barbès-Rochechouart, Paris* create a kind of space that is a copy of another space (whether it is far away or right next to the subject), and yes, it is difficult to speak about the temporal extraction of something that is there all the time. Hansen makes the important point that works such as these cannot be surrogates for the flux of consciousness – they simply make it difficult to differentiate between life and artificial time. They are 'diachronic things' because they refuse to be encapsulated as temporal objects. Hansen writes of these new digital media forms and their influence on the recipient that they do not possess agency and the opportunity to control the flux of time and our attention. The viewer is left with an extreme openness. He terms this a temporal heterogeneity. Hansen describes the diachronic things and what he calls 'their peculiar exteriority' in relation to the aesthetic experience they facilitate. Thus, he operates analytically with a distinction between life and artificial time, to point out the coincidence and the inseparability of the two in the *Empire 24/7* project and in the *Chantier Barbès-Rochechouart, Paris* scene. In Stiegler's reading of the Ekberg scene (where she watches herself), there is a differentiation between life and artificial time (the actress is watching her life in the past through artificial time (the film)). Thus, the movement of the film medium makes the experience so strong in the Ekberg scene, and the same movement is experienced in 'the porn scene', although it exists as artificial time without any relation to life, but is experienced as such by the potential viewer of the animation before whom the animated character with the swapped face moves. I have been using the statement, 'She did that', but we should instead say, 'She is doing this' because of the 'here and now' of the experience of the animation. Because of the face-swap (the identity axis) and the movement of the animation, 'the public speech' may be considered very authentic documentation, an animated *ça a été* ('this happened') and thus having a relationship to the past in its epistemic claim ('He said this'). The animated pornographic scene has another temporality: it is instead experienced in a mode of living presence. The temporal character of the deepfake face-swapped pornographic scene makes the difference between fake or real less relevant. In the deepfake face-swapped public speech, it is possible to neglect the content due to its semantic character by saying, 'I never said that', and the face stolen to confer authenticity is given back to you. In the pornographic scene, even though you may state 'This never happened', it happened in a temporal, bodily sense, where the face (identity axis) is difficult to separate from the expression axis (the bodily movements of the animated character.) As soon as something moves – takes place in time – it happens, and if something happens it is also experienced as though it happened. Thus, the deepfake face-swapped animations evokes affective authenticity. Nevertheless, 'the public speech' may be *summarized* owing to its semantic character, and may thus be denied ('I never said this'). But the movement of the animated body in 'the porn scene' is impossible to compress and hence impossible to deny. It is not possible to state, 'I never did this' when it has already happened.

Austrian media theorist Bernadette Wegenstein works with the concept of the 'cosmetic gaze' (Wegenstein, 2012:371–2). Saying that the gaze we turn on ourselves and others is cosmetic means that it is contingent on the historically available technologies for changing the body. The discovery of Botox and image-editing tools gives the changed perception of the body as incomplete because there is the possibility of improvement. For Wegenstein, the point is that this gaze, with the desire for approvements, is infiltrated completely seamlessly by technology: she calls this 'machinic sutures'. Wegenstein's text was written before Snapchat was invented, but a good recent example of how cosmetic appearances are changed by 'machinic sutures' is that plastic surgeons report the phenomenon of 'Snapchat dysmorphia' (the correct medical term is 'body dysmorphic disorder') (Hunt, 2019). Whereas people used to go to the plastic surgeon with a picture of a Hollywood star they wanted to resemble, they now come with a picture of themselves through a Snapchat filter, where their cheekbones are more marked, their skin clearer, and their lips fuller. Their experience of this technologically feasible editing of one's own image disturbs their own bodily self-image.

If beauty technologies have brought us to turn a cosmetic gaze on our own and other people's faces as something that could always be improved, one might fear how the gaze turned on a woman's face by some eyes may instantly raise the question of how she would look as an animated pornographic character, ready to be moved.

Conclusion

In contrast to the traditional movie close-up where, for instance, Asta Nielsen's face affects the viewer, deepfakes make us aware that bodies in a moving image not only affect, they are also affected. I have outlined how the assumptions regarding the face as the expresser of emotions stem from the film close-up, but the deepfake animation does not have the same 'face value', to use Deleuze's term. The fake video of Trump does not make us ask, 'What is bothering you?' Deepfake animations certainly move us and, in parallel with the fact that the face never stands still, when it comes to expression, it never stands alone. It is a part of an ecology of attention and affect. A pornographic animation is a violent act in which the predator animates, hence *moves* the victim. As I have argued, based on Stiegler's reading of Anita Ekberg watching herself, the moving image has strong affect and evokes the past by being in motion in the present. This is also the case in the filmed pornographic scene, where the movements of the face/body assemblage evoke a past, even though there is none. I have argued that this makes the act impossible to deny. Furthermore, owing to the character of ecologies of attention and their asymmetrical distribution of affect, it is probable that no attention will be paid to the victim's statement, 'I never did this'.

References

Ajder, Henry, Patrini, Giorgio, Cavalli, Francesco and Cullen, Laurence (2019) 'The State of Deepfakes: Landscape, Threats, and Impact', Amsterdam: Deeptrace, Available at https://regmedia.co.uk/2019/10/08/deepfake_report.pdf [Accessed 17 January 2020].

Balázs, Béla (2010) *Béla Balázs: Early Film Theory – Visible Man and The Spirit of Film*, New York: Berghahn Books.

Barrett, Lisa Feldman (2017) *How Emotions Are Made: The Secret Life of the Brain*, New York: Houghton Mifflin Harcourt.

Barthes, Roland (2000) *Camera Lucida: Reflections on Photography*, translated by Richard Howard, London: Vintage Classics.

Behrmann, Marlene, Scherf, K. Suzanne and Avidan, Galia (2016) 'Neural mechanisms of face perception, their emergence over development, and their breakdown', *WIREs Cognitive Science*, 7: 247–63.

Belting, Hans (2014) *An Anthropology of Images: Picture, Medium, Body*, translated by Thomas Dunlap, Princeton: Princeton University Press.

Berger, John (1990) [1972] *Ways of Seeing*, London: Penguin Books.

Citton, Yves (2017) *The Ecology of Attention*, Cambridge: Polity Press.

Citron, Danielle Keats (2019) 'Prepared written testimony and statement for the record of Danielle Keats Citron, hearing on "The National Security Challenge of Artificial Intelligence, Manipulated Media, and 'Deep Fakes'" before the House Permanent Select Committee on Intelligence', 13 June, Available at https://nsarchive.gwu.edu/sites/default/files/documents/6826697/National-Security-Archive-150-Prepared-Written.pdf [Accessed 17 January 2020].

Clarke, Yvette D. (2019) 'HR.3230: Deep Fakes Accountability Act – Defending Each and Every Person from False Appearance by Keeping Exploitation Subject to Accountability Act of 2019', 28 June, Available at https://www.congress.gov/bill/116th-congress/house-bill/3230 [Accessed 17 January 2020].

Cole, Samantha and Maiberg, Emanuel (2019) 'Deepfake Porn is Evolving to Give People Total Control over Women's Bodies', Vice, 6 December [online], Available at: https://www.vice.com/en_uk/article/9keen8/deepf ake-porn-is-evolving-to-give-people-total-control-over-womens-bodies [Accessed 26 June 2020].

Deleuze, G. (1988) Spinoza: Practical Philosophy, translated by Robert Hurley, San Francisco: City Lights Books.

Deleuze, Gilles (1991) Bergsonism, New York: Zone Books.

Deleuze, Gilles (2005) Cinema 1: The Movement-Image, translated by Hugh Tomlinson and Barbara Habberjam, London/New York: Continuum Impacts.

Deleuze, Gilles, and Félix Guattari (1987) A Thousand Plateaus: Capitalism and Schizophrenia, Minneapolis: University of Minnesota Press.

Edkins, Jenny (2015) Face Politics, Abingdon/New York: Routledge.

Ellis, Ralph D. (2005) Curious Emotions: Roots of Consciousness and Personality in Motivated Action, Amsterdam/Philadelphia: John Benjamins Publishing Company.

Fine, Debra (2014) Beyond Texting: The Fine Art of Face-to-Face Communication for Teenagers, New York: Canon Publishers.

Freeman, Elisabeth (2019) Beside You in Time: Sense Methods and Queer Sociabilities in the American 19th Century, Durham, NC: Duke University Press.

Gates, Kelly A. (2011) Our Biometric Future: Facial Recognition Technology and the Culture of Surveillance, New York: New York University Press.

Hayles, N. Katherine (2017). Unthought: The Power of the Cognitive Nonconscious, Chicago: University of Chicago Press.

Han, Byung-Chul (2017) Psychopolitics: Neoliberalism and New Technologies of Power, London/New York: Verso Books.

Hansen, Mark B.N. (2009) 'Living (with) Technical Time: From Media Surrogacy to Distributed Cognition', Theory, Culture and Society, 26(2–3): 294–315.

Hunt, Elle (2019) 'Faking it: how selfie dysmorphia is driving people to seek surgery', The Guardian, 23 January [online], Available from: https:// www.theguardian.com/lifeandstyle/2019/jan/23/faking-it-how-selfie-dys morphia-is-driving-people-to-seek-surgery

Mitchell, W.J.T. and Hansen, Mark B.N. (eds) (2010) Critical Terms for Media Studies, Chicago: University of Chicago Press.

Mules, Warwick (2010) 'This Face: A Critique of Faciality as Mediated Self-Presence', Transformations, 18, Available from: http://www.transfo rmationsjournal.org/wp-content/uploads/2017/01/Mules_Trans18.pdf

Ngai, Sianne (2015) Our Aesthetic Categories: Zany, Cute, Interesting, Cambridge, MA: Harvard University Press.

Schwartz, Oscar (2018) 'You thought fake news was bad? Deep fakes are where truth is going to die', The Guardian, 12 November [online], Available from: https://www.theguardian.com/technology/2018/nov/12/deep-fakes-fake-news-truth [Accessed 17 January 2020].

Steyerl, Hito (2014) 'Proxy Politics: Signal and Noise', *e-flux journal*, 60, Available from: http://worker01.e-flux.com/pdf/article_8992780.pdf [Accessed 20 November 2023].

Stiegler, Bernard (2009) *Technics and Time, 2: Disorientation*, translated by Stephen Barker, Palo Alto: Stanford University Press.

Tiidenberg, Katrin and Gómez Cruz, Edgar (2015) 'Selfies, Image and the Re-making of the Body', *Body and Society*, 21(4): 77–102.

Tsakiris, Manos and De Preester, Helena (eds) (2019) *The Interoceptive Mind: From Homeostasis to Awareness*, Oxford: Oxford University Press.

Wegenstein, Bernadette (2012) *The Cosmetic Gaze: Body Modification and the Construction of Beauty*, Cambridge, MA: MIT Press.

10

Deepfake Reality, Societies for Technical Feeling, and the Phenomenotechnics of Animation

Mark B.N. Hansen

Fake news as lure for feeling

A story in the *New York Times* debunking three viral rumors about the 24 May 2022 Uvalde, Texas school massacre once again begs the question: why do people 'believe' such patent instances of misinformation? And what exactly is it that they 'believe' when they credit these and like lies circulating on such online platforms as Twitter, Gab, 4chan and Reddit? (Hsu et al, 2022). Though the content of these viral rumors could take many forms, the three at issue in this story exemplify the strategy with which we have become all too familiar during Donald Trump's presidency: sowing informational chaos to create confusion and let stick what sticks. The three rumors are: one, that the shooting was a staged 'false flag' operation designed to draw local law enforcement away from the border, allowing criminals and drugs free passage into the US; two, that the shooter was transgender and the massacre the result of hormone therapy; and three, that the gunman was an undocumented immigrant who crossed illegally into the US in order to carry out the attack.

I put the word 'believe' in scare quotes in order to highlight the liminal status that these and like rumors have for their 'believers' in relation to the issue of their truth or falsity. While these claims are clearly deliberate and repugnant instances of misinformation, their truth or falsity is not what is at stake in the 'belief' they garner, at least on the part of those not blatantly exploiting them for political positioning and gain. In this sense, they are instances – albeit particularly toxic and harmful ones – of what process philosopher Alfred North Whitehead alternately calls 'propositions', or more apropos here, 'lures for feeling'. For Whitehead, propositions seek to elicit feeling rather than belief and, for this reason, they perfectly capture what is at issue in the efficacy of fake news:

> The interest in logic, dominating overintellectualized philosophers, has obscured the main function of propositions in the nature of things. They are *not primarily for belief, but for feeling at the physical level of unconsciousness*. They constitute a source for the origination of feeling which is not tied down to mere datum. (Whitehead, 1978: 186; emphasis added)

Propositions can be understood as the concrete vehicles for the non-actualized potentiality of the past to shape future process, for *what could have been but was not* to become actual.[1] The proposition, Whitehead stipulates, 'is the potentiality of the eternal object, as a determinant of definiteness, in some determinate mode of restricted reference' to the actual entities that are the 'logical subjects' of the proposition (Whitehead 1978:257). This is what Whitehead means when, in the above citation, he specifies that propositions constitute a source for feeling '*that is not tied down to mere datum*'. Propositions express the conceptual potentiality that can be brought to bear in the transition from past to future, and thereby offer feeling an important source to depart from sheer physical determinism ('mere datum'). They are potential feelings of past conceptual data prior to any conscious awareness, belief, and judgement concerning their truth or falsity.

Even though propositions are restricted largely if not wholly to human experience, they are not experienced consciously but are *felt* through what Whitehead calls the causal efficacy of the past, to which conceptual potentiality adheres. Causal efficacy is the mode of process and also the mode of perception with which Whitehead supplements Western philosophical accounts of sense perception (what he calls 'presentational immediacy'). It is the vague feeling of the total situation, and most proximately of the 'withness of the body', that is the *source* of sense perception and from which it abstracts. Propositions lure unconscious, bodily feelings about the importance of some dimension of the world. 'Subjective forms of propositional feelings', writes Whitehead, 'are dominated by valuation rather than by consciousness. Thus, [...] propositions intensify, attenuate, inhibit, or transmute, without necessarily entering into clear consciousness, or encountering judgment' (263).

In claiming that false rumours circulating on the internet are propositions or lures for feeling in Whitehead's sense – albeit toxic ones – I am seeking to localize their operation where it concretely occurs, to pinpoint how they activate responses that are, as it were, prior to and beneath the level where belief, and even more so judgement, kicks in. By so doing, I seek to account for the ways in which algorithms are always already enmeshed with human bodily activities *prior to the separation that is subsequently imposed* and whose imposition underwrites contemporary forms of critical media studies that approach media as objects of and prostheses for capacities of independent, already developed humans. On my account, the technical operations of algorithms do not engage bodily feeling from the outside as a separate process; rather, by generating a surplus of potentiality for the future, by multiplying propositions concerning what could have been but wasn't, algorithms directly affect the settled world to be felt, intensifying its potential for the future – and thereby inform feeling *from the inside*. Because they directly intensify the potentiality of the past that is felt, algorithms must be experienced through 'valuation rather than by consciousness', as the above cited passage puts it, meaning that the human share of the technical feeling, the human contribution to larger human–technical societies, takes place through bodily assimilation of algorithmically intensified potentiality, not cognitive assessment.

Algorithms are machines for generating and intensifying propositions

With its focus on propositional intensification of feeling, my account responds to Louise Amoore's injunction to conceptualize algorithms as 'arrangements of propositions' anchored in their 'experimental and iterative capacities […] to propose things in and about the world' (Amoore, 2020:20–21). Because their capacities for generating propositions vastly exceed the capacity of the human imagination, algorithms open experience to a broader potentiality of the past; they can entertain multitudinous proposals about how the past can be felt into the future and thus introduce more potentiality into process. In so doing, algorithms do not simply present an expanded repertoire of possibilities from which humans or proxies for humans choose; any such 'possibilist' conception assumes a discrete separation between the operation of algorithms and the already constituted subjects they impact. Rather than presentifying a repertoire of possibilities to be decided on by some independent agent, the algorithmic expansion of potentiality is an accomplishment of larger 'societies for technical feeling' in which the conceptual potentiality algorithms access directly informs the feeling of the past into the future.[2] Although the human share in societies of technical feeling will prove crucial, the feeling at issue here is in no way exclusively human. It is, rather, an indivisibly human–technical feeling on the part *of the larger society as a whole*.

As many sources have reported and as recent experience has time and again shown, social media and internet platforms are crucial disseminators of such toxic, predatory propositions. What I want to explore here is how the technical element informing the process of fake news matters, how the technical element facilitates an instrumental capture of feeling at a level prior to consciousness and belief. The thesis I shall entertain proposes that the technical dimension of fake news cannot be limited to how it structures the dissemination of such news, as analyses of filter bubbles and echo chambers frequently suggest (Pariser, 2011). While the repetition of the same that such structures facilitate may well reinforce the affective power of fake news, it cannot by itself explain how fake news lures feeling beneath belief and beyond consciousness. In fact, all forms of analysis which emphasize technical structures like filter bubbles assume a separation between the agent of belief (humans) and the medium that transmits content to be believed (the filter-bubbled internet). In stark contrast to such views, I would suggest that, because it produces feeling through an indivisible composition of human and technical operations, fake news operates *prior to* any such separation. On this view, far from providing a mere support to disseminate messages to already-constituted, autonomous human subjects, the technical element is a fundamental and nonseparable part of the composition of the message, of the very operativity of fake news as toxic lure for feeling.

In what follows, the deepfake image will provide a privileged example to explore the technical element in fake news more broadly: because it is generated through a clearly discernible, highly technical process, the deepfake brings to the surface the *common pattern* that characterizes all fake news, namely the deployment of technical operations to hijack the causal efficacy informing feeling. In both the generation and experience of deepfakes, the technical element transforms causal efficacy into purely actual, presentationally immediate *images*, images that are rootless and disconnected from the larger continuity of process.

This toxic deployment of the internet compromises, indeed perverts, the capacity for algorithms to expand and intensify experience: rather than opening experience to a larger share of past potentiality, it instrumentally exhausts potentiality in order to forge an image-stimulus that elicits a totally self-enclosed and self-referential, decontextualized, automatic bodily reaction. Such toxic deployment of algorithms does not figure in Amoore's 'cloud ethics', which focuses on case studies, like virtual surgery and text mining, that involve extensive compatibility and cooperation between humans and algorithms. By contrast, the toxic deployment of algorithms directly engages instances in which the hybridity of human–algorithmic societies, also central for Amoore, generates uncontainable tension between human and algorithmic elements. In the experience of fake news, the technical element is effectively *turned against* the human element; it is deployed expressly to expropriate bodily sense. Because they accelerate human–algorithmic tension to its breaking point, fake news – and the extreme instance of deepfakes – underscore precisely what Amoore overlooks: the critical necessity to functionally differentiate operations within human–algorithmic societies and, in particular, to credit the human, or rather *humanness*, for what it uniquely brings to such societies.

We must recognize that it is the human element within societies for technical feeling – and *not* some separate human *subject* – that mediates whatever relationship algorithms are able to maintain with the potentiality of process. In 'themselves', as purely technical operations, algorithms can only operate as closed systems; they function by transforming the force of potentiality, what could have been but wasn't, into 'multiplicity', a simple repertoire of possibilities. When she stipulates that there can be no 'outside to the algorithm', Amoore comes to a similar conclusion (Amoore, 2020:5). Algorithms can only operate by 'reducing a multiplicity to one' (Amoore, 2020:17); their very operationality requires the transformation of diachronic potentiality into synchronic multiplicity which, at every instance of decision, provides a repertoire of possibilities forming the basis for a 'reduction to one'.

Revisiting the 'human in the loop'

On Amoore's account no less than on mine, however, algorithms do not function 'in and by themselves'; they are not simply technical operations in isolation, but are always localized in concrete socio-technical situations that introduce elements extraneous to their technicity. For Amoore, here echoing recent trends in the humanities, this 'extra-technical' dimension of algorithmic operationality involves a congeries of agency in which humans, non-human agents, and algorithms combine to generate action. From this perspective, not only is it unnecessary to functionally differentiate the contributions of these distinct agents, it is necessary *not to do so*, since any such functional differentiation leads inexorably to some claim of human exceptionality. Put bluntly, Amoore flattens the functional differences between humans and other contributors to algorithmic systems in order to dispel the risk of human exceptionality.

By contrast, what I am seeking to theorize here is a third path between flat ontology and human exceptionalism that is capable of recognizing the unique contribution of the human element without requiring any assertion of human autonomy, let alone any separateness of the human as agent. On my account, the functionally specific role of the human is simply to keep algorithmic operationality open to what lies outside it and to which it has no access. It is the human element that can continuously feel the causally efficacious outside, the vague totality of experience, which algorithms necessarily transform into repertoires of presentational immediacy. In this sense, the human element mediates between the narrow function of the algorithm and the larger techno-social context of its real-world operationality: it is the human element that allows algorithms to be about process, about how the past is felt into the future. For this reason, the human element is fundamental to any ethics of algorithmic life.

My understanding of the human here draws on Whitehead's characterization of humans as 'amateurs of sense perception' (Whitehead, 1938:113). Unlike animals, which are completely absorbed by their sensory coupling with the world, humans are entities for whom sense perception is or can be a *known* abstraction; we are able to feel the vague totality of the causal efficacy and conceptual potentiality of process, even when we abstract from it in order to sense the world via presentational immediacy. It is precisely this capacity that we bring to societies for technical feeling, and it is only via composition with it that algorithms are able to feel the potentiality that is the processual source for the abstraction that transforms potentiality into 'multiplicity'.

The example of the deepfake captures – in extreme form, to be sure – what happens when this primordial composition with the human is thwarted. The deepfake exemplifies how algorithms become toxic when they are made to operate autonomously, separately from what should be indivisibly enmeshed with their operation, namely bodily feeling of causal efficacy.[3] On this score, the deepfake stands in for every case – predictive policing, algorithmic sentencing, and so on – in which algorithms gain their purchase by taking the place of human subjects. Such toxic, falsely autonomous operation of algorithms substitutes a 'witness of the screen' for what Whitehead calls the 'witness of the body,' thereby collapsing the vague totality of causal efficacy and potentiality into the protracted presentational immediacy of continuously reiterated decision.[4]

My account of societies for technical feeling makes a qualified argument for keeping 'the human in the loop'.[5] However, the human at issue here differs markedly from the human that Amoore envisions in her critical repudiation of arguments that centre on rendering algorithms transparent.[6] Because they overestimate the extent of machinic autonomy, such arguments overinvest the human as an autonomous counterpoint to any threat such autonomy might pose. For Amoore, it is precisely such an overinvestment that is of concern:

> the principle problem resides not with machines breaching the limit but in sustaining a limit point of the autonomous human subject – the oft-cited 'human in the loop' – who is the locus of decision, agency, control, and ethics. Such an autonomous human disavows the *we* implicated in the entangled learning of humans with algorithms. (Amoore, 2020:22)

On my account, by contrast, the very possibility for such autonomy is suspended from the get-go, since the capacity for feeling that the human element brings to societies for technical feeling is not a capacity of the human as distinct from the algorithmic, but rather a capacity of the indivisible human–algorithmic aggregate. Accordingly, far from making the human the unique 'locus of responsibility' engaging algorithms as separable operations (Amoore, 2020:5), the specific function of the human element within societies of technical feeling – to feel past potentiality into the future – is what allows algorithms to matter. The human element provides the means for their propositional expansion and intensification of worldly potentiality to directly influence how the past can be felt.

Bodily actuality and causal efficacy

In his recent discussion of fake news and deepfakes, cultural theorist Yves Citton asks us to consider an at least initially startling possibility – the possibility that fake news and deepfakes operate not by undermining the trustworthiness accorded images on account of their objectal indexicality (or any other feature), but rather by emphasizing and at the same time calling into question the capacity of images 'to resonate within the current affective state of the multitudes'. Citton means to shift our focus away from the onto-epistemic issues raised by fake news and toward their *practical* function as the 'glue' that 'keeps our attention assembled [...] around certain target issues' and that 'keeps together our social aggregates' (Citton, 2021:50). Channelling the causally efficacious wisdom of popular culture – in this instance, singer-poet Thom Yorke's *Harrowdown Hill* – Citton suggests that what makes images effective or efficient is their capacity to recruit followers or believers, and he specifies that this capacity is wholly independent of their content. It is only the count itself that counts:

> In the nightmarish world of *Harrowdown Hill*, images [...] become *wirklich* (i.e., true because efficient) as soon as enough of us *think the same things at the same time* and *there are too many of us so you can't count* – and this, independently of the factor that pushed us to aggregate around a particular belief[...]. The 'objective' adequacy between the representative image [...] and the referent it is supposed to represent is literally *discounted* within an echo chamber where all that counts is the count itself. (Citton, 2021:51)

If Citton's analysis places fake news and deepfakes squarely in the domain of causal efficacy – they are engineered both to serve needs that are pre-perceptual and to produce effects that are extra- or post-perceptual – the question remains whether his analysis does justice to their impact on the bodily experience that, as we have seen, is absolutely central to the operation of causal efficacy.[7] By presenting the efficacy of the deepfake as a choice between two apparently mutually exclusive options – its capacity to simulate the real versus its capacity to foster attachments – Citton suggests that these two aspects of its operation can be separated and can operate independently from each other. However, what if the collective attachment Citton seeks to emphasize is in fact only made possible by a hijacking of bodily feeling? What if collective attachment is the product of the image's repurposing as technical catalyst rather than the simple voiding of its objective adequacy?

Such questions literally haunt – and I shall claim, effectively compromise – Citton's optimism regarding a more positive deployment of deepfakes, which he expresses by way of a series of questions. 'What if', he asks, the media that controls our thinking, the 'Slime' that Frank Zappa conjures in his song 'I am the Slime',

> was precious [precisely] for its stickiness? What if it provided the glue that keeps our attention assembled [...] around certain target issues, and around certain possible responses? [...] [S]hould the glue keeping together our social aggregates be attributed to the mediarchic Slime fed to them? Or wouldn't it be more accurate (and more promising) to locate the stickiness on the side of our subjective affects as receivers, rather than on the side of the content (images, ideas, stories) distributed through our ubiquitous screens? (Citton, 2021:50)

Appealing as such a possibility may be, Citton's effort to redeem the deepfake fundamentally misrecognizes what is at issue in today's Slime. As the exemplar of the latter, the deepfake underscores the profound tie binding the image as toxic stimulus with its power to generate 'stickiness', to catalyse collective attachment. The content of the deepfake *is* its technical element, and the fact that this technical element co-participates in the genesis of a feeling is what explains how deepfakes – and fake news more generally – produce affective responses. Without the technically generated stimulus, there would be no affective response.

If Citton's analysis risks undervaluing the danger algorithms pose, that is because, in viewing them exclusively as lures for concrete collective attachments, he simply brackets the negative side of their operation. He thus neglects to explore how their technical genesis and operation co-opts the very process of bodily feeling, the witness of the body, that generates collective attachment when indivisible human–technical societies take up lures for feeling and experience causal efficacy and its adherent conceptual potentiality. What is ultimately at issue in Citton's undervaluation of the toxicity of fake news is a lack of attention to the crucial role that algorithms play *as technical operations* which operate generically by 'reducing multiplicity to one', thereby collapsing causal efficacy into the protracted presentational immediacy of the engineered image or filter bubbled fake news story.

If we are to redeem algorithmic processes as means to generate positive collectivities, we will accordingly need to criticize the reduction that informs their toxic deployment and relocate them outside the closed space generated through such reduction. Contra Citton, *this cannot be done without reckoning with the fundamental link binding the technical and any affective, bodily response*. What is needed is a transformation – not an elimination – of the technical dimension.

Deepfake reality

The irreducibly technical operation of algorithms is made manifest in a particularly nefarious way by the recent phenomenon of animated deepfakes, understood as *the extreme instance* of the toxicity of fake news. By bringing the fusion of animation and live-action cinema to a culminating point, deepfakes hyper-accelerate the toxic logic of simulation, made famous by Jean Baudrillard's provocative claims about mediated reality, to a point of no return.[8] For what informs the cultural operation of deepfakes is not simply their power as *visual* illusions that substitute mediation for directly lived reality but, far more fundamentally, their exploitation and instrumental appropriation of the very logic of bodily motricity. By appropriating the logic of bodily motricity, deepfakes hijack the causal efficacy that informs bodily experience, the witness of the body, and makes it serve what is in effect a contextless, *ex nihilo*, presentationally immediate lure for feeling. Because they are the most extreme examples of this algorithmic process, deepfakes constitute a blueprint and ideal type for exploring how fake news works generically. They illustrate simply and concretely how fake news hijacks bodily feeling, detaches it from its causal efficacy, reattaches it to a presentationally immediate stimulus that engages an alternate, solipsistic history of causal efficacy, and thus redirects it to serve nefarious ends.

Towards the end of 2017, the first so-called deepfake image appeared on the internet (Cole, 2017). The content of the first deepfake, like that of the vast majority that have followed in its wake, is banal and predictable: it displays the face of a movie star fused onto the body of a pornographic actress, just as one would expect. The techno-aesthetics informing the deepfake, however, are certainly not simple and straightforward. As its name reveals, the deepfake is an image composed using advanced machine (so-called 'deep') learning and is thus a highly engineered, synthetic image.[9] For this reason alone, deepfakes fit squarely within the trajectory of cinematic and technical image culture toward an increasingly 'perfect' realism, a total triumph of opticality as the medium for the perfect simulation of reality. Deepfakes mark an *epochal* shift in the configuration of image and embodiment – a shift from capturing images of already extant movement to expropriating the logic of movement-perception itself. Deepfakes point to a moment when the image and the body will have been made 'inseparable', to invoke Giorgio Agamben's suggestive conception (Agamben, 1993), but in a configuration that, unlike what Agamben imagined in 1990, is instrumental and techno-rationalistic, and hence anti-human as well as anti-process: that is, violently reductive of the injunction against 'defac[ing] the value experience which is the very essence of the universe' (Whitehead, 1938:111).

The development of deepfakes is a testament to the astounding rapidity of technical change. No more than five years ago, deepfakes would have been the exclusive prerogative of well-resourced institutions such as advertising agencies and Hollywood movie studios; today they can be produced in a matter of hours by amateur web surfers using freely available, off-the-screen software.[10] What explains this massive shift is the application of deep learning techniques to the problem of image production, and in particular, the deployment of generative adversarial networks (GANs). Introduced in 2014, GANs mobilize the competition between two machine learning computers – a generator and a discriminator – in order to accelerate and improve, that is, *to optimize*, machine learning outcomes. Although the first deepfakes were made with applications drawing on other deep learning techniques, it is the use of GANs that opened the spectre of deepfake *perfection*. As journalist Ian Sample explains, the use of GANs to produce deepfakes heralds the advent of the artificial synthesis of embodiment itself:

> A GAN pits two artificial intelligence algorithms against each other. The first algorithm, known as the generator, is fed random noise and turns it into an image. This synthetic image is then added to a stream of real images – of celebrities, say – that are fed into the second algorithm, known as the discriminator. At first, the synthetic images will look nothing like faces. But repeat the process countless times, with feedback on performance, and the discriminator and generator both improve. Given enough cycles and feedback, the generator will start producing utterly realistic faces of completely nonexistent celebrities. (Sample, 2020)

By combining the generator's capacity to synthesize *new* images on the basis of patterns it discovers in noise with the discriminator's rapid learning on a massive amount of cultural data, GANs set up a process that, in the words of journalist Rob Toews, gives 'neural networks the power not just to perceive, but to create' (Toews, 2020).

Because of its power to catalyse toxic reactions, the deepfake illustrates the negative underside of our contemporary status as 'phenomenotechnical' beings, beings whose experience – that is, whose bodily experience – is fundamentally mediated by explicitly *technical* phenomenotechnical interfaces.[11] We ever increasingly *live* our vague implication within the totality of causally efficacious process, within nature, by way of technologies that expand access to the conceptual potentiality of process, that multiply the possibilities for what is not but could be, and that allow them to matter for the future. This generalized operation of technologies to mediate and intensify process marks both an expansion and a generalization of 'phenomenotechnics', the notion which philosopher Gaston Bachelard introduced to describe the reality of experimental science following the microphysical revolution.[12] No longer restricted to the domain of science, today's phenomenotechnical operations involve indivisible human–technical aggregates that undergird the vast majority of our everyday activities, from scheduling a doctor's appointment or buying a plane ticket to simply searching the internet or reading a daily news feed. Along with this expansion, there has occurred a shift in the locus of phenomenotechnical operations: the primarily cognitive result of restricted experimental phenomenotechnics has given way to primarily bodily results that, far from being the prerogative of scientists, are the common experience of (most of) humankind. Deployed in relation to our digital reality, phenomenotechnical operations yield the indivisibly human–technical feelings that constitute the basis for experience in our world today.

As the epitome of algorithmic capture of process, the deepfake illustrates the toxic side of our phenomenotechnical constitution. It marks the extreme instance of the displacement of the 'witness of the body' by the 'witness of the screen', as I put it above. In the wake of this displacement, causal efficacy is itself 'presentified', made into a purely synchronic repertoire that, as I have shown, loses touch with potentiality, that simply transforms diachronic potentiality into synchronic multiplicity.

Dissolving the uncanny valley

It is precisely by hijacking the embodiment informing movement, by reducing embodied potentiality to a static possibility space, that GANs are (or soon will be) able to produce images so realistic that *they will no longer fall into the so-called 'uncanny valley'*. 'Until recently,' observes one scholar,

> even the most expensive alterations have tended to fail. CGI and motion-capture faceswaps draw unwelcome attention to themselves, falling into the 'uncanny valley' of almost, but not quite and triggering a vague unease or revulsion in viewers. Deep-learning AI changes the game. The multidimensional complexity of transforming one person's face into a seamless mask for another actor is just the kind of discrete

task that deep neural nets excel at conquering. Bridging the uncanny valley is just another kind of board game for an AI to learn. (Fletcher, 2018:463)

This milestone – bridging the uncanny valley – gives some objective measure to the slippery notion of perfection that the deepfake has elicited. What it shows is that the deepfake is, at least potentially, the *perfect* simulation: the deepfake combines the extraction of the embodied logic underlying the visual fluency of images with the 'processing fluency' that makes humans particularly susceptible to lending credibility to moving images.[13] The result is an automaticity of bodily *response* that effectively transforms the thick, causally efficacious history of process into a purely presentist *reaction*. It is precisely this capacity of the deepfake to dissolve the uncanny valley that produces the *epochal* shift it introduces: because it can lure feeling by directly hijacking embodiment, thus dispensing with any need for adaptation on the part of the human, the deepfake radicalizes the power of simulation. Specifically, it collapses bodily feeling into an animated image and thus, in an inversion of how process *should* operate, following Whitehead's injunction against defacing the value experience of the universe (Whitehead, 1938:111), makes feeling a function of the abstraction of presentational immediacy. By detaching feeling from its bodily source and history of causal efficacy, the deepfake renders feeling rootless and vulnerable to manipulation.

As its name indicates, the uncanny valley, first theorized by Japanese robotics researcher Masahiro Mori, designates a liminal space between the human and the technical that is infringed when robots are too real seeming, too like their human models. The uncanny valley has long guided work in robotics, functioning as an injunction against making robots too verisimilar. That is beginning to change, however. The practical work of more recent roboticists, for example Dave Hanson, and the critical work of theorists like Jenny Rhee, challenges the consensus that has made the uncanny valley taboo. In this more recent vision, what the uncanny valley marks is less a hard limit on the possibilities for simulation of humanness than a space of negotiation between humans and machines where what is at issue is humanness itself. In her effort to retheorize the uncanny valley as a 'boundary-*making*',[14] not a 'boundary-identifying', practice (Rhee, 2013:309), Rhee effectively transforms the uncanny valley into a *phenomenotechnics of embodiment*: a space of open-ended negotiation – an open 'affinity,' not a pre-framed 'familiarity' – between human and machine.[15] Rhee shows that, far from marking out a forbidden space, the uncanny valley defines an experimental terrain for retraining the human through practical renegotiation of the boundary separating humans from machines. The repetitive labour of training required by such renegotiation forges commonality where none existed before.[16]

Considered in the context of deepfakes, Rhee's argument takes on a markedly different significance. For if deepfakes do succeed in bridging the uncanny valley, their success will come not through an embodied training of humans but, as we have already observed, *simply through the wholesale, brute-force expropriation of our embodiment*. Foregoing the need for any acclimation period on our part, deepfakes directly engineer the dynamics of the image to make it coalesce perfectly with the neurophysiological processes informing our conferral of credence to images. In this respect, deepfakes are like – or perhaps simply *are* – movement-images that elicit mirror neurons; they directly capture – and indeed might be said to weaponize – the neurophysiology of audiovisual perception such that images of movement can take the place of, can elicit the *same response* as, actual movements. When they process massive amounts of data as purely actual data, GANs reduce the *generativity* of environmental potentiality into an inert database for generating one new image. GAN-generated deepfakes literally exhaust the possibility space of mass quantities of data, leaving behind data husks whose potential has been converted into a hyper-immediate stimulus. In the process – and this is what is truly *epochal* here – GAN-generated deepfakes literally expropriate *our embodied sense of movement*. Deepfakes, Schick poignantly observes, 'effectively steal [...] our biometrics' (Schick, 2020:141).

From animation to algorithm

Insofar as they epitomize the toxicity of fake news, deepfakes occupy one extreme of a continuum of algorithmic abstraction. As we have seen, they involve the instrumental expropriation of the processual logic of bodily feeling in the service of a selectional principle that has no aim other than to produce the perfect simulation, a pure presentationally immediate image created through a process of abstraction that literally *destroys its own causally efficacious basis*. Such an abstraction is a bad abstraction, what Didier Debaise has recently called a 'predatory abstraction' (Debaise, 2021). What makes an abstraction bad or predatory is its self-enclosure and pretention to autonomy: bad abstractions, Whitehead tells us, 'function in experience so as to separate them[selves] from their relevance to the totality' (Whitehead, 1938:123). If this means that a bad abstraction is an abstraction that is cut off from the broader causal efficacy and potentiality informing it, then the deepfake is the very epitome of bad abstraction.

When algorithms decide on potentiality in the service of an endogenous selection principle, they are repeating a gesture whose origin can be traced back to cinematic animation. What is at stake in both cases, as I shall now show, is the *scope of value* that informs selection: just as cinematic animation forecloses the potentiality of drawing that remains *external* to the self-enclosed space in which it operates, algorithms foreclose the potentiality of the larger environmental situation they capture by restricting it to what their endogenously generated selectional principle recognizes and includes as 'data'. One need only think of the basic protocol of today's most experimental machine learning systems: the quest to categorize unorganized data operates in the service of a constantly evolving endogenous selectional principle, which is nothing other than the evolving-emerging, sought-for category itself. In the case of cinematic animation and algorithmic governance alike, an endogenous, instrumental principle of value substitutes for the 'existential' value generated by the feeling of broader causal efficacy and potentiality.

Because it requires that the generativity of drawing be subordinated to a rigid technical principle, animation encapsulates the operation that is also, though in more complex ways, at issue in today's algorithms. In this way, cinematic animation provides a simple and schematic picture of the violence algorithms perform. The comparison of algorithms with cinematic animation makes patent how efficaciously algorithms deploy their endogenously generated principle of value to foreclose any environmental potentiality that cannot be enfolded into their operation. In so doing, algorithms take the cinematic principle of 'imposition' to its extreme and render it dynamic, making all potentiality – 'generativity' as such – a function of a constantly updating actuality. Cinematic animation thus provides an anticipation and a simplified blueprint for how algorithms generate images by hijacking the generativity of animation and constraining it via an endogenously generated principle or value.

Yet cinematic animation also differs from algorithmic operationality in consequential ways. As we shall see, cinematic animation leaves intact an outside – the potentiality of drawing – even as it constrains it by submitting it to the cinematic principle of imposition. It is precisely such an outside that, as Amoore has suggested, is foreclosed when algorithms are made to operate autonomously. For this reason, when we re-embed algorithms in the larger social contexts in which they operate, when we correctly position them as elements of indivisible human–algorithmic societies capable of feeling the impact of their intensification of potentiality, we effectively *rediscover* and *restore* the potentiality of the animatic outside that their narrowly technical operation has effectively eliminated.

From 'transfer' to 'generativity/imposition'

In its cinematic form, animation combines a technical operation – the mechanical repetition of the any-instant-whatever – with the drawn image. William Schaffer centres his insightful exploration of the specificity of cinematic animation around a passage from Gilles Deleuze's *Cinema 1*.[17] Deleuze writes:

Any other system which reproduces movement through an order of exposures [*poses*] projected in such a way that they pass into one another, or are 'transformed', is foreign to the cinema. This is clear when one attempts to define the cartoon film; if it belongs fully to the cinema, this is because the drawing no longer constitutes a pose or a completed figure, but the description of a figure which is always in the process of being formed or dissolving through the movement of lines and points taken at any-instant-whatevers of their course. (Deleuze, 1986:5)

In unpacking this passage, Schaffer distills four 'preconditions' of the technical possibility of cinema. These are (1) instant photos or snapshots; (2) temporal equidistance between snapshots; (3) transfer of this temporal equidistance onto the spatial equidistance of the filmstrip; and (4) an automatic mechanism for projecting the frames of the filmstrip following the temporal equidistance informing the capture of snapshots. The first two of these preconditions pertain to the production side of cinema – image inscription; the second two pertain to the reproduction side of cinema – image projection.

Cinematic animation breaks with the first two of these preconditions, which, Schaffer tells us, do not obtain or, more precisely, do not *need to* obtain in its case. If cinema would be impossible using long exposures, he observes, the 'same is not true […] of the animation process. Despite the obvious and immense advantages of the snapshot for the working animator, effective animations could be created using long-exposures for the recording of frames, since the individual frames take the form of photographed drawings' (Schaffer, 2007:457). Animation's break with the first two preconditions interrupts the technical operationality of cinema *as a whole*. What is thereby exposed is nothing less than animation's *non-cinematic* ontology:

It cannot, however, be a matter of merely subtracting the first half of Deleuze's formulation of the conditions of cinema – conditions 1 and 2 – leaving us with conditions 3 and 4 to define animation as a 'truncated' form of cinema. Since the four conditions taken as a whole are logically sequential, the 'subtraction' of the first two conditions *necessarily and radically changes the status of the third*. Instead of a transfer, which refers to the movement *of already existing bodies*, as with the Deleuzian account of cinema, there is in animation a double movement of *imposition* and *generation*. From the point of view of individual cels, considered in isolation, recording onto a film strip *involves the imposition of an indifferent measure*; from the point of view of the moving image, this same process involves a pure act of generation, a veritable 'giving of life' to animated bodies. (Schaffer, 2007:458; emphases added)

With this distinction between 'transfer' and 'imposition/generation', Schaffer pinpoints quite precisely how animation is rooted in a different extraction from the body than the cinematic one. Whereas conventional or live-action cinema extracts movement from already existing bodies, animation *extracts movement from the manual power of drawing itself.* It is this power that accounts for animation's capacity to generate movement, to 'give life' to animated bodies.

In its cinematic deployment, however, this power of drawing – this 'pure act of generation' – is constrained by the technical demands of the cinematic apparatus in which it is enclosed. By imposing the indifferent measure of the any-instant-whatever on the generative power of drawing, cinema constrains the potentiality of drawing, rendering it a function of cinematic continuity rather than animatic generativity. It is in this sense, precisely, that cinematic animation both anticipates and provides a simple blueprint for algorithmic operationality: it resolves the tension between open generativity (the potentiality of drawing qua causal efficacy) and the principle of imposition (the indifferent cinematic measure) in favour of the latter, just as algorithms exhaust potentiality in the service of an endogenously generated principle of value.

Algorithms beyond animation

Indeed, with the development of algorithmic culture, animation is both emancipated from its constrained *cinematic* operation and made more ubiquitous as a cultural operation. Yet far from liberating its open generativity, this process submits animation to an even more rigorous cleansing of its potentiality. We can grasp the extent of this cleansing by comparing the nearly identical formulas for cinematic animation and for algorithmic operationality. In the generic formula of cinematic animation – *generativity* + *imposition* = *cinematic animation* – the two terms or 'addends' maintain a degree of tension with each other and the 'sum' is a result of the resolution of this tension. By contrast, in the generic formula for algorithmic processing of environmental possibility into decision – *generativity* + *imposition* = *algorithmic animation* – the 'sum' is the result of the subsumption of one 'addend' by the other. In algorithmic animation, imposition subsumes generativity entirely, filtering it through and making it a function of imposition. In the process, any tension between actuality and potentiality is dissolved in favour of the former.

Algorithmic operationality incrementally processes potentiality by submitting it to an endogenously generated principle of value. Because this latter rigidly determines the bounds of what has value (or, to return to Citton's argument, of what counts), it effectively depotentializes the very potentiality that informs its operation. In Whiteheadian terms, it reduces the causal efficacy from which it abstracts to a continuously re-iterated series of presentationally immediate decisions that over and over again reduce multiplicity to one. This means that the generativity involved in algorithmic animation is a false or simulated potentiality. *Itself constituted as a function of an endogenously generated principle* (for example, relevance of key image features), such false potentiality compromises the animatic tension between generativity and imposition from the very get-go. In developing from its cinematic form into the basis for today's algorithms, animation effectively exchanges one constraining principle of imposition for a yet more constraining one, the cinematic 'any-instant-whatever' for the principle of algorithmic optimization. This wholesale subsumption of generativity by algorithmic optimization operates what I call the *algorithmic collapse* of animation.

In light of this longer genealogy of algorithmic imposition, we can now more clearly appreciate what is at stake in the deepfake. As the culmination of the algorithmic subsumption of animation, the deepfake is *at one and the same time* the apotheosis of the process of generativity *and* the epitome of algorithmic collapse. It is both the product of a total openness to and exhaustive inclusion of the whole of possibility *and* what results when possibility is comprehensively evaluated by a myopically instrumental, endogenously generated, self-enclosed principle of imposition or value. What is singular here is precisely how, in the deepfake, the operation that embraces possibility in its fullness and totality *coincides absolutely* with its wholesale instrumental mobilization. This is precisely why the deepfake is the *perfect instance* of algorithmic collapse: deepfakes result from and express a process in which the complete exhaustion of potentiality itself serves the instrumental end of expropriating the processual logic of embodiment in order to produce perfect, self-enclosed simulations that operate to lure feeling as automatic reaction.

The technicity of fake news

With the exception of some politically targeted instances, including deployments to protect the identity of witnesses and more nefarious ones to catalyse geopolitical conflicts (Schick, 2020), deepfakes have largely operated in the realm of the personal and, one might even say, the trivial. In this sense, what makes them epochal – their expropriation of the processual logic of embodied feeling – does not immediately translate into any pressing 'existential' danger. Yet as the epitome of the toxicity of fake news and pinnacle of the technical engineering of animated images, deepfakes foreground what is often overlooked in analyses of fake news: the reality that algorithms act beyond our knowledge and control, and in ways that can open experience to a larger share of worldly sensibility, but that can also foreclose this potential in the service of narrowly instrumental ends. Precisely because of their extreme toxicity, deepfakes exemplify the agency that algorithms as specifically technical operations wield as elements in larger societies of technical feeling. On account of this radicality and technical 'simplicity', deepfakes help shed light on the far more complex technicity of fake news.

Both deepfakes and fake news operate by depotentializing causal efficacy. For this reason, both are toxic, predatory abstractions. Deepfakes operate by *exhausting* the causal efficacy informing movement in order to condense it into a presentationally immediate image capable of hijacking the feeling, the potentialized causal efficacy, that viewers bring to it. The lure for feeling they offer is thus a false one, an invitation to participate in experience that is somehow discontinuous with the past the viewer brings to the situation. Such experience catalyses embodied response in the service of ends unconnected to what we might call its cosmological situation: by harnessing the 'energy' informing the viewer's past for myopic, presentationally immediate release, it transforms diachronic embodied response into simple, immediate, depthless reaction.

Although fake news involves a different technical element and a different redeployment of extracted energy, it likewise operates by expropriating viewer-reader feeling. However, in the case of fake news, the technical element catalysing reaction is not a specific technique of machine learning, but the internet itself, understood not as mere support for feeling, but as an indivisible element of feeling. By the 'internet itself', I thus mean more than the algorithmic selection processes that are responsible for creating echo chambers and filter bubbles. I mean more than the social and political agendas that manipulate these algorithms. And I mean more than the internet's continuous creation through ongoing user interaction. All of these features suppose the separation of human and technics that I would like to think beyond and beneath. By the 'internet itself', I thus mean the aggregate of algorithms that brings together, in an indivisible feeling, these and other technical and non-technical elements, including the distinctly human capacity to feel conceptual potentiality, into larger societies that can directly feel the propositionally expanded and intensified potentiality long before it take forms as consciously held beliefs.

In its work to expropriate the feeling of its users, fake news leverages two constitutive 'technical' components of internet activity – depthlessness and simplicity of content, and speed of transmission or time criticality. Yoked together, and sharing in a larger feeling in concert with the users they recruit, these components produce hyperbolic, contextless messages that obtain their catalytic force from what we might call their 'informational freshness', their apparent *ex nihilo* appearance as hyper-simplified abstractions of the potentiality of complex situations. Fake news, like the three viral rumours I invoked at the beginning of this article, must be there, as it were, *always already*, as if arising with the event itself. It must be readily available, *pre*-available, as an alternative narrative, an alternative proposition, about an event. It must offer narratives or propositions that do not engage users as lures for feeling to continue ongoing causally efficacious processes but rather as false, predatory lures that tap into alternative, extremely narrow lineages of causal efficacy, namely users' solipsistic histories of feeling, which is to say, of bad feelings – be these racist or homophobic or transphobic or misogynistic or anti-authority or anti-immigrant or… Fake news operates by overwriting the complex situation it purposely misrepresents with such alternative, solipsistic histories of feeling. It quite literally *uses* events – for example, a racially motivated massacre like the recent one in Buffalo, NY, or a school shooting like the recent one in Uvalde, Texas – as triggers to activate these alternative histories of feeling.

The ineliminable technicity of attachment

The comparison with deepfakes helps us pinpoint the limitation of analyses of fake news, Citton's included, which focus on the internet as support for communicational activities rather than as a component in a larger composition fusing technical and human elements, an element in a larger society of technical feeling. Again, the crucial issue at stake here is whether the production of collective attachments that Citton and others would like to ascribe to the internet can be separated from the concrete technical images that catalyse such attachments. With respect to both the deepfake and fake news, the technically engineered image or news story works to hijack bodily response rather than to channel it to forge collective attachments. As we have seen, the deepfake concentrates the generic causal efficacy of the witness of the body into a hyper-immediate witness of the screen. Fake news achieves a similar end by expropriating the causal efficacy and conceptual potentiality of events and relocating them within a different lineage of feeling – the solipsistic lineages of the bad feelings of certain users. Users who are taken in by fake news fall prey to a technically engineered lure for the feeling; their feeling, accordingly, serves as warrant for them to 'believe' that they are part of a veritable collective attachment (that is, a society with an ongoing, shared history of feeling) when in fact they are solipsistic units in a falsely collective count. Like the deepfake, fake news is a perfect simulation.

What I have been here describing perfectly captures the process of recruiting believers through the count. Citton, you will recall, disengages the efficacy of images from their content, arguing that it is only the count itself that counts. Yet what is the count, if not the construction of a false collectivity? What is the count, if not a mere aggregation of separate, fully individuated feelers brought together by their liability to be lured by propositions about events that connect, that are made to connect – always for disparate, individualized reasons – to their own solipsistic lineages of feeling?

What the foregoing analysis pinpoints is the common pattern characteristic of toxic, predatory propositions disseminated on the internet: the hijacking of the feeling of causal efficacy by a technically catalysed, hyper-immediate and disconnected pseudo-feeling. Accordingly, when Citton discounts the content of the image, he effectively discounts the technical element itself. For the content *is* the technical element – the reduction of potentiality to a hyper-immediate stimulus. In so doing, Citton not only jettisons a key element of the indivisible human–technical society that he is seeking to describe, but he argues as if the alleged 'good' operation – 'the affective congruence with the multitudes' – can be separated, and deployed separately, from the 'bad' operation, namely, the toxic propositional lure itself.

Put another way, what the common pattern of toxic, predatory propositions underscores is that the two allegedly independent operations – triggering by technically generated image or fake news story; recruitment of users into collective, affective attachments – are in fact neither separate nor separable. Because deepfakes and fake news recruit 'feelers' by hijacking the affective, bodily experience of the causal efficacy of the world, whether by distilling it into hyper-immediate images or displacing it in favour of solipsistic lineages of feeling, whatever collective attachments they generate cannot but be toxic ones, false attachments cut off from the continuity of experience that redirect affective embodiment to nefarious ends. The bodily feeling at work in these toxic attachments is without connection to the effaced causal efficacy and potentiality – specifically the potentiality of bodily life to experience the self, others, and the world, as Whitehead puts it (1938:110) – whose instrumental expropriation and exhaustion quite literally composes the deepfake image.

Humanness, or why algorithms matter

I have already suggested what would be needed for algorithms to participate non-toxically in indivisible human–technical societies: their constitutive partiality must be recognized and celebrated, and their openness to being modified by that which lies outside their always actual operation must be affirmed. Algorithms must never be taken to be autonomously acting operations, closed in relation to any outside, but must rather always be approached through their participation in the operation of larger indivisible human–technical societies. There is no algorithm-in-itself, no algorithm-by-itself. Algorithms simply do not and cannot operate in insolation, separated from the human element that composes reality with them. They need humans to value their results by keeping open the potentiality that they process but that they themselves can only experience through the abstraction of their technical operationality – as a continuously iterated, temporally flattened, presentationally immediate 'multiplicity reducing to one'. This means that algorithms, when considered narrowly as technical operations, are fundamentally incomplete: algorithms always operate within larger societies that involve a functional differentiation, as discussed above. According to this differentiation, it is the human element within the larger society that brings in the capacity to evaluate and to value the propositions that algorithms multiply and intensify. Moreover, just as there is no algorithm-in-itself, there is no human-in-itself; rather, what we might call 'humanness' arises in 'intimate cooperation' with that 'portion of nature' that is the body (Whitehead 1938:115).

What makes humans unique without being exceptional – our capacity to grasp the partiality of our own abstractions and to sense the vague totality from which they abstract – is precisely what makes our contribution to algorithmic culture so imperative. We are unique among entities because we both participate in *and* observe and design the happening of feeling, the process through which feeling the past produces the future. We are the vehicles through which the potentiality of the past not only remains alive (which it does for all levels of process) but through which it can be differentially or selectively drawn upon. In their vocation to multiply and intensify propositions – proposals about how the potentiality of the past can shape the future – algorithms provide vastly more conceptual possibilities than can be generated by the human imagination, including ones that, like AlphaGo's legendary 37th move in its March 2016 match against Go master Lee Sedol, are absolute surprises to us (Metz, 2016a, 2016b). However, it remains the human share that can evaluate and value these possibilities. My broad claim here is that when humans do this, we value and evaluate algorithmic propositions as proxies for process itself, for the process in which we share, and not in our own self-interest or through self-reference.

When algorithms operate toxically, it is precisely because this human share gets foreclosed or impeded. Accordingly, in order to invest in the positive potentiality of algorithms as proposition machines, we must intervene critically and practically in their operation and thereby interrupt their instrumental closure. We must provide a larger context and space which can keep them open to the potentiality that lies beyond their grasp. With her account of how doubt can be built into algorithms, Louise Amoore provides some concrete examples of how this might work (Amoore, 2020: chapter 5). What she doesn't emphasize nearly enough, however, is the role played by humans – or perhaps we better say, by *humanness* – in designing and participating in systems capable of integrating doubt understood as proxy for differential and potentially incompossible potentialities that the past carries with it into the future.

The imperative to accord humanness such a central role manifests clearly when we ask how we humans *know* that algorithms are always partial, that the propositions they generate concern differential valuations of the unrealized potentiality for the past to be felt into the future. If we do not and cannot know algorithms on the basis of an understanding of how they function, this is not simply because their layers and procedures are too complex to be known (as contemporary machine learning protocols readily admit, even celebrate). Rather, it is because *no analysis from the algorithmic perspective can grasp how algorithms engage a potentiality that is outside their operationality and beyond their mode of 'experience'*. For that, the human share is needed. And indeed, it is not so much knowledge that the human share brings in, but rather feeling: if we can *know* that algorithms are always partial, that is because we *feel* the openness of potentiality they multiply and intensify. When we maintain critical vigilance about the operationality of the human–algorithmic societies in which we increasingly find ourselves enmeshed, we are *acting on* our necessarily *prior* feeling of the potentiality expressed by algorithmically generated propositions. Such propositions are not evaluated by us as cognitive possibilities; rather they engage experience as lures for feeling, and whatever feeling results from such engagement, even though it takes place through our contribution, is not *our* feeling, but a feeling of the larger society – of the society for technical feeling – within which it is generated. On this account, algorithms matter not because they engage reality separately from humans, but because they directly and causally influence how the past is felt into the future by multiplying and intensifying the propositional potentiality informing the larger societies in which their agency and ours fuse.

Notes

[1] In his exposition, Whitehead distinguishes propositions from 'eternal objects', which he introduces to account for the potentiality of process at the most generic level. Eternal objects are the potentiality of the past: the 'pure potentiality' that is 'referent to *any* [...] entities, in the absolutely general sense of *any*' (Whitehead, 1978:256). Eternal objects, for example colours or shapes or mathematical relationships, are what determine the *how* of process, the manner in which an actual entity concresces or becomes concrete. In simpler, less technical terms, eternal objects provide a fully generic source for potential – *what could have been but was not* – to become relevant in future process.

[2] 'Society' is Whitehead's term for any enduring object. An enduring object is a composition of actual entities and of sub-societies of actual entities that come together and persist in their togetherness through their sharing of some pattern. It is important to bear in mind the divergence of Whitehead's technical notion from the ordinary, more restricted sense of society.

[3] This autonomous mode of algorithmic function makes common cause with the 'technical solutionism' so rampant in our culture. Consider the examples of predictive policing or algorithmic sentencing systems, where algorithms supposedly achieve their 'objectivity' from their autonomy in relation to biased, human judgement.

[4] The notion of 'withness of the screen' builds on my earlier analysis of 'machinic reference'. The latter designates the substitution of a technical operation for the *impure* mode of perception that Whitehead calls 'symbolic reference'. Symbolic reference is the normal or typical mode of human experience in which sense perceptual experiences are referent to causally efficacious ones (and vice versa) via a common element. The notion of machinic reference, like that of the withness of the screen, designates the possibility

that this *correlational* operation could be performed by technical operations rather than embodied human ones. See Hansen (2015).

5   For Amoore, it is 'the human in the loop' and not the 'degree of autonomy afforded to machines versus humans as a locus of decision' that impedes cloud ethics (2020:21). Claiming that the human in the loop can only be an autonomous human, Amoore argues that this 'disavows' the algorithmic 'we'. My argument, in contrast, is that the 'we' at stake here can only be truly achieved through a feeling-together that happens at a more fundamental level of process than 'entangled learning'. This level, of course, is that of causal efficacy with its adherent conceptual potentiality.

6   Amoore rightly criticizes arguments that link the opacity of algorithms to the solidification of a 'black box society' and propose transparency as the solution to algorithmic bias. Her position, with which I fully concur, is that algorithms necessarily involve bias, and that we should seek to design their operation with that in mind, so that their bias becomes a resource rather than a liability (Amoore, 2020:5). What I question, however, is whether criticizing such a position requires a flattening of the specificity of the human contribution.

7   Citton turns to Simondon's conception of the image cycle, developed in his 1965–66 course on the image, for an account of the pre- and extra- or post-perceptual operation of images. For Simondon, the cycle of the image proceeds through three moments or stages. The first, which concerns an *a priori* image that is already present, in embryonic state, within the body, correlates with instinctual movements and reflects Simondon's conviction that 'motricity precedes sensoriality' (Simondon, 2008:20). The second moment relates the body to an external object and generates an *a praesenti* image that is the vehicle for informational exchange with the external environment. Finally, the third moment concerns the continued activity of the image even after the object is no longer perceived by the subject and involves an *a posteriori* image within the psyche, a memorial imprint that prolongs the activity of the second moment in a manner similar to Whitehead's conception of feeling as the activity through which past potentiality gives rise to future experience.

8   Without a doubt, the pinnacle of this trajectory, thus far at least, is the fusion of animated with live-action cinema that takes a host of forms in our contemporary culture. With the appearance of films like *Pirates of the Caribbean: The Curse of the Black Pearl* (2003), *Sky Captain and the World of Tomorrow* (2004) and *Beowulf* (2007), a corner of cinematic production turned fully digital; heavily invested in quickly changing and improving technologies of body capture, notably the process of 'universal capture', these films and the industry they exemplify seek to extract the 'know-how' of embodied bodily movement and deploy it as the principle for the production of what I want to think of as a new kind of realism. While they may look realistic in all ways, what makes these films and similar productions believable, what compels us to take them for real, is their success at simulating the deep bodily logic of movement that in some ineliminable sense lies beneath the surface of appearance and the image (see Telotte, 2010, chapters 9–10).

9   Most of the deepfakes currently circulating in our infosphere are pornographic in nature, typically involving the overlaying of a (female) celebrity's face on the body of a (female) porn performer. Deepfakes have also been widely deployed as forms of personal revenge and celebrity worship, and in a few cases, as political stunts or means of protecting vulnerable witnesses. See Schick (2020).

10   Consider the case of iFake, an anonymous YouTuber, who in December 2019 released a video in which they used free AI software to solve the de-ageing problem that so troubled the SFX crew working on Scorsese's film *The Irishman*; what in 2015 required a team of professionals, millions of dollars, and days of computational run-time had become, by the end of 2019, easily replicable by an individual with no special training or skills using typical applications downloadable from the internet.

[11] I would argue in fact that we have always been phenomenotechnical beings, and that the primary meaning of *technical* in phenomenotechnical concerns our generic need to supplement our limited perceptual access to reality, including our own bodily reality, with indirect means. Rituals and magic practices thus constitute phenomenotechnical interfaces just as much as algorithmic systems do, even though the latter can be said to be technical (and the former not) in an additional sense.

[12] French philosopher of science, Gaston Bachelard, introduced the *phenomenotechnical* interface in order to describe the operations of the experimental sciences, and above all physics, which from the scientific revolution to the microphysical revolution, have ever increasingly involved the instrumental deployment of technological apparatuses and platforms capable of making contact with dimensions of physical reality or 'nature' that could not be accessed via (human) sense perception. In Hansen (2021), I have shown how the algorithms informing much of everyday experience in our world today, including experience on the internet, constitute an omnipresent phenomenotechnical interface. The crucial difference that characterizes our situation is the sheer scale of cultural phenomenotechnics: no longer restricted to the domain of experimental science, or any other specialized endeavour, the phenomenotechnical interface now plays a role in many, if not most, of the mundane tasks we carry out in everyday life. In this respect, it furnishes an opportunity for us to excavate and theorize what it means for cultural agency to be shared across the human–technology divide.

[13] Commentators have noted the susceptibility of humans to lend credence to audiovisual moving images. Summarizing research on image perception, Schick claims that 'we are wired to want to believe audiovisual material that "looks" or "sounds" right. Psychologists call this "processing fluency", referring to our unconscious cognitive bias in favor of information that our brain can process quickly. We do it a lot more quickly with visuals than with text' (Schick, 2020:29). The notion of *looking or sounding right* aptly captures what is at stake in the *perfection* of the image, what characterizes the deepfake as perfect simulacrum. What 'perfect' means here is that the image actually takes the place of what it is an image of: perfection means that there is no way perceptually, on the basis of neurophysiologically embodied perception, for humans to discriminate synthetic images from captured ones.

[14] Rhee describes her aim as follows: 'I offer an alternative reading of the uncanny valley as a site of entanglement – one that highlights and challenges constructed boundaries between human and nonhuman, as well as opens up these boundary-constructions for critical engagement and historicization' (Rhee, 2013:302).

[15] 'Affinity' and 'familiarity' are the two different translations that have been given for the Japanese word, *shinwakan*, in English renderings of Mori's work. The former appears only in a 2012 translation and for Rhee, and I concur, it marks a reorientation of the uncanny valley into an experimentation with the flexible boundaries of humanness, rather than accommodation within a fixed space of difference. See Rhee (2013:311–12), where she characterizes the new translation as the basis for a reconsideration of the uncanny valley as a 'site of destabilization' (311).

[16] Rhee cites Lucy Suchman's observations about the irreducible significance of embodied training in her encounter with Cynthia Brezeale's robot, Kismet. What for Suchman seems jarring and indeed uncanny is hardly so for Brezeale, who enjoys a history of interaction with the robot that makes her experience of it mundane and for all intents and purposes seamless: 'The contrast between my own encounter with Kismet and that recorded on the demonstration videos [with Breazeal] makes clear the ways in which Kismet's affect is an effect not simply of the device itself but of Breazeal's trained reading of Kismet's actions and her extended history of labors with the machine' (cited in Rhee, 2013:306).

[17] Schaffer stresses that this passage is the sole invocation of animation in Deleuze's entire two-volume study of the cinema.

References

Agamben, G. (1993) *The Coming Community*, translated by Michael Hardt, Minneapolis, University of Minnesota Press.

Amoore, L. (2020) *Cloud Ethics: Algorithms and the Attributes of Ourselves and Others*, Durham, NC: Duke University Press.

Citton, Y. (2021) 'Could Deep Fakes Uncover the Deeper Truth of an Ontology of the Networked Images?', *Nordic Journal of Aesthetics*, 30(61–62): 46–64.

Cole, S. (2017) 'AI-Assisted Fake Porn Is Here and We're All Fucked', Vice, 11 December [online], Available from: https://www.vice.com/en/article/gydydm/gal-gadot-fake-ai-porn [Accessed 2 February 2021].

Debaise, D. and Keating, T.P. (2021) 'Speculative Empiricism, Nature and the Question of Predatory Abstractions: A Conversation with Didier Debaise', *Theory, Culture & Society*, 38(7–8): 309–23.

Deleuze, Gilles (1986) *Cinema 1: The Movement-Image*, translated by H. Tomlinson and B. Habberjam, Minneaopolis: University of Minnesota Press.

Fletcher, J. (2018) 'Deepfakes, Artificial Intelligence, and Some Kind of Dystopia: The New Faces of Online Post-Fact Performance', *Theatre Journal*, 70(4): 455–71.

Hansen, M.B.N. (2015) *Feed-Forward: On the Future of Twenty-First-Century Media*, Chicago: University of Chicago Press.

Hansen, M.B.N. (2021) 'The Critique of Data, or Towards a Phenomeno-technics of Algorithmic Culture', in E. Horl, N.Y. Pinkrah and L. Warnsholdt (eds) *Critique and the Digital*, Zurich: Diaphanes, pp 25–73.

Hsu, T., Frenkel, S., and Thompson, S.A. (2022) 'Debunking 3 Viral Rumors About the Texas Shooting', *The New York Times*, 26 May [online], Available from: https://www.nytimes.com/2022/05/25/technology/texas-shooting-misinformation.html

Metz, C. (2016a) 'How Google's AI Viewed the Move No Human Could Understand', Wired, 14 March [online], Available from: https://www.wired.com/2016/03/googles-ai-viewed-move-no-human-understand/.

Metz, C. (2016b) 'In Two Moves, AlphaGo and Lee Sedol Redefined the Future', Wired, 16 March [online], Available from: https://www.wired.com/2016/03/two-moves-alphago-lee-sedol-redefined-future/.

Pariser, E. (2011) *The Filter Bubble: What the Internet is Hiding From You*, New York: The Penguin Group.

Rhee, J. (2013) 'Beyond the Uncanny Valley: Masahiro Mori and Philip K. Dick's *Do Androids Dream of Electric Sheep?*', *Configurations*, 21(3): 301–29.

Sample, I. (2020) 'What are deepfakes – and how can you spot them?', *The Guardian*, 20 January [online], Available from: https://www.theguardian.com/technology/2020/jan/13/what-are-deepfakes-and-how-can-you-spot-them.

Schaffer, W. (2007) 'Animation 1: The Control Image', in A. Cholodenko (ed) *The Illusion of Life 2: More Essays on Animation*, Sydney: Power Publications, pp 456–85.

Schick, N. (2020) *Deep Fakes and the Infocalypse: What You Urgently Need to Know*, London: Monoray/Octopus Publishing Group.

Simondon, G. (2008) *Imagination et invention (1965–66)*, Chatou, Éditions de la Transparence.

Telotte, J.P. (2010) *Animating Space: From Mickey to Wall-E*, Lexington, KY: University Press of Kentucky.

Toews, R. (2020) 'Deepfakes Are Going To Wreak Havoc On Society. We Are Not Prepared,' Forbes, 25 May [online], Available from: https://www.forbes.com/sites/robtoews/2020/05/25/deepfakes-are-going-to-wreak-havoc-on-society-we-are-not-prepared/.

Whitehead, A.N. (1938) *Modes of Thought*, New York: Free Press.

Whitehead, A.N. (1978/1929) *Process and Reality*, edited by D.R. Griffin and D.W. Sherburne, New York: Free Press.

Index

References to images appear in *italics*. References to endnotes
show the page number and the note number (231n3).

A

abstraction
  algorithms and 232–3
  deepfakes and 218, 225, 228–9, 230
  facial recognition and 174, 176
  human perception and 64, 65–6, 71, 73, 76
  image-formation process incompatibility 6
  motion capture and 173
  predatory 225, 230
  temporamentalities and 183
  things as 103–4
A Bug's Life 116
actualities
  about 17
  animators, constructed by 78
  feed-forward loops 19
  in pre-classical films 119
  and reality 15–16
aesthetics
  about 80n1
  neuroaesthetics 36–7, 73, 94
  nine laws of 73
  questions of CGI 118, 126, 127–8, 129
  types of (analogue / digital) 13, 62
affect / affectivity
  about 2–4, 12, 80n11
  and actuality (realism) 18–19
  attention and 205–6
  biosemiotics and 71–2
  data set for, incomplete 72–3
  and depersonalization 16
  effects, affective 18, 22n1, 63, 67–9,
    72–3, 79
  emotions and 80n11, 187–8
  human perception and 63–4
  and incomputability 20
  mimesis 64, 67–8
  nonconscious 6, 54
  and phenomenology 17–18
  and temporality 20–2, 23n9, 201

theories 6–7, 71, 88
  of video games 132–3
  See also 'special affects'
affectio (to move) 10, 196
affective effects 18, 22n1, 63, 67–9, 72–3, 79
affective perception 2, 22n1
affective trans-subjectivity 69
agency
  of algorithms 229–30
  in gameplay 8
  human 3–4
  in matter 30
  in video games 8, 134, 138, 143, 144
AI (artificial breeding) 33
AIA (Atmospheric Imaging Assembly) 171–2
Alberti 156
alchemy, political 167–8
Aldred, Jessica 139
algorithmic visualization 63
algorithms
  animation and 225–6
  collapse of animation 228–9
  dangers posed by 220–1
  deepfake / fake news reliance on 10,
    215–17, 222–3
  human element to 217–19, 232–4
  limitations of 20
  research on 131–2
alienation 77, 78, 137, 139
Alpers, Svetlana 163, 165
ambience act 145
Amoore, Louise 215, 216–17, 218, 226, 233,
  235n5–6
Anable, Aubrey 132, 146
analogue animation *See* hand-drawn animation
animation
  about (archaic sense) 161
  algorithms and 225–6
  military 153–4
  See also animation (moving images)

animation (moving images)
  about 2, 13–14, 22n1, 23n9
  algorithmic collapse of 228–9
  brain and 96–8
  cinema and 65–6, 67, 227–8
  computer–generated (See CGI
    (computer-generated imagery))
  conceptual (See conceptual animation)
  in data processing 8
  deepfakes (See deepfakes)
  frames per second (fps) 42, 43, 52, 56,
    87, 183
  hand-drawn (See hand-drawn animation)
  military training using 154–5
  mimesis 64, 67–8, 80n9
  noise and 172–3, 174, 188
  perceptual (See perceptual animation)
  punctums (See punctums)
  real-time 171–2, 173, 174–5, 177–9, 182
  stillness and 42, 50, 51–6
  stop-motion 112, 115, 117, 171–2
  structurally coupled systems 7, 95
  theses on 98–100, 100–4
  touch in 116–17, 122–6
animators 64–7, 69, 78, 80n2, 81n24,
  111–12, 115–17
Anselm (Saint) 184
anticipation 19, 22, 226
Apple 32
arcades 133, 145
archives, digital 2
artificial breeding (AI) 33
artificial intelligence 3
Artificial Smile camera 197–8, 197
'As We Become Machines' (Lahti) 132–3
Atmospheric Imaging Assembly (AIA) 171–2
atoms 5, 37–9
attention, ecologies of 196, 203, 204–5, 210
audio 22n1
auto-affection / auto-affective processes 17–18,
  20, 21, 77
Autopoiesis and Cognition (Maturana and
  Varela) 43, 49
Avatar (Cameron) 64, 80n3–4, 173
avatars
  about 139
  embedded 143–5
  ideological 92, 95, 96–7
  player, identification / relationship with 8,
    18–19, 137, 140–1
  sexualized images of 139
  types of 141–2
axes (expression / identity) 10, 200, 205,
  206, 208–9
Azéma, M. 90

B

Bachelard, Gaston 236n11
backgrounds 76, 115–16, 189n2

Bacon, Francis 164, 165
Balázs, Béla 200–1, 202
Barker, Jennifer 122
Barré, Raoul 189n2
Barrett, Lisa Feldman 202
Barry, Susan R. 13, 81n20
Barthes, Roland 86–9, 90, 99, 100, 102,
  103–4, 107, 206–7
Baudrillard, Jean 221
Bazin, Andre 14–15
Beccario, Cameron 177
Behrmann, Marlene 202
Beil, Benjamin 139–40
Beller, J. 188
Bellour, R. 181
Belting, Hans 51, 161, 203
Bergson, Henri 12–13, 16, 23n7, 95,
  96–100, 203
Bertalanffy, Ludwig 48–9
Beyond Texting (Fine) 203
Biederman, Irving 74
biorobotics 3
biosemiotics 6, 71–2
Bishop-Stephens, William 104
bits 71
Blomberg, Johan 135–6, 137
body, the
  about 3–4, 23n6
  CGI, challenge of producing in 63
  as data 5, 32, 37
  as embodied intelligence 3
  face (See face; faciality)
  image, with / without 138–9
  longitude / latitude of 111, 114–16, 117
  as mode 115, 117
  motion-capture suits 172–3
  and perception 12–13, 22n1
Bonehill, John 157
Bongard, Josh 3
Borst, A. 183
brain
  Bergson's position on 96–8
  cognitive science and 11–12
  imaging studies of 3
  information processing 76
  (un)measurability of 71
  mind control 94–5
  neurocinematics 93–5
  neuroscience research 23n2
  plasticity of 7, 11, 12, 44, 45, 56–7,
    58n2, 91–3
  recursive architecture of 5–6, 43–6, 70
Brassett, Jamie 70
Bray, John Randolph 189n2
breath / breathing 36
Brezeale, Cynthia 236n16
Broadfoot, Keith 121
Brothers: A Tale of Two Sons 137, 146
Brouwers, Henrietta 55

Bruns, Daniela 7, 8, 18
Buddha *See TV Buddha* (Paik)
Burroughs, William 50
Butler, Rex 121

C

Cainthus 33
cameras
  Artificial Smile 197–8, *197*
  camera obscura 8–9, 156, 163–6, *164*
  multiplane 116–17, 172
Cameron, James 64, 75
capital 185–8
The Capture 174
caricature 118, 121–2
Carr, Nicholas 57
cartographic grids 156–7, 175
causal efficacy
  about 214, 235n5
  algorithms 10, 216, 218, 228–9
  bodily actuality and 219–20
  deepfakes, reality of 221–3, 224, 225–6,
    230–2
CGI (computer-generated imagery)
  about 6, 63
  hand-drawn animation, compared
    to 111–12
  intersections 116, 122–4, 125, 126
  'special affect' of 8, 113–14, 118–22
  3D 38, 62, 64–5, 114–16
  ubiquitousness of 62
  See also animation (moving images)
Chakrabarty, Dipesh 185
Chantier Barbès-Rochechouart, Paris (Huyghe) 208
ChatGPT 1
chronoclasm
  about 9, 19, 171
  debt crisis and 185–8
  real-time animations 178–9
chrono-technologies 183
cinema
  animation and 7, 65–6
  technical possibilities of 227–8
Cinema 1 (Deleuze) 201, 226–7
cinema of attractions 119, 180
cinematic animation *See* animation
  (moving images)
Citizen Kane 182
Citron, Danielle 195–6
Citton, Yves 196, 204–5, 219–21, 228,
  231–2, 235n7
Clark, David 13–14
clay
  digital, pixel sculpture as 38
  likenesses in 8–9, 160–1, 166
  mud, hardening of into 30–1
close-ups, filmic 201–2
cloud ethics 216, 235n5
code 13–14, 131–2, 145–6

codec *See* MPEG codec
cognition 69–70
  See also conscious cognition;
    conscious–nonconscious cognition;
    nonconscious cognition
cognitive assemblages 73, 78–80, 82n25
cognitive science 11, 167
Cohen, Jonathan 140
Cole, Samantha 206
computation, digital 2, 20, 64, 71, 77
computer-generated imagery *See* CGI
  (computer-generated imagery)
computerization 2, 4, 77
conceptual animation 6, 46–8, 50–1, 53–4,
  56, 58n4
conscious cognition
  about 11–12
  conceptual animation and 47–8, 52–3
  information processing 5–6, 21
  presubjective 3, 21–2, 80n12,
    88–9, 105
  subjective 17, 22
  time and 23n9
  See also conscious–nonconscious cognition;
    nonconscious cognition
conscious–nonconscious cognition
  affectivity and 18
  recursive dynamics of 5–6, 43–6, 70
  See also conscious cognition;
    nonconscious cognition
controllers 133, 134–6, 137, 146, 147n2
conventional animation *See* hand-drawn
  animation
corporations 185
cortisol 34–5
cosmetic gaze 209
cows 5, 32–5
Cracknell, Ryan 120
Crafton, Donald 189n2
Crawford, Garry 133
Critical Terms for Media Studies (Mitchell and
  Hansen) 202
crystals *See* liquid crystals
Cubitt, Sean 8, 9, 19–20

D

dairy cows *See* cows
Damasio, Antonio 52
Daniels, Stephen 157
Dargis, Manohla 119–20
Dash *(Incredibles)* 123
data
  about 160
  animation 159
  body as 5, 32, 37
  incomplete, for affect 72–3
  noise as 172, 173
  truth as 179–82
  visual 156, 159, 160, 165

data processing 8, 9
data visualization 8–9, 174, 175–6, 179, 187–8
da Vinci, Leonardo 161
Deacon, Terrence W. 45
Debaise, Didier 225
debt 9, 185–6
deepfakes
  about 195, 221–2
  algorithms, reliance on 10, 215–17,
    222–3, 229
  causal efficacy 219–20, 221–3, 224,
    225–6, 230–2
  consequences of 9–10
  face-swaps 10, 195–6, 198–9, 205–6,
    208–9
  fake news and 216–17
  pornography 206, 208–9, 210, 235n9
  public speech 208–9
  transmission speed of 174
  uncanny valley, bridging of 223–5
Deeptech 195
Deeptrace 195
Dehaene, Stanislas 11, 46, 74
de la Perrière, Guillaume 154
Deleuze, Gilles
  on the actual and virtual 15, 23n8
  on animation 226–7
  on dividualization 128
  on faciality 10, 198, 199–200, 201
  on movement images 98–100, 111
  on perception 68
  on the body (longitude / latitude of) 111,
    114–16, 117
depersonalization 15, 16
De pictura (Alberti) 156
de Piles, Roger 161, 162
Derrida, J. 180
determinism 4, 22, 92, 214
Detroit: Become Human 145–6
Dickinson, Emily 45
Diderot, Denis 160
digital
  archives 2
  computation (See computation, digital)
  health 2, 31–3, 36–7, 44
  humanities 2
  media (See media)
  objects 115–16, 117
Disney 91, 120–1
dividualization 128
DNA 39
Douglas, Mary 172
Dragon Age 141
Dreyfus, Hubert 20
Duchamp 90
Dumbarton Castle (Scotland) 157,
  158, 158–9
dynamic propositions 114
dynamics See recursive dynamics

E
ecologies of attention 196, 203, 204–5, 210
The Ecology of Attention (Citton) 204–5
Edelman, Gerald 43–5, 46–7, 49, 70, 75
Edkins, Jenny 199–200, 201
Eisenstein, Sergei 91, 113, 120–1
Ekberg, Anita 207, 208
ek-stasis 17
Elastigirl (Incredibles) 113, 120, 123–4,
  125, 126
Electronic Superhighway (Paik) 50–1
embodied intelligence 3
embodiment
  phenomenotechnics of 224–5
  video games 138, 139, 140–1, 142, 144
E-mini market 178
emotions
  about 52, 80n11
  affect and 80n11, 187
  close-ups, filmic 201–2
  facial movements and 202
  and feelings 6, 52, 54
  mirror neuron and 68–9
  neurocognitive theories of 3
  portrayal of on film 53–6
  in still images 201
  See also feelings
Empire 24/7 (Staehle) 208
empty anticipation 22
Encyclopédie (Diderot and le Rond
  d'Alembert) 160
engagement 136, 144–5
Ernst, Wolfgang 183
expectation See protention (expectation)
expression axis (how are you/what are you
  doing?) 10, 200, 205, 206, 209
expressive, the See hand-drawn animation

F
face
  about 198–9
  as a medium 202–3
  close-ups, filmic 201–2
  identity axis (who are you?) 10, 200, 205,
    206, 208–9
  See also faciality
FaceApp 197–8
Face Politics (Edkins) 199–200
face-swaps, deepfake 10, 195–6, 198–9,
  205–6, 208–9
Face Visualizer (Manabe) 199–200
faciality 10, 198, 199–200, 205
facial recognition 80n3, 80n10, 174,
  176, 179
fake news 10–11, 195, 213–14, 216, 219–21,
  229–32
Featherstone, Mike 138–9
feedback 44–5, 132, 133–4, 178, 187
feed-forward loops 19

feel (Pixar) *See* Pixar
feelings
  about 80n11
  and bodily emotions 6, 52, 54
  facial movements and 202
  organic, creation of in CGI 63
  See also emotions; 'special affects'
Fine, Debra 203
fire-flames 78, 81n24
Flusser, V. 185
Flynn effect 57
fMRI *See* MRI (magnetic resonance imaging)
Foucault, Michel 154, 172, 183
frames per second (fps) 42, 43, 52, 56, 87, 183
Frankfurt School 91, 92
Freeman, Elisabeth 201
Freud, Sigmund 12, 43, 174
Furuhata, Yuriko 90, 91–2, 95

G

gait (analysis / capture / recognition) 172,
  174, 179
Galloway, Alexander 131, 145, 147
gaming *See* video games
Gaming at the Edge (Shaw) 140–1
GAN (generative adversarial network)
  animation 9, 174–5, 182, 222, 223–5
gaps
  and perception experience 107, 172, 175,
    181, 182, 183, 188
  perforations 75–6
Gardner, Alexander 206
Gates, Kelly 202
Gee, James Paul 143–4
generalized proletarianisation 77
generative adversarial network animation
  See GAN (generative adversarial
  network) animation
genetics 33–4, 92
Giddings, Seth 8, 132
Gilbreth, Frank 172
Gilbreth, Lillian 172
Giraud, Jean (Mœbius) 66
Gitelman, Lisa 180
Gödel 179
Google 37
Grand Theft Auto V 144
The Greeting (Viola) 52–3
Gregersen, Andreas 134, 138, 141
Gregg, Melissa 3, 12
grids (cartographic / perspectival) 156–7, 161
Grodal, Torben 134, 138, 141
Guattari, Félix 10, 198, 199–200
Gunning, Tom 119, 180

H

Han, Byung-Chul 205
hand-drawn animation
  about 6, 62

backgrounds 115
CG animation, compared to 111–12
and emotions / senses 63
layers in 116–17
longitudinal relations in 115
movement 66
realistic, advantages over the 64–5
Hanhardt, John G. 51, 52
Hansen, Mark B.N. 9–11, 19, 20, 196,
  202, 207–8
Harrowdown Hill (Yorke) 219
Hasson, U. 93–4
Hayles, N. Katherine
  on biosemiotics 71–2
  on cognitive assemblages 73, 78–9,
    81n14–15
  cognitive neuroscience theory 12
  on computational media 19
  on meditation 204
  on noise 75
  on nonconscious cognition 69–71
  on recursive architecture of the brain
    5–6, 21
health, digital 2, 31–3, 36–7, 44
Hellblade: Senua's Sacrifice 142
Henry, Michel 17–18, 20–1
Holzer, Jenny 205
homophily 141–2
Horkheimer 24n11
HRT (hormone replacement
  therapy) 34
human intelligence 3
humanities, digital 2
Human Longevity, Inc. 39
human perception
  about 4, 22n1, 63–4, 203–4
  abstraction and 64, 65–6, 71, 73, 76
  and affective effects 63–4, 67–9, 72–3, 79
  body, and the 12–13
  enactive concept of 167
  mirror neuron (*See* mirror neuron)
  of movement in animation 65–6, 183–4
  noise and 64, 75–6
  recursivity and 64, 70, 78–9
  selectivity in 73–4
  structurally coupled systems 7, 95
  studies of 3
Hurd, Earl 189n2
Husserl 17, 19, 21–2, 24n11, 207
Huygens, Constantijn 163–4
Huygens Jr., Constantijn 164, *164*
Huyghe, Peter 208

I

'I am the Slime' (Zappa) 220
iconoclasm 179
identification (with / as the avatar) 140–2
identity axis (who are you?) 10, 200, 205,
  206, 208–9

ideological avatars 92, 95, 96–7
images
  about 23n7–9
  hand-drawn (*See* hand-drawn animation)
  impact 113, 122, 124–6
  moving (*See* animation (moving images))
  optical 63
  from perception to production of 91
  pictures, compared to 165
  punctums (*See* punctums)
  still 42, 50, 201
  virtual (*See* animation (moving images))
imagination 9, 38, 75, 112, 165, 174–5
immersion 136, 137, 139
impact images 113, 122, 124–6
incompleteness 6, 64–5, 73, 138–9, 187, 188
The Incredibles 113, 118
Incredibles 2 7–8, 113–14, 119–20, 122–6,
  126–8
Ingold, Tim 80n8
intelligence *See* artificial intelligence;
  embodied intelligence; human intelligence
intentionality 17–18, 21
internet 51, 185, 198, 215–16, 230, 231–2
interoception 204
intersections 116, 122–4, 125, 126
Intervista (Fellini) 207
The Irishman (Scorsese) 235n10
Ishii, Hiroshi 37
Isoda, K. 80n10
isolation, law of 73

J

Jack-Jack *(Incredibles)* 123, 124
Jacob, Christian 156
James, William 15, 103
Jeaurat, Edme-Sébastian 163
Jenkins, Eric 6, 7–8, 86–8, 107

K

Kane, Carolyn L. 63
Kaplan, Caren 159
Kelly, Andy 146–7
Kemp, Martin 163
Keogh, B. 135
Kepler, Johannes 164–5
Kerimov, Ferdinand *(Grand Theft Auto
  V)* 144
keyframes 176, 184
Kimura, Bin 15–16, 23n10
kinetic propositions 114
Kirkpatrick, Graeme 134–5, 137
Kismet 236n16
Klaus, Frank 34
Klevjer, Rune 143
Kosovichev, Alexander 173
koto (way of appearing) 16, 18
Kramnick, Jonathan 167
Kuspit, Donald 53

L

Lahti, Martti 132–3
Lasseter, John 80n6, 115, 116, 121
latitude (of the body) 111, 114–16, 117
Lazzarato, Maurizio 81n17
left-to-right movement 136, 147n2
le Rond d'Alembert, Jean 160
Leslie, Esther 5
Life is Strange 146
liquid crystals 5, 29, 31, 37, 39
longitude (of the body) 111, 114–15
Lost Dimension (Virilio) 181
Lowe, Victor 102
Luhmann, Niklas 48–9, 58n5

M

magnetic resonance imaging *See* MRI
  (magnetic resonance imaging)
Malabou, Catherine 11, 91–3, 95, 96–7, 103
Manabe, Daito 199, *199*
Man of Sorrows 53
Marey, Étienne-Jules 90, 172
margin of indeterminacy 77
markets, economic 177–8
'marvellous astonishment' (Pixar feel) 7–8,
  113, 118–22, 122–3, 126–8
Marx, K. 180, 187
Massumi, Brian 23n9, 114, 127
matter 30–1
Matter and Memory (Bergson) 12, 95, 96, 97, 99
Mattern, Shannon 30–1
Maturana, Humberto 43, 49
Mays, W. 103
media
  as bridge 202–3
  digital 2, 4, 13–14, 18, 19, 35, 208
  new media studies 2
mediation hypothesis 182, 186–7
meditation 204
memory *See* retention (memory)
mentalités 183
Merkwelt (perceptual world) 72
Merleau-Ponty, Maurice 1, 2, 20, 138, 143
meta-consciousness 6, 47, 48
Metal Gear Solid 137
micromovements 145–6
Mihailova, Mihaela 119
military
  animate, definition of 153–4
  Scotland survey (1700s) 156–9
  training environments, synthetic 154–5,
    166–8
mimesis 64, 67–8, 80n9
mind control 94–5
mirror neuron 37, 68–9, 80n10, 81n18, 225
Mitchell, J. 57
Mitchell, W.J.T. 202
Miyazaki, Hayao 63, 66–7, 75–6, 77–8,
  80n5–6, 81n24

mo-cap (motion capture) 64, 90, 172–3
modes, bodies as 115, 117
Mœbius 66
Mona Lisa 174
mono (things that appear) 16
MooMonitor+ 32–3
Mori, Masahiro 224, 236n15
motion *See* movement
motion capture *See* mo-cap (motion capture)
movement
  animated, human perception of 65–6, 183–4
  early images of 89–90
  false illusion of 96–9
  human bodies in CGI, challenge of 63, 80n8
  left-to-right, controller 136, 147n2
  motion capture (mo-cap) 64, 90, 172–3
  in pre-classical films 119
  punctums (*See* punctums)
  and rest 114–15
  stillness and 42, 50, 51–6
  universal context 184
  vision and 13
  See also animation (moving images)
moving images *See* animation
  (moving images)
MPEG codec 172, 176, 184–5, 187
MRI (magnetic resonance imaging)
  about 3, 23n2
  fMRI (functional MRI) 93, 94–5
Mr Incredible *(Incredibles)* 123–4, 125, 126
mud 29–31, 32, 39–40
Mules, Warwick 202
multiplane cameras 116–17, 172
Mumford, L. 183
Muriel, Daniel 133
Murray, Janet 134

N

Nagai, Yukie 23n3
NASA 171–2, 173
Natural History (Pliny) 160
naturalism 17, 64
nature, designed 37–9
negative space 181
Neitzel, Britta 138, 140
neural Darwinism 44
neuroaesthetics 36–7, 73, 94
neurocinematics 93–5
neuroreductionism 3, 4, 22
new media studies 2
Ngai, Sianne 205
Nintendo Wii 134, 135
Noë, Alva 167
noise (incompleteness / ambiguity)
  capital and 186–7
  data as 171–3
  facial expressions / motion as 174
  and perception 75–6
nonconscious affect 6, 54

nonconscious cognition
  about 42–3, 45–6, 69–71
  information processing 5–6, 21, 43
  perceptual animation and 47, 52–3
  time and 23n9
  See also conscious cognition;
    conscious–nonconscious cognition
nonphenomenological approaches 6–7, 21,
  89, 95, 98, 100
North, Dan 119

O

O'Connell, Kelly 116
Oculus Go 36
One World Terrain 154–5, 166–8
O'Pray, Michael 121
optical images 63
over-animation 113

P

P-actions 134
Paik, Nam June 5–6, 42, 46–7, 48, 50, 51,
  56, 57
Palaeolithic art 90
The Passing (Viola) 53
Passions (Viola) 53, 57–8
patents 189n2
Payne, Lewis 206
peg system 189n2
perception *See* human perception
perceptual animation 5, 47, 48, 50–1, 53, 56
perforation (gaps) *See* gaps
Perov, Kira 53–4
personality (of avatars) 140, 141, 142
perspectival grids 156–7, 161
Petty, William 167–8
Pfeifer, Rolf 3
phenomenological approaches
  affectivity and 17–18, 91–2, 95
  critiques of 24n11
  movement images 96, 98, 99–100
  punctums 6–7, 89
phenomenotechnics 10, 222–3, 224,
  236n11–12
Philips, Trevor *(Grand Theft Auto V)* 144
photorealism 113, 118–19, 121–2,
  123–6, 127
picnolepsia 181, 182, 184–5, 188
picturae 165
Pitts-Taylor, Victoria 11, 12, 23n6
Pixar 7–8, 112–13, 115–17, 118–22, 122–6,
  126–8
'Plan of the Castle of Dunbarton'
  (Sandby) 157, *158*
plasmaticness, protean 91, 113, 117–18,
  120–1, 123
plasticity
  brain 7, 11, 12, 44, 45, 56–7, 58n2, 91–3
  of the real 155–6, 166–8

players (human)
  actions by in video games 133–4
  avatars, identification / relationship with 8,
    18–19, 137, 140–2, 143–5
  controllers and 135–6
Playfair, William 175
Playing with Feelings (Anable) 132
PlayStation 135
Pliny 160–1
political alchemy 167–8
pornography 10, 195, 206, 208–9, 210,
  221, 235n9
positivism 17
Poulaki, Maria 94–5
Power, Pat 64, 75, 76
predatory abstractions 225, 230
presubjective consciousness 3, 21–2, 80n12,
  88–9, 105
  See also conscious cognition
primal impression 22
primitive actions (P-actions) 134
projections 156–7, 161, 163, 166, 174
prolepsis 185
proletarianisation, generalized 77
propositions
  algorithmically generated 232–4
  dynamic and kinetic 114
  'lures for feeling' 10, 214–16, 231–2, 234n1
protean plasmaticness *See*
    plasmaticness, protean
protention (expectation) 19, 22, 207
protoself 52, 92
  See also nonconscious cognition
'Proxy Politics' (Steyerl) 198
Psycho Mantis *(Metal Gear Solid)* 137
Psychopolitics (Han) 205
punctums
  about 86
  movement (new punctum) 6–7, 86, 88–9,
    103, 107
  still images (Barthes's punctum) 86–7, 87,
    88, 89, 90–1, 101–2, 107
Putades 160–1, 166

Q

Quade, Rich 115
Quintet of the Astonished (Viola) 54–5

R

radical atoms 5, 37–9
Ramachandran, V.S. 68, 73
rare earth elements 31, 39–40
realism
  cinematic 14–15, 18, 65, 235n8
  of deepfakes 221–2, 223–5
  photorealism 7, 118, 119, 121, 122, 123, 126
reality 15–16
real-time animation 171–2, 173, 174–5,
  177–9, 182

recursive dynamics 5, 6, 21
  brain plasticity and 58n2
  and cognition 43–6, 46–8
  human perception and 64, 70, 78–9
  stillness and motion 42, 51–6, 58n4
  systems theory and 48–51
reentrant connections (reentry) 44, 45, 47,
  49, 70
Reeves, Bill 115
relational temporal thickness 104
rest 114–15
retention (memory) 19, 22, 207
'Rethinking Plasticity' (Furuhata) 90
Rhee, Jenny 224–5, 236n14–16
Rise of the Tomb Raider 146
Rivère, F. 90
Rizzolatti, Giacomo 68
role (of avatars) 140, 141, 143, 144–5
Rosenberg, David 160
Roy, William 157
RPGs (role-playing games) 141–2
rubber (in animation) 113, 118, 123–6, 126–8
Rules of Play (Salen and Zimmerman) 140

S

Salen, K. 140
Sample, Ian 222
Sampson, Tony D. 5, 6–7, 21
Sandby, Paul 8–9, 156–7, 158, 159, 160,
  161, 165–6
Schaffer, B. 99
Schaffer, William 65, 112–13, 114, 117–18,
  121, 127–8, 226–8
Schallegger, René 141–2
Schick, N. 225, 236n13
Schmelas, Andreas 197
Schumacher, Thomas 122
Schutz, Alfred 15
Scotland survey 156–9
screen-devices 5, 29, 31, 37, 39
Seigworth, Gregory J. 3, 12
seismographs 176–7
selectivity 6, 64, 73–4
Sellers, Peter 55–6
semiotic operator 81n17
Senua *(Hellblade)* 142
Serres, Michel 75
sex videos *See* pornography
Shadow of the Tomb Raider 135
shadows, tracing 8–9, 160–1, 163–4, 165, 166
Shannon, Claude 75
Shaw, Adrienne 140–1, 143
Sheets-Johnstone, M. 80n8
shells (avatars as) 140, 141, 172–3
sight *See* vision
Simondon, Gilbert 6, 70, 76–7, 79, 81n21,
  81n23, 235n7
skillful coping 20
smartwatches 32

Smith, George 153–4, 159
Sobchack, Vivian 121
Sonic the Hedgehog 145
Sørensen, Mette-Marie Zacher 9–10
sound effects 22n1, 80n13
sparks 120, 125, 129n1
Special Affects (Jenkins) 116, 119, 120, 129n1
'special affects' 8, 113–14, 118–22
Spinoza 10, 88, 111, 114–15, 196, 200, 203
Staehle, Wolfgang 208
Statistical Breviary (Playfair) 175
Stengers, Isabelle 22, 104, 205
Steyerl, Hito 198
Stiegler, Bernard 10, 57, 76–7, 207–8, 210
Stoichita, Victor 161
stop-motion animation 112, 115, 117, 171–2
structurally coupled systems 7, 95
Stubbe, Stefan 197
subjective consciousness 17, 22
sub-universes 15
Suchman, Lucy 236n16
sun 171–2, 173, 176
Sutherland, Ivan 37
symbolic reference 234n4
synaptogenesis 44
systems theories 48–50, 58n5

T

Tamari, Tomoko 5, 6, 20
Tanaka, Keiji 74, 81n19
Taussig, Michael 67
technical mentality 6, 70
temporal heterogeneity 208
temporality 10, 19–20, 90–1, 182–3, 199–201, 206–8
temporal thickness, relational 104
temporamentalities 182–5, 187, 188–9
temporealities 183–4, 185, 187, 188–9
tertiary retention (memory) 10, 207
Terzidis, Kostas 64–5
Tetris 139–40
The Thinker 47–8
3D computer animation 38, 62, 64–5, 114–16, 154–5
Thrum II (Bishop-Stephens) 101, 104–5
Thrum III (Bishop-Stephens) 104–5, *105*, *106*
ticks 114–15
time
  animation techniques and 8
  and cognition (conscious / nonconscious) 23n9
  perceptions of 9, 207–8
  real-time animation 171–2, 173, 174–5, 177–9, 182
  truth and 179–82, 183
  units of, graphs with 175, 177–8
time-consciousness 19, 21–2
Toews, Rob 222

Tononi, Giulio 43–5, 46–7, 49, 70, 75
topography 154–5, 157–9, *158*, 160, 164, 166
Torre, Dan 56
torture 144
touch, in animation 116–17, 122–6
Toy Story 115, 118, 122, 127–8
tracing shadows 8–9, 160–1, 163–4, 165, 166
Traité de perspective à l'usage des artistes (Jeaurat) 163
transferability 116
trans-subjectivity, affective 69
Tronstad, Ragnhild 141, 142
Trump, Donald 203, 205–6, 213
truth 179–82, 183
TV Buddha (Paik) 5–6, 46–7, 57
TV Rodin (Paik) 47, 57

U

Umwelt 4, 72
uncanny valley 223–5
unconsciousness 12, 43, 67, 68, 78, 135, 188, 204, 214, 236n13
An Universal Military Dictionary (Smith) 153, 159
US Army 154–5, 166–8

V

Väliaho, Pasi 8–9
VaM software 206
Varela, Franco 7, 43, 49, 95
vector predictions 184, 186
vectors 159, 184–5
Venter, Craig 39
vestibulo–ocular effect 81n20
video games
  about 131–2
  actions of players 133–4
  as affective systems 132–3
  agency in 8, 134, 138, 143, 144
  arcades 133, 145
  avatar–player relationship (identification with) 8, 18–19, 137, 140–2, 143–5
  controllers 133, 134–6, 137, 146, 147n2
  embodiment 138, 139, 140–1, 142, 144
  engagement 136, 144–5
  face-swaps with pornographic content 206
  immersion 136, 137, 139
  micromovements 145–6
  military training using 154
  See also avatars; players (human)
Viola, Bill 6, 42, 48, 51–6, 57, 207
Violet *(Incredibles)* 123, 124–5
Virilio, P. 181, 184
virtual, the 15
virtual images *See* animation (moving images)
virtual realities
  and cows 34–5
  face-swaps with pornographic content 206

military training using 154–5
  perception of 15
Visible Man (Balázs) 200–1
vision 13, 202
visualizations
  algorithmic 63
  data (*See* data visualization)
von Uexküll, Jakob 4, 72
Voronoff, Serge 34

W

WALL-E 120
Watson, David 159
wearables 32, 37
weather 177, 178, 182
Wegenstein, Bernadette 209
Wells, Paul 121
Whalen, Zack 136
'What the Frog's Eye Tells the Frog's Brain'
  (Lettvin et al) 49
Whitehead, Alfred North
  on causal efficacy 10, 214, 216, 218, 223,
    225, 228–9, 231–2
  on feeling 235n7
  movement images, thesis on 100, 101–4

nonphenomenology 7, 21
  propositions ('lures for feeling') 10,
    214–16, 231–2, 234n1
  on society 234n2
  on symbolic reference 234n4
Wirkwelt (effector world) 72
Wolf, Gerhard 161
Wotton, Henry 164–5

X

Xsens MVN bodysuit 172

Y

'Year Zero: Faciality' (Deleuze and
  Guattari) 198, 199–200
Yorke, Thom 219
Yorō, Takeshi 76

Z

Zao app 195
Zappa, Frank 220
Zimmerman, E. 140
Zur Phänomenologie der Depersonalisation
  (Kimura) 15